LE NID

HOUSES AND GARDENS
ARTS AND CRAFTS INTERIORS

M. H. BAILLIE SCOTT

ANTIQUE COLLECTORS' CLUB

This edition © Antique Collectors' Club 1995
Reprinted 2004
First published in 1906 by George Newnes Ltd.
World copyright reserved

ISBN 1 85149 234 8

British Library Cataloguing-in-Publication Data
A Catalogue record for this book is available from the British Library

Printed in England
Published by Antique Collectors' Club Ltd.,
Sandy Lane, Old Martlesham, Woodbridge, Suffolk IP12 4SD

CONTENTS

5

CONTENTS

HOUSES ILLUSTRATED

CONTENTS

COLOURED PLATES

MACKAY HUGH BAILLIE SCOTT
(1865 –1945)

CRAFTSMAN ARCHITECT

AMONG the half a dozen architects of the Arts and Crafts movement whose names have survived into modern times, M.H. Baillie Scott's looms large. He is not as well known as Charles Annesley Voysey, W.R. Lethaby or Ernest Gimson, and has never achieved the same international fame as the father of the modern movement, Charles Rennie Mackintosh. These figures played very different roles in the early years of this century, Voysey as an all round designer, W.R. Lethaby as a theoretician and Gimson principally as a furniture designer. Scott combined all these talents, together with some of the European acclaim of a Mackintosh, and his presence has endured through his books. He was the only one among these named architects to publish a complete collection of his 'work early in his career and to argue his philosophy of architecture persuasively through its pages.

M.H. Baillie Scott was very much a figure of his time, the 1890s, when the arts were sublimated by symbolism and in many cases fused together by a desire to explore myth and origin in elemental terms. The wish to make the material speak was emphasised by Scott in an article in *The Studio* in 1903: 'Architecture considered in this way [as an expression of structural facts] becomes a kind of sculpture, and is concerned rather with the modelling of masses than the adornment of surfaces. In dealing with these the claims of the structure to supply its own decoration in the stonework of the walling or the beams of the ceiling are not disregarded, and if these are partially concealed by superficial decoration it is always realised that in so obscuring the structural facts and the history they have to tell, a certain loss is sustained which must be replaced by something of equal, if not greater, interest of a superficial nature.'[1] Scott was a child of the Arts and Crafts movement and these ideas had been carefully laid down by William Morris many years before. Scott's approach, however, was less dogmatic and more accessible to a middle-class public.

M.H. Baillie Scott was born at St. Peter's, Ramsgate, Kent, on 23 October, 1865, into a prosperous middle-class family. He showed artistic inclinations at an early age, but was forced by his father to take up an agricultural education at the Royal Agricultural College, Cirencester. This may have

9

been a turning point in his life, for he probably assimilated, as well as the farming, the craft traditions of Gloucestershire and must have been aware of the county's vernacular buildings. It is interesting to note that many of the leading Arts and Crafts architects and designers had a Gloucestershire or West Country background, Lethaby and Gimson designing there and C.R. Ashbee setting up his Guild at Chipping Campden.

Scott chose architecture rather than agriculture as a career and moved to the office of Major C.E. Davis, the City Architect of Bath, in 1886. He seems to have learnt little from Davis's ponderous style of building but probably liked Somerset for its rural setting and craft traditions. Even at this stage he seems to have been acquainting himself with the progressive ideas of William Morris, Phillip Webb and Norman Shaw through the pages of the architectural magazines. He was developing a very spontaneous style of creating buildings, ideas stemming from his innate sense of materials, local features and a flowing unstructured plan, all sketched rapidly on the back of an envelope. He must have been aware of the houses of the slightly older Voysey, simple rational structures with steep roofs, published in *The British Architect* 1890-1.

Scott married at Bath in 1889 and shortly after left the city with his young wife for a new life in the Isle of Man. There he was employed by the surveyor Fred Saunderson and obtained a number of commissions that enabled him to break away on his own in 1893 with an office in Douglas. His work was beginning to be published, particularly the designs of a small bungalow at Douglas, strongly influenced by American architecture and a tile hung villa in the Norman Shaw tradition illustrated in *The Building News* in November 1893. Scott had also received a commission to build a large house at Onchan, Isle of Man, for a wealthy Lancashire industrialist and this may have given him the opportunity to build a house for himself at Douglas in 1892-3. This was the Red House, which still survives and is a good statement of Scott's genius for innovation. It is picturesque but has no fussy ornament and its interior eliminates corridors and partitions, opening up the spaces for communal family living in an entirely new way.

In April 1893, Charles Holme founded *The Studio*, an illustrated magazine of fine and applied art for a cultured but fairly wide audience. It is only necessary to look at the other architectural and artistic journals of that time to see how new and original were the aims of this magazine. It catered for an emerging class of art conscious people in a middle-income bracket, those who would not commission a mansion but might easily aspire to an architect-designed home. They were the patrons of the New Art, they might

A ROADSIDE HOUSE. THE HALL

very well live in one of the newly planned garden suburbs, and they visited craft exhibitions. They were exactly the clientele with whom Scott wished to make contact and for whom he could design a house for an art lover or for a musician. Scott published his first article in the magazine just over a year later, entitled 'The Ideal Suburban House.'

This tentative proposal may have been the link between Scott and an artistic patron, Carl St. Amory of Bedford, musician and writer of operettas, who commissioned a house from him on these lines in 1895. It was the first design exhibited by the architect at the Royal Academy. The scheme was published in *The Building News* rather than *The Studio* and shows a half-timbered residence, its eaves sweeping down to the garden, a mixture of local brick and plaster, the fingers of chimneys above. The drawings of the interior are moody and highly wrought, with the quality of illustrations in a child's book. They show a very carefully considered 'hall place' at the centre of the house and running through two storeys. It is decorated with old oak furniture, metalwork and textiles, friezes of murals inset above the staircase arch in the tradition of William Morris. This house was never built, but it pointed the way to Scott's conception of the architect as the designer of the whole house down to its last detail and it also provides the link with the town of Bedford.

Scott may have come into contact with Bedford in the mid-1890s through the nationally known workshops of John P. White who ran the Pyghtle Works on the outskirts of the town. From small beginnings, White had established by the last decade of the century a joinery business that was used by most of the major architects of the time. The Pyghtle was sited by the railway and had excellent communications with the whole country, more significantly its craft-based structure with shops for metalwork, stonework as well as woodwork was exactly in tune with the times. The firm was providing joinery for the architects Sir Raymond Unwin and Barry Parker at their newly projected Letchworth Garden Suburb, it was used by the Arts and Crafts architects C.H.B. Quennell and C.E. Mallows, and was in contact with illustrators such as F.L. Griggs who had close associations with C.R. Ashbee's Guild.

Scott settled at Bedford in 1901, opening an office at 4 Windsor Place, St. Cuthbert's Street. The close link with J.P. White's Pyghtle Works was an attraction, but so too was the excellent and reasonably priced education at the Bedford schools for Scott's children. His Bedford period was highly productive, it saw him branching out into furniture design and fabrics as well as being the birthplace of his important book *Houses and Gardens*.

Scott's credo in an age of jerry-building was unusual; his concern was to design a house for a family rather as a tailor might fashion a suit of clothes. Rooms had to be conceived for the family needs first and then for each individual grouping in that family second. In an article on 'A Country Cottage' he writes: 'The hall or house place as it was called . . . consisted chiefly in the formation of special cells for special purposes.'[2] The rooms for adult use had to be conveniently but not harshly separated from those of the children and both from those of the servants (Scott's families still had servants). But above all, there was the spiritual consideration that the whole household would work well together in an atmosphere of harmony and continuity. This was why his halls were so important, meeting places for families where music, conversation and stories could be enjoyed together.

As a focal point in this shared experience was the fireplace about which Scott had strong views. He advocated fixed benches in ingle-nooks, the fire embrasure formed from one side of an outside wall and therefore not stuck unnaturally outside the room space. Woodwork should be exposed and structural: 'Here as elsewhere we have to contend with that mechanical ideal which is the mark of almost all modern work, and which takes no account of textures or surfaces, but reduces every thing to one monotonous dead level. Those who have felt the charm of an old beam with its adzed surface will be able to appreciate how all this is lost under the modern joiner's plane, and this is but one example among many of the degradation of modern craftsmanship in this respect.'[3] Scott saw the dining room as an adjunct to this hall rather than as a separate room: 'For such a household it seems reasonable that the partial incorporation of the dining room in the general house place should be adopted, so that during meals the family share in the warmth and spaciousness of the hall instead of being confined within a separated cell, which it hardly seems worth while to warm merely for its intermittent uses.'[4] He also expresses the forebodings of the architect who sees his designs ruined by his client: 'It is a painful thing for an architect to design a mantelpiece for which he dares not hope to choose the ornaments, and which may become a resting place for he knows not what atrocities in china and glass.'[5]

With this concern in mind Scott moved from the design of the house to the design of those things that went in it, furniture, textiles and ornamental metalwork. Aided by J.P. White's excellent workshops and smooth running publicity machine, Scott was able to create household objects that were exhibited in international fairs, widely illustrated and capable of being reproduced in quantity though not mass-produced. In the year of his arrival at Bedford he issued with J.P. White *Furniture Made At The Pyghtle Works,* 1901, with his own designs for chairs, chests and cabinets manufactured by the firm. These were avant-garde by virtue of their clean, clear lines and their use of traditional woods like oak and mahogany blended with less usual ones like holly. The forms of the furniture were based on earlier European models, the vaguano from Spain and court cupboard from England, but some like the cabinet exhibited at Dresden in 1903[6] seem Japanese in origin. Like Frank Lloyd Wright, Scott was influenced by Japanese art and advocated Japanese prints in some of his interiors. His furniture was more notable for its bold decoration than its shape and many of the designs have elaborate inlays in their doors and flaps, themes of blue birds and flowers in stylised art nouveau curves inset with pewter, pearl and ivory.

Scott's omnivorous interest in the house extended to textiles and embroideries. Writing in 1903 he said: 'In the consideration of the place of needlework in the house, it is necessary to remember that the embroidery should be made for the house, and not the house for the embroidery.'[7] He was against pictorial representations and preferred stylised ornament and 'broad appliqué' for the walls. He was concerned to break up the space for temporary needs and so advocated embroidery on curtains, *portières* and screens (several of his houses had movable wooden screens). He designed bedspreads, cushion covers and overmantel panels of repeating flowers, some of these worked for him by Mrs. Scott.

Scott's exposure abroad, particularly in Germany and Austria where the Wiener Werkstëtte and the Vereinigte Werkstaetten of Munich were gaining ground, brought him important foreign patrons. Between 1897 and 1898 he had designed interiors in the Palace, Darmstadt, for the art-loving Grand Duke of Hesse. At about the same time he created interiors for a forest retreat for the Crown Princess of Roumania. Scott, bohemian to the last, would turn up at these royal residences in casual clothes with little more luggage than a knapsack! His most perfect surviving dwelling was for another foreign patron, Theodor Buhler, the Swiss industrialist, in 1909 at Uzwil. The Landhaus Waldbuhl had all the Scott characteristics of careful planning, scrupulous woodwork and furniture and ornaments designed for their exact positions within the space, and Scott's correspondence and drawings for this house (a rare survival) were published by the Gesellschaft für Schweizerische Kuntsgeschicte in Bern in 1979. Scott's popularity on the Continent enabled J.P. White to open warehouses in Frankfurt and Dresden to meet the demand, where they remained in operation until 1914.

It was as well that Scott found such support in Germany, for he had

TERRACE HOUSE. THE LIVING HALL

precious little encouragement at Bedford where townsfolk were too stodgy to accept his democratic plans and unornamented spaces. He built two delightful cottages in the neighbouring village of Biddenham and a sprinkling of houses in Cambridge and Hertfordshire, not to mention some paired cottages and detached artist houses in Letchworth.

Living in a converted cottage at Fenlake near Bedford, Scott concentrated on the compilation of his master work *Houses and Gardens,* 1906. He illustrated it with his beguiling watercolours, deceptively simple in appearance but using subtle shades and washes to bring out the strong contrasts of his interiors. He took the reader through basic theories of design and planning 'Houses As They Are and As They Might Be', 'Some Forms of Plan' and then the needs of the householder room by room. It was an ingenious system, not blinding his readers by styles and science but seducing by reason and requirement. Simple modules were shown that any householder could understand and sections on 'The Soul of the House' and 'Colour'. Gardens were to be naturalistic and not 'at war' with nature, the siting of the house in its garden or landscape being the most important consideration.

In his classic work *Das Englische Haus,* 1905, Hermann Muthesius set the seal on what pioneering architects like Scott were doing: 'The end of the nineteenth century saw a remarkable spectacle of a new departure in the tectonic arts that had originated in England and spread across the whole field of our European culture. England, the country without art, the country which until recently had . . . lived on the art of the Continent, was pointing the way to the world and the world was following.' Scott was to write a further book in 1933, but *Houses and Gardens* was to be the benchmark of his success, almost the benchmark for his age, a time when there was leisure to consider every detail in a building and an abundance of craftsmanship to carry it out.

Simon Houfe
June, 1995

1 *The Studio,* Vol. 28, 1903, p. 191.
2 *The Studio,* Vol. 25, 1902, p. 86.
3 *The Studio,* Vol. 6, 1896, p.104.
4 *The Studio,* Vol. 32, 1904, p. 120.
5 *The Studio,* Vol. 6, 1896, p.105.
6 *The Studio,* Vol. 31, 1903, p. 57.
7 *The Studio,* Vol. 28, 1903, p. 283.

TERRACE HOUSE. VIEW OF PERGOLA. SHOWING USE OF WATER AND REFLECTED LANTERN, ETC.

INTERIOR OF A FLAT

A HOUSE IN POLAND. BEDROOM

TRECOURT. VIEW FROM SOUTH-EAST

ROSE COURT. THE PERGOLA AS SEEN FROM GARDEN ROOM

WHITE NIGHTS. HALL OR HOUSE PLACE SHOWING DINING RECESS

HEATHER COTTAGE. VIEW FROM WEST

HEATHER COTTAGE. VIEW FROM NORTH-EAST

HEATHER COTTAGE. THE HALL

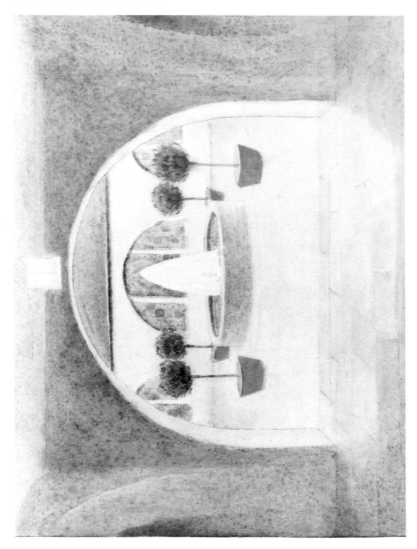

EVERDENE. THE INNER COURT FROM ENTRANCE

EVERDENE. VIEW FROM SOUTH-WEST

EVERDENE. VIEW FROM SOUTH-EAST

FALKEWOOD. THE DINING-HALL

FALKEWOOD. THE DRAWING-ROOM

INTRODUCTION

ONE of the most prominent features in the literature of the last few years has been the garden book, and so numerous have these publications become that every one may learn how a garden should be formed and how maintained. All the gardens described in these books are necessarily attached to houses, and the house as an appendage to the garden meets with a certain degree of attention; but the problems involved in house-building, furnishing, and decoration have hardly been treated with the consideration they seem to deserve. If this increased study of gardening is but the prelude to the consideration of the house, it may be taken as an augury from which much may be hoped. For just as one finds that the buildings of an agricultural community are generally well conceived, so the kindly influence of the garden may lead to the realisation of houses which may possess some of the kind of beauty which flowers and trees have. For the building and adornment of the house is surely the most important as well as the most human expression of the Art of man. We are apt to consider it in these utilitarian days as a trite formula – a matter of drains, wallpapers, and bay-windows – and we are apt to forget the possibilities of beauty which lie in mere building – possibilities which do not necessarily demand great expenditure for their development, but which may be realised in the simplest cottage. Those who dwell amidst the vulgar and impossible artistry of modern villadom may visit now and then some ancient village, and in the cottages and farm-houses there be conscious of a beauty which makes their own homes appear a trivial and frivolous affair; but such beauty is generally held to be incompatible with modern ideas of comfort and sanitation, and the lack of real comeliness in a modern house is often held to be a necessary concession to practical demands.

And so the art of building as practised in modern times is not so much an Art as a disease. In the early stages of the Victorian era it took the form of a pallid leprosy. Nowadays, it has become a scarlet fever of red brick, and has achieved a development of spurious Art expressed in attempts to achieve the picturesque, which in its smirking self-consciousness has made the earlier candid ugliness appear an almost welcome alternative. There is no town or village but is being gradually disfigured by this plague of modern building, and one has almost forgotten that houses have been and may yet be an added beauty rather than a disfigurement to the land. And in matters of furniture and decoration one finds the same spurious art on all sides, so that the modern house of the average citizen has reached a stage of degradation which might be a subject for ironic laughter if it were not for the pity of it. The serene and earnest beauty of the old house is everywhere being replaced by a superficial smartness posing as art. It is difficult to know where to turn to escape from this oppressive nightmare of hideous building. Here and there one may find houses built and furnished with sincerity, but these are comparatively so few that they appear but as drops in the ocean. It is doubtful whether education will provide relief, for it is mainly the modern Board-school which provides the most convincing object-lesson of the degree of depravity of which building is capable. Nor is it possible to hope for much from the Church, where building activities have recently been mainly concerned with the disfigurement of the ancient glories of its buildings and in the construction of elaborate and unconvincing forgeries of an obsolete art.

It might be supposed at least that all this ugly building would be attended with some compensation of a practical kind, and that the modern villa would at least possess utilitarian qualifications. But here again one finds that so far from being in any way adapted to the real requirements of its occupants, it is designed in accordance with a tradition which is based on the life and habits of the occupants of a mansion. The best part of its limited space is set apart to impress the neighbours, and the family is confined in some plastered rectangular cell which is already crowded with unnecessary and pretentious furniture.

But enough has been said, perhaps, to show that there is an urgent need for reform in the plan of the average modern house, and, apart from artistic considerations, it is at least desirable that it should be rationally designed. It has often been urged that a house should express and conform to the special needs of those for whom it is built. But while this is certainly desirable it may be questioned whether houses of special type should be extensively built. A house has to meet the requirements of many occupants, and it seems reasonable that one should bear in mind in its construction as to how far it is adapted for general demands.

In the design of houses for various clients of moderate means, I have been led to conclude that it is possible to deduce a normal plan which meets the requirements of the average family, and that variants from this constant type of plan are to be found rather in appendages to the plan than in any essential modification of its central features. Instead of a conception of the house which presupposes the collocation of a number of compartments which in the smaller houses become each too small for comfort, it is suggested that the house rationally planned should primarily consist of at least one good-sized apartment, which, containing no furniture but that which is really required, leaves an ample floor space at the disposal of its occupants.

The private apartments for the individual members of the family may then be considered as subsidiary to the central dominating room, and in some cases some of these may take the form of recesses in it. In cases where limited means demand a smaller type of house this should still consist of its central ample floor space, and restrictions should be met by giving up secondary rooms, while the bedrooms should constitute the private apartments of the various members of the family group. In this way even the labourer's cottage still retains its hall, which has now become kitchen, dining-room and parlour. In thus aiming at realising completely a simple type of plan rather than in striving to attain a cheapened version of a more complex design is salvation to be found for the small householder.

That the principles of house planning thus briefly suggested, and which are further developed and exemplified in the following pages, are something more than impracticable dreams, may be partly shown by the evidence of those who have built houses designed on these lines, many of which are illustrated and described here.

Since January 1895, when I first illustrated in the *Studio* a scheme for a house, I have been flattered by many realisations of my plans for houses in various parts of the world. While some have had the justice to realise that an artist should be given the opportunity of developing his own conceptions, others less scrupulous have consigned the matter to other hands, and the plans have suffered much from unsympathetic treatment in this way. So much depends on the careful working out of the details to meet each particular case, so much in the choice of materials and in adaptations to local conditions, that a plan realised in this way must necessarily differ widely from the original conception; and inasmuch as it is not the reputable architect who is willing to appropriate the plans of his contemporaries, these houses have been for the most part merely caricatures, which have done much to bring undeserved discredit on the principles they profess to follow.

So much has been ably written on the subject of the Garden, that I have confined my remarks here chiefly to a few broad principles with a special reference to the economic question. To those who wish to study the subject I would recommend a careful perusal of Miss Jekyll's books which may be taken as an infallible guide.

HOUSES AND GARDENS

In the chapter "on making the best of it," I have endeavoured to show how a suburban house may be mitigated by judicious treatment. The man who lives at St. Mildred's or The Pines might, after re-christening his house more appropriately as "The Crime," seek to reduce its pernicious influences by some such means as I have endeavoured to describe.

In the design of the modern flat I have tried to show how the same principles advocated in the plan of the ordinary house are applicable.

In the discussion of the terrace house it is shown, I think conclusively, that the universal standard plan is based on irrational fallacies, rather than on real requirements, and that the question of varying aspect alone demands a corresponding variation in planning.

In the consideration of cottages it is urged that their cheapness should only be such as may be consistent with comeliness and comfort, and that the plan should be the outcome of actual requirements based on the habits of life of their occupants.

Some types of holiday houses are illustrated, and it is suggested that in such buildings a greater fancifulness is admissible than in houses for every day occupation.

It has always seemed to me impossible to consider the matter of furniture and decoration apart from house building with which they are so intimately related, and the architect who attempts to achieve a satisfactory interior must necessarily to some extent control these important factors. While in the space at my disposal I have been unable to deal with these matters in detail, I have endeavoured to indicate a few guiding principles.

In conclusion, it may be well for me to anticipate certain criticisms by stating that I profess no expert knowledge in the arts of literature or illustration. It is my business to design houses and their appointments, and the work of preparing this book has been done in leisure moments snatched from the time which must be devoted to the labours of the architect. It is my hope that this may afford some excuse for the manifold shortcomings of a work which necessarily constitutes a very limited and inadequate treatment of a subject of such illimitable scope.

CHAPTER ONE

HOUSES AS THEY ARE AND AS THEY MIGHT BE

THE popular conception of the artistic house is that it is a fancy dwelling in which the claims of Art override practical requirements. It is often held to represent indulgence in the æsthetic faculties which can only be obtained at the expense of material comforts. Like those early prints which were sold at "a penny plain and tuppence coloured," houses are broadly divisible, it may be supposed, into two classes – the plain and every-day house, unattractive and practically useful, which may be obtained for a penny or its equivalent; and the Art house, which is only for those who can afford the luxuries of life, and who, living amidst the coloured glories of the tuppenny house, cheerfully accept these beauties in exchange for mere material advantages, or as a costly addition to these.

That such a conception is not without a basis in facts must be admitted, and the demand for spurious Art, which the little knowledge of modern Art education so readily inculcates, is met on all sides by those who cater to the wants and the whims of the public.

The house which, for want of a better word, we must continue to differentiate from the ordinary house as "artistic," bases its claims not on its frillings and on its adornments, but on the very essence of its structure. The claims of common-sense are paramount in its plan, and its apartments are arranged to secure comfortable habitation for its inmates, and to reduce labour in service or cleaning to a minimum. No dusty carpets cover its floors. Its windows are not cloaked with elaborate curtains and blinds. Its apartments are not crowded with useless and unlovely furniture. It aims at fulfilling no popular conception of what a house should be, follows no fashion, and apes not its neighbour mansion. If restricted resources necessitate that it should be small, there is yet no sense of cramped accommodation, because restrictions have been met by frank concessions. It is a roomy and commodious cottage, not a mansion in miniature, while under more generous conditions it attains the true dignity of the country house, and does not ape the cottage.

In its construction the exposure of every feature of the building is not necessarily involved, and though the structure indeed largely contributes to the beauty of the house, it is often obscured to meet practical requirements, or to supply surfaces for plain spaces of pure colour or thoughtfully conceived decoration. The furniture, too, reveals little trace of conscious effort. It does not pose or smirk or in any way insist on our attention to its artistic perfections, but is modest and serviceable, and rests its chief claim for existence on the possession of those qualities. It is fitted for its purpose, and is not necessarily made of expensive or highly-finished materials. In such a realisation of a house, that same reasonableness which is claimed as a basis of the whole fabric forbids the attempt to achieve many of the beauties which belonged to the houses of the past. Old work is, indeed, carefully studied, and the principles which governed it followed. Old models are often taken for the features of the house and its furniture, but these are necessarily changed and modified to meet modern conditions and limitations. The Art of the people which flourished in the past is now extinct, and so we can no longer enrich our houses and furniture with carving and painting. The wit and fancy of the old workman which found such a field for its display in the woodwork of old houses is no longer available; and only those who can afford to employ the few surviving artist craftsmen, or those incapable of discerning the gulf fixed between the old work and the new, may dare to decorate their houses in this way. In the meantime, and until Art again revives, whitewash represents a temporary expedient which has much to recommend it, and "when in doubt, whitewash" might well be taken as a maxim to be followed in the decoration of the modern house.

Before proceeding to consider the possibilities of the house as it might be, it may be well to glance for a moment at the house as it is. Every one who has experienced the disappointments of a search for a dwelling will probably willingly concede that the average modern house is not remarkable for convenience or beauty, and under the conditions which govern its production it is not strange that this should be so.

The majority of small houses especially are designed and built by men who have no knowledge or skill in planning, and whose notions and habits of thought are entirely commercial. The higher skill has been mainly employed on the larger houses, and the small ones have been consigned to the jerrybuilder, who has built them as we see them, so that one is led almost to forget that a small house can be made both comfortable and comely, and that in its expression of modest homeliness and simplicity it may often put to shame the pretensions of its larger neighbours.

Not alone, however, it must be confessed, is the builder to blame for the demerits of the small house. It may be said that he is the wise man who builds houses for fools to live in, and too often the occupier of a small house is in love with its very defects. He admires the front elevation with its bay window and the leaded glazing in the front door, and hangs his pictures and arranges his furniture with a touching assurance that all this is as it should be, while his wife receives her friends in her little drawing-room with a rooted conviction as to its undoubted elegance. Or again, it would appear that the modern householder, like the hermit crab, is the outcome of a series of concessions, and has finally become adapted to a dwelling designed less with a view to his comfort than to the profit of its possessor. But still there is a section of householders who have no illusions as to the beauty of their dwellings, and who cannot reconcile themselves to their defects, and this class, it may be hoped, is a growing one.

There is yet, however, a further stumbling-block to be found in the blind, irrational following of tradition in house-planning. The modern cottage almost invariably strives to include within its restricted space the features of the mansion. So it misses the excellence within its easy reach in its futile attempt to ape its larger neighbours, and, like the dog in the fable, is left bereft of the substance while it grasps at the shadow. This method of house-building is still further encouraged by the commercial classification of houses in the market. There is the house with two reception-rooms, and next above it in the scale of excellence the house with three reception-rooms. A bay window is a further asset; and so houses are valued, not in relation to the skill and thought displayed in their planning, but by the degree in which their interior has been subdivided into rectangular compartments, and again by the number of excrescences in the shape of bay windows, &c., which they possess.

Houses which might have been much more reasonably and economically built as a terrace are thus placed a yard or two apart in order that they may be described as detached; and the space in the plan, which might have been devoted to a much-needed pantry or added to the dining-room, is partitioned off to form the third sitting-room, which will raise the house a step in the house agent's scale of excellence.

While urging that improvement in the plan of the modern house, and the small house especially, must chiefly consist in the converse of this commercial evolution, and that conventional ideas must be sacrificed to secure at least one room of reasonable size, I do not advocate the pushing this principle too far. In a neurotic age it will not be wise to try and emulate the simplicity of the earliest types of plan, where all the various functions of the domestic life were discharged in one apartment; and the desk for the student, the grand piano and the cooking-range are necessarily incompatible occupants of the most commodious "house place;" and when used simultaneously one may well imagine that the view from the open gallery, which overlooks and in overlooking destroys the privacy of the whole, would not be entirely harmonious. The whole problem of the modern house is thus necessarily an attempt to secure those opposing qualities of privacy and spaciousness, and the plans illustrated show various methods in which this has been more or less successfully achieved.

It must not, however, be too hastily assumed that a rational reform in the planning of houses will be readily welcomed by the occupants of the modern villa, for no subject is so surrounded by every kind of cant and illusion. Those who exclaim against the restrictions and inconveniences of the modern house would be the first to object to the sacrifice of its imaginary qualifications for the real comforts of life. The greater part of the inconvenience and discomfort of the modern house is due partly, it is true, to the ignorance of its builders, but mainly to the prejudices and conventional standard of its occupants. The small house is regarded not as a roomy cottage but as a mansion in miniature. Like the immortal Mrs. Wilfer, its occupants are anxious that we should believe that though they live in a small house, "male domestics are no rarities to them;" and so we find the modern house, with its tissue of pretentious absurdities and inconveniences, chiefly explained, inasmuch as it is the exponent of the ideals of its occupants, who have set the possession of that gorgeous male domestic as a sort of counsel of perfection, an impossible and long hoped-for ideal to which all must be sacrificed.

And so the drawing-room is made worthy of his presence by imitations of French furniture, and the dining-room is duly enriched with its appointed carved and fumigated oak. The shadow of the flunkey broods over the whole establishment.

The man who is sincere enough to see the unworthiness of such ideas, and who is wise enough to regard the small house as a large cottage rather than a restricted mansion, will demand planning and furniture on totally opposite principles to those usually followed. He has no wish to emulate his neighbours in the matter of fashionable furnishings and methods of life. He has a settled conviction that the simplest form of life is the worthiest and most reasonable, and that true progress lies not in multiplying and complicating the appointments of the house, but in reducing them to the lowest effective limit. He does not consider the house to be a place for the display of furniture and bric-à-brac, but primarily a home for human beings, planned for their comfort, convenience, and pleasure. He demands in the planning of his house, besides practical comforts, that kind of beauty which is inherent in the structure, which depends largely on proportion, and does not require furniture for effect. And so in the broad simple spaces of his roomy cottage he disposes his few belongings. He has no wish to reproduce the departed glories of any of the popular styles. These fantastic and histrionic revivals find no place in his home. He is content with simple and straightforward joiner work. Neither is he anxious to cover every square inch of his walls and ceilings with pattern, and he is quite unimpressed by the wares of the trade decorator, with his embossing and stamping and gilding. These things are familiar to him in the houses of his friends, in his club and his hotel, and at home he would have rest. Not that he has entirely abjured decoration in his home, but it must be for him not the seductive cleverness of the trade artist, but the best product of the heart and brain; something, too, individual and peculiar. In the meantime, white-wash will do well enough.

For the rest, he has an eye for detail, and as far as possible he tries to secure good and thoughtful design, not only in his house but in all its appointments, and so his knives and forks, his china and glass, all bear the impress of thought and feeling in design and manufacture. Nor does he stop here. The very simplicity and unpretentiousness of his surroundings are eloquent in suggestions for the ritual of his daily life, and just as he does not wish to imitate the mansion in his modest dwelling, so is he less willing to ape the habits of its occupants. When he asks a friend to dinner, he does not seek to impress his guests by the multitude of his courses or the magnificence of his plate. He may indeed be quietly proud of the homely beauty of his surroundings, but it is a pride which is based not on their costliness, not on their price in the market, but rather on such qualities as fitness for their uses and beauty of line, colour, or texture.

In the furnishing of his house he has been careful to exclude all but the absolutely essential. He does not buy a table because he thinks it will "look well" standing in a bay window, and then proceed to find some ornament which will "look well" standing on the table. He might as reasonably first buy a mouse-trap on æsthetic grounds, and then a supply of mice to enable it to fulfil its functions. He knows better than to occupy valuable space with unnecessary articles of furniture, and is not without experience, perhaps of that strange and dreadful tyranny which these mere inarticulate objects are capable of exercising over their so-called possessors, now become their slaves. But here he touches on the confines of a great cult, a religion whose votaries are to be found in almost every family. These household gods are enshrined in rooms willingly given up for their occupation and sacred to their worship. They have no use, they have no beauty even. They are gods, and it remains but to worship them, keep them clean and hidden from the vulgar gaze. From this idolatry the modern householder must be set free before it becomes possible to achieve domestic surroundings which are rational and beautiful.

In seeking for a basis for a plan the governing factor will necessarily be the requirements of the average family, and if the matter is considered carefully, it will be found that these requirements represent a fairly constant quantity. It is important that the plan should be adjusted to meet these requirements, and that the accommodation provided should neither be too large or too small; for the large house is not always a thing to be desired. It necessarily involves not only expenditure in building, but also expense in maintenance, and so it is apt to become a costly incubus to its occupants. On the other hand, a house which is small and cramped is still less to be wished for, involving as it does a loss of privacy and much friction both physical and mental between its inmates. A house should be spacious enough to allow of its occupants to move easily about without getting into each other's way or tumbling over the furniture, and compact enough to make it easily and economically cleaned and worked. More than this, the average family should not require, nor should it be contented with less, and while the house should contain all the best appliances for saving of labour it should also minister to the mind, and represent the striking of a nice balance between the utilitarian scientific ideal on the one hand and the æsthetic on the other. Whatever beauty it possesses should be based on sound and rational planning and construction. In its features it should not aim at realising the latest things in doors, fireplaces, or windows, but the simplest and most rational type of these, and its beauty will largely depend in the omission of much which is vulgar, unnecessary, and expensive in the ordinary house. In gloomy weather, it must provide an interior in which one will not find it irksome or unhealthy either for mind or body to be confined, and a haven which will go far to compensate for sunless days.

If, with a view to secure these good ends, the family unit is subjected to analysis it will be found to be capable of division into two factors, the family and the servants representing two alien communities to be sheltered under the family roof. No longer do the early conditions obtain which made it possible for these to co-mingle, and for the comfort and wellbeing of each it will be well that they should each have a certain degree of privacy. Again, the family itself is divisible into parents and children, and outside the family itself the claims of the visitor must be considered. It is, indeed, the claims of the visitor in the traditions of the mansion applied to the smaller house which has played such havoc with house planning, and which has led to the conception of the family rooms as reception-rooms, arranged primarily to impress the guest of the hour, and which has made the best sitting-room too fine for daily use, and has set apart the best bedroom as a spare room, perhaps hardly ever occupied.

The average house should not be a place primarily for the reception of visitors, but a dwelling for a family, and the only impression the unfortunate visitor will receive segregated amidst forbidding furniture in an unaired and obviously unused room will be mainly one of discomfort. The house should then be designed essentially for its occupants, and should consist mainly of one good sized apartment, with plenty of floor space and elbow room, and with only such furniture as may be actually required. This room or house place, with its ample fireplace and broad spaces of floor, may, perhaps, be carried up nearly twice the height of the other rooms, which may be low and small. If, however, a gallery is introduced, it should be provided with shutters to secure privacy and freedom from draughts. The dining-room may either be a small separate room, or it may consist of a recess arranged as shown in the plans illustrating these remarks, and described fully later on.

The other appendages to this central room, inasmuch as they are for the occupation of separate members of the family, may be reduced considerably in size. Those which demand an absolute privacy will be completely cut off from the house place, while others in which privacy is not so essential may be included in the central idea of the house, screened from the house place as required by sliding doors or curtains only.

There will thus be a ladies' room or boudoir, which will also be used for the reception of those visitors who are not received in the house place itself, a room for the children, and a man's room which may be devoted to the particular hobbies of the master of the house, and christened accordingly as a "den" or "study." Many modifications of such a scheme may be made to meet limitations of cost; but the essential principle insisted on is that the smaller kind of house, instead of being subdivided to the greatest possible extent into tiny compartments, should at least contain one good-sized room, which, by such devices as sliding-doors, can be made on occasion still larger. The arguments advanced in favour of such a reform have designedly been entirely practical ones; but from the artistic point of view it may be urged that success in planning can only be achieved by a conception which has a focus. The house which merely consists of a series of separate compartments conveys to the imagination no definite coherent expression. To the family crowded into one of these rectangular cells, the house for the time being is limited by the walls of the room they are occupying, and the remaining rooms, some perhaps rarely inhabited, are each distinct and separate, bearing no relation to the whole scheme.

It is not alone necessary, however, that the apartments of the house should be well designed and arranged in due relation to their functions. It is important also that the routes of passage of the various members of the family units should be carefully studied and arranged without undue waste of space in passages. The hall or house place, while forming the central idea of the plan, must not be a passage-room for servants or visitors. The servants should be able to reach all the other rooms and the front entrance without passing through it, and the room appointed for the reception of visitors who may not be on terms of intimacy which would warrant their reception in the house place itself, should be reached from the front entrance without infringing on the privacy of the family. In some cases the children may have their special entrance from the garden and special staircase, and a separate staircase for the servants is often desirable. The extent to which this isolation of routes may be carried out in the plan depends greatly on the particular circumstances of each case. It must not be pressed too far, and in that judicial balance of advantages and disadvantages of which the plan is the outcome, it may often be to some extent deliberately ignored.

So far I have dwelt on the economical side of house-planning, mainly because it is in the house for the average family that reform is most urgently required. Where space is necessarily limited and precious, it is of great importance that it should be made the most of. The defects of the present house, it has been shown, are chiefly due to a blind and unreasoning adherence to obsolete traditions and to the abortive attempts to produce on a small scale the appointments and apartments of the mansion rather than to realise on a large scale the cottage plan. It has been urged that the number and arrangements of the subdivisions of the whole house space covered by the roof should be governed by actual requirements, which, in the case of the average family, represent a fairly constant quantity, and the house evolved on these principles should be at least approximately suited to actual uses, expanding into spaciousness where the members of the family meet together, and contracting to a minimum in rooms occupied by its individual members. In cases where the uses of such smaller apartments do not demand an absolute privacy, these may take the form of recesses in the central common room, and the application of these principles to the plan suggests at once the dining recess. In other cases, where the intermittent use of a room occurs for purposes which do not demand absolute isolation from the common room, sliding-doors or even curtains may be found sufficient to give the required privacy, while in such rooms as those devoted to the play of the children or the work of the master of the house, a more complete isolation is demanded, in the one case to shut noise in and in the other to shut it out.

While it is probable such a conception of the house will not recommend itself to the followers of an irrational tradition, on the other hand the dawning spirit of a more rational era tends to a utilitarian ideal no less to be deplored. The house here represents a congeries of conveniences, and in its wholesale rejection of the beauties of the old world refuses to admit features and principles which belong to all the ages. It is the part of the modern architect to fall into neither extreme, but to study and weigh the qualities and defects of the old houses, and, having inwardly digested the lesson they have to teach, to use the knowledge gained in a rational way.

But if it is undesirable that the dweller in the small house should aim at a cheapened version of his richer neighbour's abode and manner of living, it is still less the part of the man who is able to build and maintain a large house to imitate the cottage qualities, and achieve the cottage "with the double coach-house."

The curious affectation which has led to the reproduction of the farmhouse kitchen, with dishes and domestic utensils displayed instead of vases and knicknacks in a household where such a room is a sort of artistic toy, is but an extreme example of many such conceits. The importation of milking-stools and spinning-wheels into our drawing-rooms are but other examples of the same tendency to bring the cottage into the mansion. One feels at once a sense of the incongruous in such affectations, just as one would in an assumed artlessness of manner in the mistress of such an establishment. And examples might be multiplied of a like inconsistency of varying degrees of affectation. One of the least to be condemned is possibly the building of a large house as a magnified cottage, a method for which precedents are not wanting in many modern examples of domestic architecture. In the old days, a large house was usually a dignified structure. It expressed a certain quiet stateliness of planning and furnishing, and in the old English manor house one found the straight vista of the carriage-drive leading to the square forecourt, with the front entrance of dignified aspect. Without vulgar ostentation the whole effect was one of quiet, homely dignity, not rejoicing in expense for the sake of expense, but for the sake of beauty and fitness.

The large house will be chiefly marked by the number of its specialised rooms, which, however, should still combine to form an ensemble focussed in its central hall. It will further be distinguished by the use of materials which are beyond the means of the occupant of the cottage, and by the introduction of ornament of real beauty in design and workmanship. It will admit of the realisation of decorative schemes, which still retain their quality as a background and setting to life.

Too often, the large house with its collections of furniture and ornaments degenerates into a private museum, of which its owner is merely the custodian, and which in many cases drive him to seek escape to more congenial surroundings, leaving his house unoccupied for the greater portion of the year. In such excursions he indulges further that vice of indiscriminating acquisitiveness which has already crowded his house with objects of Art. It becomes a show place exhibited on the appointed day to the hushed and admiring groups of tourists, who absorb with interest the parrot-like utterances of its custodian.

Such a development of the house may have points in its favour when its treasures are of real worth and arranged and chosen with discretion. But at its best it is not a home in the true sense at all. Like the public museum, it represents a kind of workhouse of the Arts, where furniture and china made for every-day use, and claiming our admiration chiefly in their adaptability to definite functions in the domestic life, rest like able-bodied paupers on a bench in inglorious idleness.

The true place of Art is in the service of every-day life, and beautiful furniture should be found fulfilling its function in the home rather than crowded in the museum, where the worship of its beauties becomes a kind of dilettante cult.

In the days when beautiful things were made every day as a matter of course, there were no museums and no Art Galleries, and the whole art force of the nation was beneficially spent in the construction, adornment and furnishing of its buildings.

Instead, then, of founding a private museum, it may be urged that the man who builds a large house should resolve to achieve the highest degree of fitness and beauty in all its appointments, and in doing so he will be getting far nearer to the real qualities of the houses of the past than if he aims at a mere histrionic reproduction of the ancestral hall which gives him merely the outward semblances of a body from which the soul has fled beyond recall.

To consciously aim at achieving "style" in design, either old or new, is to follow a Will of the Wisp. For the pursuit of style, like the pursuit of happiness, must necessarily lead to disappointment and failure. Both alike are essentially by-products, and the quality of the by-product is in direct ratio to the worthiness of the ideal pursued. One may liken style to a jewel in the hilt of a sword, which flashes brightly when the blade is drawn in a worthy cause, and to which the warrior absorbed with the matter in hand will give but slight attention. It is a quality of the "flower of things" only to be gained by root culture, and he who aims at style is he who would paint the lily instead of watering it.

To produce a stately modern apartment, it is not necessary to disinter the Corinthian column, or to set the modern workman once more to carve that oft-repeated formula of acanthus leaves at the bidding of some blind pedant who has no eyes for the beauty of the flowers and trees which surround him. Such vain repetitions do but destroy our sense of the beauty of their originals.

It is well that the apartments of the mansion should be of stately and dignified aspect, but let it be a stateliness and dignity which is vital, local and modern, the new thought of a new age wrought with eagerness and care, instead of the trite and stale copyism of the forms of the past. It is not necessarily true, as many seem to imagine, that the only alternative of this copyism is a bizarre striving after originality and eccentricity of design, and which, posing as the "new art," is justly condemned by the judicious. New work which is based on the study of the past, which is sane, reasonable and vital, will only be considered eccentric from the point of view of those whose thoughts revolve round obsolescent centres. Apparent eccentricity is the necessary concomitant to every advance in thought, and new ideas revolve round a centre which is constantly moving forward. The impressions of the surrounding country reported by the vanguard must necessarily seem untrue to those in their rear, but gradually as these are pushed and hustled forward they reach the same standpoint and recognise the truth of the picture. Architecture as expressed in house building and adornment is like all human affairs, necessarily in a state of flux – to live is to advance; and so, while holding fast that which is good, let us still hope for that which is better, and not let our admiration for past glories blind us to the undreamed possibilities of the future.

CHAPTER TWO

SOME FORMS OF PLAN

IN making the plan for a house it will be necessary to banish from one's mind the conception of its interior as a mere group of isolated compartments, and to think of it rather as a central room surrounded by subordinated ones, some of which may in many cases form either recesses in the central apartment or communicate with it either by folding or sliding doors. In a house of average size it has been suggested that this central room may often be made two storeys in height, thus giving a large central air space and counteracting any feeling of confinement which might be experienced in a house where all the rooms should be as low as possible.

In economic building it will be wise to make the house itself of simple rectangular form, covered with a single span of hipped roof. A plain house

Fig. 1

Fig. 2

Fig. 3

is not necessarily an ugly house, and thus simplicity of form coupled with good proportions and unbroken eaves lines will often be more telling in its effect than unsuccessful attempts to achieve the picturesque. The site when this is much restricted will determine to a great extent the form of the house plan, but in cases where the conditions are fairly liberal it may be a question as to whether the plan should be square or long and narrow. The square house is warmer, as there is not so large a proportion of outside walls. It also covers more space with an equal amount of walling than the longer type of plan.

But it does not admit of a long south front, and so its rooms are not so sunny. Generally speaking, it is best to follow a middle course and to make the house long enough to secure a south aspect for the principal rooms, and wide enough across to keep the rooms with not too much exterior wall, and so to secure as far as possible the advantages of both types of plan.

In order to get that low snug effect which is so characteristic of the old English house, and which always seems desirable and appropriate in the country especially, the eaves of the roof are sometimes brought down to about the window sill level of the upper rooms, making the bedrooms partly in the roof. This may be desirable in certain cases, but as a rule it is better to keep the eaves at such a height that they are unbroken by the windows, and thus secure a simple outline and a larger attic space, which whether developed or not into rooms is always useful as a possible means of extension.

In departing from the rectangular form of plan, the first step consists in making an L-shaped plan by adding a projecting wing at one end, and this is often a very suitable form for a small house, while a further development of this is the T-shaped plan. If this form is then made symmetrical by adding a similar wing to the opposite end of the main roof and perhaps by also adding a central projecting porch the form arrived at would be as shown in Fig. 6, and this is often to be found in old English manor-houses, while a further extension of this form leads to a house built round a court (Fig. 7). Another form of plan which is without precedent in the past but yet has some special advantages is that shown in Fig. 8, and which is described fully later on.

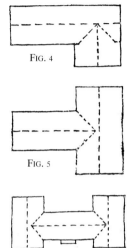

FIG. 4

FIG. 5

In all these forms it will be observed that the form decided on for the ground plan involves at once the plan of the roof, and these two factors of ground plan and roof plan are the primary factors in designing a house.

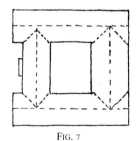

FIG. 6

Next to them the most important consideration is the height of the ceilings and the number of storeys; and in order to secure the horizontal proportions which are generally desirable, it is important that the ceilings should be as low as possible and the house not more than two storeys in height. The larger the house the less difficulty there is in this matter, as the extension of the ground plan makes the horizontal dimensions preponderate even with high ceilings; but in small houses, unless the ceilings are kept low, it is best to give up the

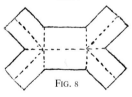

FIG. 7

FIG. 8

horizontal idea and to accept verticality as the characteristic of the design, although in the country especially this is an undesirable alternative.

Conditions of plan and the desire to achieve picturesque arrangements of roofing will often lead to more complicated outlines in the form of the house, though they will generally be traceable as developments of the types I have sketched. The success of such schemes will mainly depend on the balance of the roof plan and the satisfactory grouping of the masses of house from all points of view. It will also depend on the extent to which picturesqueness appears to be the outcome of practical requirements, rather than a quality pursued for its own sake.

In the consideration of house plans there is a tendency to consider only seriously the large house on the one hand and the labourer's cottage on the other; but, as I have already pointed out, the house which the average citizen requires has hardly met with the attention it deserves, while its plan is the outcome of a tradition which belongs essentially to the large house. The study of house planning, it is contended, may best be approached by considering the central type of plan required for the ordinary type of house, and showing how this may be expanded into the larger house and contracted if need be to its minimum dimensions. It is suggested that the hall as the central focus of the house would, in most cases, persist through the whole scale from cottage to mansion, and that changes in plan will chiefly consist in the modification of subsidiary apartments, the rooms required for the various members of the family, the guests and the servants. The family group, consisting of the parents and children, will demand for its members, besides the necessary bedrooms, &c., private sitting-room for master, mistress and children, while the accommodation for servants and visitors will vary in direct ratio to the size of the house. A reduction in size from a central type of plan will involve the elimination of separate private family rooms, in which case it is desirable that the bedrooms in some cases should be specially adapted for use as bed-sitting-rooms.

As the house expands in size, and includes the almost continuous presence of guests, the central hall with its adjoining rooms become more public in their character, so that separate suites of rooms may be required for family and guests, while the servants' quarters become correspondingly increased and subdivided. These large houses, however, are not possible for the average man; and these and the labourer's cottage represent the extremes of a scale of building of which the central type is the house of average size for more than which few should seek, and which it should be the triumph of the architect to make as perfect as restricted conditions may admit.

CHAPTER THREE

THE HALL

The room we came into was indeed the house, for there was nothing but it on the ground floor, but a stair in the corner went up to the chamber or loft above.

It was much like the room at the Rose, but bigger; the cupboard better wrought, and with more vessels on it, and handsomer. Also the walls, instead of being panelled, were hung with a coarse loosely-woven stuff of green worsted, with birds and trees woven into it.

There were flowers in plenty stuck about the room, mostly of the yellow blossoming flag or flower-de-luce, of which I had seen plenty in all the ditches, but in the window near the door was a pot full of those same white poppies I had seen when I first woke up; and the table was all set forth with meat and drink, a big salt-cellar of pewter in the middle, covered with a white cloth.

"A Dream of John Ball." William Morris

BEFORE considering the hall in the modern house it is necessary to return to the most primitive form of plan, when the house itself was the hall and served for every function of the domestic life. It was there the family cooked and ate their food. It was there they talked. And when night came it was on its rush-strewn floor that they slept.

Gradually, however, as civilisation advanced, special cells were developed from this unicellular type of plan, each adapted for its special function. And so the original simple organism became complex, and, as each cell became differentiated, the hall lost one by one its functions. There were parlours for talking, bedrooms for sleeping, dining-room for eating, drawing-room for withdrawing; and thus the hall itself became a superfluous and unnecessary adjunct – its occupation gone.

And so, like the tail of the crab, it began to dwindle, or, at most, it persisted like the buttons on the back of a coat, as a useless part of the plan, merely serving to connect the other portions of the house.

And thus we find this atrophied form of the hall in the shape of the narrow lobby with the staircase in it, which even in the smallest villa is still dignified by the ancient title. In modern times the revolt against the sordid ugliness of the Victorian house led those who aimed at recreating beauty in domestic surroundings to turn with an enthusiasm which was almost passionate to the study of the earlier types of plan, where the hall played such an important part. And so, amidst other features and details of the past, the hall became again a somewhat notable feature in the plan, and was considered almost an essential adjunct to the artistic house.

In the large house, where economic conditions of planning may give way to the fancy of the individual, this revival of the hall may perhaps be justified, and a sitting-room may well be sacrificed for the sake of a fine focus to the plan; but in the smaller houses, where every inch of space must be made the most of, such a hall was a somewhat expensive luxury, though, inasmuch as it is the mark of the modern mind to be incapable of conceiving beauty except apart from usefulness, the hall in this connection helped to give what is considered "artistic character" to a house. It was at least useless enough for that! In nearly all cases the hall so revived was essentially a passage room for the family, the servants and the visitors, and so whatever functions it might have performed as an additional sitting-room were lost. With its numerous doors, its open staircase and gallery, it was draughty and comfortless. And yet this revival of the hall, in spite of its obvious drawbacks and its practical uselessness, seemed to point to some dissatisfaction with the type of plan blindly evolved under economic conditions. In such an evolution it is not necessarily the fittest which survives, but only the fittest which man is capable of achieving step by step in an empirical way. It has been shown how by such a process, the house from a single room became gradually subdivided into a number of boxes connected by the dwarfed remains of the original room which now fulfilled the only function left to it and became a passage merely.

It has also been shown how such a house lacks coherence and consistency, and in the smaller houses how it leads to cramped conditions. Advance in planning no longer takes the form of a blind evolution; for the modern architect, with his essentially modern historical sense, looks back on the houses of the past, and consciously studies the plan of the modern house so that it shall be adapted for the real needs of its occupants.

And his first step is to revive the hall, but to revive it with a difference. It is to be a room where the family can meet together – a general gathering-place with its large fireplace and ample floor space. It must no longer be a passage, and the staircase must either be enclosed or banished from it. Whether it is called hall, house place, or living-room, some such apartment is a necessary feature as a focus to the plan of the house (see colour illustration p.11).

Of all the functions which such a room originally possessed the last to go was the function of feeding; and even when it became desirable for the ladies to retire to their withdrawing-room, and privacy in sleeping apartments was felt to be essential, the hall still remained a dining hall, and as such it might well remain in the modern house, where the function of dining is still the central and typical feature of the domestic ritual; for home life, even if conducted on the most approved principles of plain living and high thinking, is still to a large extent, it must be confessed, a question of meals. The family may or may not meet to talk or to study, but it is almost universally the custom to meet to eat. And so, to put the matter in another way, the central room may be obtained by an enlargement of the dining-room in the ordinary house and by a corresponding reduction in the other apartments.

But this reduction in some cases will make these secondary rooms somewhat small if they are entirely self-contained, and so it is further suggested that those which do not demand a strict division from the hall should be divided from it by folding or sliding doors, or even by curtains, so that they share in its spaciousness and appear rather as recesses than rooms claiming a separate individuality. If it is considered desirable that dining should not be the central function of the hall, the dining-room may form a recess which will be described later on. The process, in short, involves an examination of the evolution of the house, and consists in substituting a partial for a complete differentiation from the hall in cases where the functions of cells make it possible and desirable.

It is felt that to merely reduce the various special rooms to their minimum size and then to add a hall or living-room is not only expensive in that it adds to the already large number of special rooms yet another room, but that this room, so added, being deprived of all its functions by the special rooms, hardly justifies its existence as a dominant note in the plan. The term living-room for such an apartment is misleading; for life in the home is composed of so many functions, and when these are all provided for by separate compartments the hall or living-room must necessarily dwindle away. By retaining, therefore, those original functions of the hall which do not demand a complete isolation from it, either in the hall itself or where means allow in the form of recesses, the hall regains its ancient place and constitutes to a great extent the house.

It is only in the large house, indeed, that the spacious hall may still justify itself, although it still remains a passage. Here, as in the hotel, it constitutes an expansion of the route plan of the house, where one may observe, as it were, the full current of the household life. It bears much the same relation to the private rooms as the busy market does to the homes of the people who meet there.

CHAPTER FOUR

THE DINING ROOM

I entered the door, and started at first with my old astonishment with
which I had woke up, so strange and beautiful did this interior seem to
me, though it was but a pothouse parlour.

A quaintly carved sideboard held an array of bright pewter pots and
dishes and wooden and earthen bowls; a stout oak table went up and
down the room, and a carved oak chair stood by the chimney-corner,
now filled by a very old man dim-eyed and white-bearded. That, except
the rough stools and benches on which the company sat, was all the
furniture. The walls were panelled roughly enough with oak boards to
about six feet from the floor, and about three feet of plaster above that
was wrought in a pattern of a rose stem running all round the room,
freely and roughly done, but with (as it seemed to my unused eyes)
wonderful skill and spirit. On the hood of the great chimney a huge rose
was wrought in the plaster and brightly painted in its proper colours.

"A Dream of John Ball." William Morris

IF we assume the case of a family who meet in the evenings in one large
room with its comfortable fireside, and adjourn to a separate room for
dinner, high tea, or supper, or whatever form the evening meal may
assume, where a certain degree of economy in labour and fuel is
necessary, it becomes undesirable to light a fire in the dining-room, which
is only used for a short period. In many cases the difficulty is met by using
the dining-room as a sitting-room in the evening, and for this purpose it is
not always adapted. The dining-table is usually unnecessarily large, and the
available floor space is reduced to a narrow strip round this table, and this,
again, is further restricted by the sideboard and the chairs. And so a chain
of circumstances may have driven the unfortunate owner of the suburban
house to spend his evenings inexorably wedged between the dining-table
and the fire. In the whole space covered by the roof and enclosed by the
walls of his house there is room enough, if thoughtfully disposed, to afford
him a more spacious setting for life than this. The thoughtless application
of an obsolescent tradition has, in fact, ended in his being pushed into a
corner by insistent and triumphant furniture; and there for the present we
may leave him.

In the smaller types of house it may be, first of all, considered how far it
is desirable to use the central hall as a dining-room, or, in other words, to

make the dining-room large enough to serve as a hall or house place as well. This enlargement of the room will reduce considerably the main objection to such a scheme, and the lingering odours of the food will not be so much in evidence as in a small room.

By following an ancient usage, the table may be of the trestle or gate type, and may then be removed when not required and placed against the wall. But the arrangement which seems to meet the case most satisfactorily is the introduction as an appendage to the hall of a dining recess, of which several examples are given in the plans illustrated.

When the dinner is being laid the curtains which screen the recess from the room may be drawn across the opening, the table being laid from the small serving-room adjoining the dining recess, and so it is not necessary for the servant to pass through the hall at all. When the dinner is ready one may imagine the curtains drawn, displaying the table bright with dainty glass and flowers, lighted by a central hanging lamp or candles against the dark background of the seats. And so, apart from the obvious practical advantages, the effect would be far more artistic than the ordinary arrangement of the dining-table, which lacks focus, and from any point of view hardly composes pictorially. There would be something also specially charming from the dimly lighted hall, in the effect of the suddenly parted curtains, and that suddenly revealed brightness of glass and silver. Not only is an internal effect gained in this way, which is more interesting than the ordinary arrangement of the dining-table, but everything may be worked with a minimum amount of labour and with that quiet orderliness which may have been felt to be an impossibility in the cramped conditions of the small house. The position of the recess would be such as to allow of ample ventilation, and the serving would be done from the front unoccupied side of the dining-table, while, if on special occasions the recess proved too small to accommodate the guests, it might be supplemented by an additional table in the hall.

In seeking so to satisfy the claims of the imagination as well as the practical needs, one is tempted to take a step further in the process, and to dream of a table thus arranged, further adorned with piles of luscious fruit and nuts, rather than with steaming joints.

Vegetarianism, in a meat-consuming world, is yet for most of us a counsel of perfection. It is only those cast in heroic mould who can accept what Mrs. Earle, in her fascinating book, describes as "servants' cheese" as a substitute for tempting dishes. The non-meat eater at the board is in much the same position as the non-cannibal at a feast of "long pig;" but as it has been possible to wean the cannibal from preying on his fellow-man, so it may also be possible to wean the civilised man from devouring his fellow-animal, and the dining-table of the future household will no longer be disfigured by the family joint, or the streets of the future town by the butcher's shop.

In the further development of the dining-room as a separate apartment, it may appear as a room adjoining the hall, and preferably connected with it by a wide doorway. It should be so placed that service can be effected from the kitchen without passage through the other parts of the house. If it is still occasionally used as a sitting-room, a recessed fireplace is a desirable feature, especially when the room is not very large. The fire will not then scorch the backs of those seated at the table, and an ample space will be provided for a fireside circle.

Professor Kerr has insisted that a dining-room should be of northward aspect, and he has characterised a dining-room with a southern aspect as "oven- like." This dictum is largely due to the tradition of over-windowing rooms, which is still so much practised, for if the south dining-room is oven-like, all other southern rooms demand the same description. This matter will be pursued further when the windows of the house are specially considered; but this objection to the south dining-room is considerably modified in a house where the windows are of the horizontal rather than the vertical type, and where, while large enough to admit ample light, they are not so large as to make the room susceptible to every change in the external temperature. Modern science has shown that sunlight is the great health-giver and germ destroyer, and few rooms should be deprived of it.

A northward dining-room seems not unreasonable in large houses, where the number of other apartments confine its uses to luncheon and dinner merely.

THE DINING HATCH

Many objections have reasonably been made to the ordinary type of hatch between a dining-room and the kitchen premises. It often affords a passage for sounds, smells, and draughts, and also demands the services of two servants for its use. These difficulties may, however, be got over by making it in the form of a good-sized cupboard, having doors opening into the dining-room, and a little side door opening into a passage adjoining the kitchen premises or a pantry. The plan sketched here shows how this may be arranged. In such a cupboard a great many of the table appointments would be permanently kept, while the whole of the dishes containing the food for a

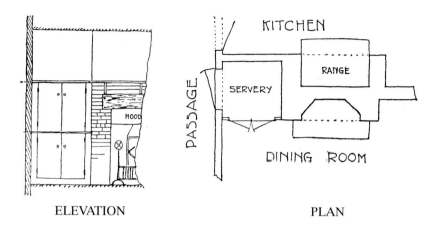

ELEVATION   PLAN

course would be placed in it from the side door. The servant would then enter the dining-room, and from the cupboard doors at the side of the fireplace the dishes, &c., would be removed and placed on the table. In many cases such an arrangement would involve a considerable saving of labour.

If the cupboard were made in two parts, as shown in the sketch, the lower part might then be devoted to the coal and wood for the dining-room fire, which would be put in from the side door.

CHAPTER FIVE

THE DRAWING ROOM

THE title of "drawing-room" is perhaps a little misleading in view of the uses of the modern apartment called by this name. It was used originally as a withdrawing-room for the ladies from the revelry of the dining hall, and this traditional usage still lingers. But since it was given its original title, the other members of the family have also been allotted their withdrawing-rooms, and the name as applied today is hardly sufficiently distinctive. It will be better to think of it as the ladies' or mistress's room, just as the study is the master's room, and it is here that the mistress of the house receives visitors, as it is in the study that the master receives his. Inasmuch, however, as it is usually the mistress who

55

presides over the social functions of the house, it is the drawing-room which becomes essentially the apartment for the reception of visitors. Its size and relative importance on the plan will depend largely on the extent to which the reception of visitors is practised by the family. It may safely be assumed that in most cases this will vary directly with the size of the house, and that those whose means are limited will not be prepared to entertain on an extensive scale.

To begin with the smallest kind of house, it may first be desirable to consider under what circumstances the drawing-room may be omitted altogether. The complete conception of a normal house plan would allot to each member of the family group, besides a share in the common room or hall, two private apartments, a bedroom and a sitting-room. The next reduction in the plan would be to substitute for these a single apartment – the bed-sitting-room. Let us assume then that the bedroom of the mistress of the house is so placed and so arranged that it is adapted for use as a sitting room. It may possibly, under these circumstances, be placed on the ground floor. As such, if properly planned, it might still to a certain extent be used as a private reception room. But how far is the hall adapted for the reception of visitors in such a household? It may be assumed that the master will be engaged during the day, either in his own room or at his business, and that the children will either be in the nursery or schoolroom or at school. During the whole day then the hall remains unoccupied; and there seems to be no reason why, except on special occasions, it should not be used as a reception room. It is by such deliberate concessions that the smallest kind of house can still retain its spaciousness, and there is no reason in clinging to the cramped drawing-room simply because somewhere in the remote past our ancestors were unduly merry over their wine.

The next step in the house where economic conditions are not quite so rigorous will be the consideration of the drawing-room as partially differentiated as a recess or appendage to the hall. This rudimentary treatment is to be found in the old Scotch cottages, where the working end of the single room was called the butt and the reception end the ben, and where a visitor was invited to "come ben."

It helps to preserve that wholeness of the plan which is so helpful in securing beauty in the home. Such a form of drawing-room I prefer to call the "bower," which admirably suggests its daintiness of treatment, and later on will be found an example illustrated and described. Open as it is to the hall it shares in its spaciousness, and in the warmth of the central fire, and its occupants do not feel that sensation of confinement which makes the small room so oppressive. It bears indeed the same relation to the hall as the verandah or garden room does to the outside world.

It has already been pointed out that the hall itself during the hours of the more formal calls will probably be unoccupied, and so the visitors in the bower need not be entertained in a separate apartment, while those more intimate friends who may pay a later visit require no isolation from the family circle in the hall.

In the larger establishment the drawing-room may be considerably increased in size, though the wholeness of the plan may still be retained by the use of sliding doors dividing it from the hall, giving on special occasions a large apartment. Or again it may become specialised as a reception room, so constantly used that it no longer fulfils its function as a private sitting-room for the mistress of the house. And so a boudoir is added to the plan for this purpose, and in special cases the germ of the bower develops into a series of state reception rooms, till the whole establishment becomes given up to the guests, and the family take refuge in a private suite of apartments.

CHAPTER SIX

THE STUDY

HAVING considered the mistress's withdrawing-room from the central hall, we must now deal with the master's withdrawing-room – the study or "den." In the first instance, considering the smallest kind of house, to what extent, it may be asked, is this a necessary extension of the plan? To the average occupant of the small house, who spends his days away from home and his evenings in the room occupied by the family, the study is not always necessary and would probably be seldom used. It would be, at any rate, worth giving up to secure a central apartment of ample size. If we assume a house already shorn of its drawing-room, with the bedroom of its mistress appropriated as partial sitting-room, where shall the master of the house betake himself on those occasions when he desires privacy and solitude? With the special retreats already provided for the other members of the household he may possibly claim the hall itself on these occasions, but the most suitable position for his retreat seems to be in the attics. Here a picturesque and attractive room can be formed with little expense. With a good roof, boarded and felted under the tiles, such a room will not be greatly affected by extremes in external temperature, and it will be sufficiently remote to ensure him an absolute quiet.

If, however, the study adjoins the hall, it may be separated from it by a solid wall, and possibly by double doors. It is in the development of the master's room that the special plan chiefly consists. For the literary or scientific man it will require a complete isolation from noise, and its constant use will justify the appropriation on its behalf of a somewhat greater portion of the house space than would otherwise be allotted to an individual member of the family group. For the artist it will expand into a studio, for the medical man into a consulting room, and perhaps a waiting-room, with their separate entrance. In the case of the artist, especially when a somewhat large room is desirable as a studio, under economic restrictions the central hall may perform this function during the day, when the other members of the family are engaged either in their own special retreats or outside the house, and thus this central hall will become the family room in the evening.

CHAPTER SEVEN

THE CHILDREN'S ROOMS

THE full complement of children's rooms required for the family will, besides the sleeping apartments, consist of three – the day-nursery for the younger children, the schoolroom and playroom for their elders. It is unfortunate that incomes do not vary directly with the size of families, and so the streets of a town often present the anomalous condition of large houses occupied by small families and small houses overcrowded with large ones. On a winter's night in London, for instance, one may observe the tenements of the poor crowded to overflowing with their occupants, while the streets, too, are occupied by those who have not even these apologies for homes; and yet there are thousands of empty rooms in the larger houses untenanted.

Restricted means make it necessary to substitute a single apartment for the night and day nurseries, in which case, if possible, the beds should be placed in a recess. Or, again, a single room may fulfil the functions of playroom and schoolroom. More rigorous conditions will demand that the elder children prepare their lessons in the hall, and will deprive the children of their private apartment, as it has already deprived the parents of theirs. It is still maintained, however, that these successive deprivations should be faced in the reduction of the plan, rather than the household be cramped by making the house consist of a number of small boxes, and in these cases its members should fall back on the bedroom for occasional use as a sitting-room. In many cases a portion of the roof-space affords a place for the children's playroom, and the form and position of the attic is very well adapted for this use. The children can make as much noise as they like without disturbing the other members of the family, and it is easy to adapt the structural timbers of the roof to support a swing and other furnishings of the gymnasium. A children's room on the ground floor may have its separate entrance to the garden through a sunny verandah, which will enable them to keep as much as possible in the open air.

It may be well to reconstruct our conception of the home and to consider it not so much a place for the reception of visitors as for the rearing of children; and in its planning the inclusion of at least one large room will be of the greatest benefit to the health of their bodies and minds. In houses where circumstances do not allow of ample accommodation for special children's rooms, it is urged that the central apartment should become to a great extent a place for their work and play.

It is no part of the scheme of this book to discuss the planning of schools, but it is so intimately connected with my present subject that I hope to be excused a brief digression. The private school is too often a building planned, and not well planned, for a house, and rooms intended for occupation by members of an average family are overcrowded with children. In Board schools special rules govern the planning and limit the occupants of its rooms, but in the average school no such rules are enforced or observed.

But even in the Board school an excessive zeal for light and air has led to an unnecessary expanse of windows, so that its rooms are subjected to every variation of the external atmosphere, and can neither be readily warmed in winter or cooled in summer. In warm fine weather children should be taught in the open air in sunny verandahs or garden-rooms. In winter they should be able to feel really indoors in the school, and not confronted with the glare of large walls of glass. Light and air they should have in plenty from windows of reasonable size placed in right positions; but an excessive expanse of window area, while it does not materially increase the light, destroys the whole function of a room as a shelter from external conditions.

CHAPTER EIGHT

THE KITCHEN AND OFFICES

THE planning of the kitchen premises, especially in small houses, is a subject which does not always receive the attention it deserves. In the early part of the nineteenth century the kitchen premises, even in country houses, were commonly placed in an ill-lighted basement, and the house was planned with a callous indifference to the great question of labour saving.

But the growing scarcity of servants, as well as the growth of democratic ideas, have led in recent years to a more careful consideration of the working of the house. It is now usual to place the kitchen premises on the ground-floor level, and where this is difficult, as in town houses, the basement is better lighted and provided with a lift. For the house of average size it is not desirable either to cramp or to unduly extend the kitchen premises. They should be the best size for their purpose, and the multiplication of offices, apart from the question of expense in building, means so much the more to clean and keep in order. The fittings of a first-class yacht might well be studied to show what can be done in a limited space; and although a more liberal space may be allowed in the house, all contrivances which make for compactness and simplicity are worthy of study.

In the smallest houses in this country it is usual to provide a kitchen which is the cooking-room and sitting-room for its one or two servants, adjoining which is the scullery; and these two apartments, often both very small, form the main portion of the kitchen premises. In modern American plans for small houses it is quite usual to combine kitchen and scullery into one apartment. The English tradition in this respect dates from the period of insanitary sinks, and the scullery was justly regarded as a place to be severely isolated on account of its offensive odours. But fitted with its white-glazed sink, its white-tiled dado, and its pipes properly disconnected and exposed, the well-ventilated and well-lighted modern scullery may in the small house at least, form a recess in the kitchen, and thus add to the simplicity of the plan. Besides kitchen and scullery, the small house should contain at least a good pantry, larder, coal store, and servants' w.c., all compactly and conveniently arranged – the pantry, with its shelving of scrubbed deal, the larder, with its slate shelves and ventilation of wire gauze, the coal store, large enough to contain a winter supply of coals if possible, and the w.c., with its door opening into the open air.

While the kitchen proper, which is not also a sitting-room, should generally have a northern exposure, in the small house its uses suggest a compromise, and a more cheerful aspect is desirable. South-east may be recommended, and assuming that it is not over-windowed, its temperature will not be unduly influenced by exterior conditions. The larder should face north, and not open off the kitchen, and the kitchen premises as a whole should be placed near enough to the living-room for convenience of service, and yet be completely isolated, so that even in the small house the noise and smell from the kitchen should not penetrate to the sitting-rooms. Although thin partitions may be used between certain rooms, the division between the sitting-rooms and kitchen premises should be at least of nine-inch brickwork. In the internal finishing of the kitchen premises, that structural finish which has been suggested for certain portions of the living-rooms will be specially appropriate. Such superficial finishings as varnished sanitary wall papers and linoleums may be suitable for the house built in the usual modern way, but tiles and the liberal use of whitewash are better. It may be desirable in the sitting-room-kitchen that the floor should be of wood. If so, the boards should be laid on concrete with no spaces for insects. Red tiles or stone are, however, better materials for the floor, and with a few rugs or mats will not have a cold appearance.

For the walls there is nothing quite so cleanly as white-glazed Dutch tiles. The harsh glaring tiles made by English firms have the same forbidding glare which sheet glass has, while the Dutch, with their soft uneven glaze, have an inviting and homely appearance. When means will allow, the lower part of the walls at least should be finished in this way, with whitewash above. For the woodwork green paint varnished and flatted is recommended. White paint shows marks too readily to be quite suitable for kitchen premises, or the woodwork may be in white wood specially selected and left unpainted. The tiled treatment of the walls should be extended as far as possible in the kitchen premises; but, where it is unadvisable, whitewashed brickwork will form the best finish for larders, pantries, &c., although, if the house is of stone, it will be desirable to plaster or cement the walls. For the ceilings whitewashed plaster or, where the joists are shown, whitewashed woodwork left rough from the saw will be the best finish. All pipes in the kitchen premises should be left exposed, and neither buried in plaster or concealed in casings. Everything should be capable of easy cleansing, and there should be as few corners as possible to collect dust and dirt. Without mentioning any special make of kitchen range, I should recommend that this important apparatus should be of a type which admits the use of the open or closed fire, and which has an arrangement for raising or lowering the fire as required.

CHAPTER NINE

THE BEDROOMS

THE position and size of the bedrooms if, as is usually the case, they are placed on an upper floor, will depend largely on the disposition of the ground floor. This, however, should not result in a haphazard arrangement, but ground floor and first floor should react on each other until an arrangement is arrived at which fulfils the conditions of plan required by each. The bed should be placed in such a position that it is free from draughts, and not exposed when the door is opened. It is desirable where possible that the bed should be placed in a recess, so that the room can, if required, be adapted as a bed-sitting-room. It is also an advantage, especially in a room where windows on two sides are possible, that the bedroom should have two windows – one of which, long and low, and provided with a window seat, may be left unobstructed. The other may be placed in such a position and at such a height that it will light the dressing-table which stands against it (see colour illustration p.19). Or where the windows are in one wall only, the dressing-table may stand in the space between two windows, neither of which is thus obstructed.

The fireplace will not take the dominant place in the plan which it enjoys in the sitting-room, and the bed instead will form the focus of the room. The fire, too, will be of a type which can be kept in all night without attention, and for this purpose the fire on the hearth is the best. For the average family a minimum of three bedrooms will be required. In the absence of a special dressing-room, a recess in the parents' bedroom may answer this purpose, or it may be arranged that the master of the house should use the bathroom as a dressing-room. In addition to the parents' room, there will also be a boy's bedroom and girl's bedroom, neither of which need be very large, and besides these a night nursery and a day nursery may be required, with one or more spare bedrooms. If a single apartment, specially planned, is used for a night and day nursery, and the spare bedroom not considered justifiable under restricted conditions, the requirements of the family can be met by a house containing four bedrooms.

In addition there will also be the one or more bedrooms required for servants. This it will generally be most convenient to place on the attic floor, and where the other attic space is not used a servant's attic can be arranged by dropping the kitchen floor a few steps below the general level, with a room over it correspondingly lowered, and thus an attic may be gained without raising the whole roof. It is generally desirable, however, to leave a certain amount of space in the roof which can be developed as bedrooms if required, not only to meet subsequent requirements of the family, but in the event of the house changing hands to admit of its accommodation being readily capable of being increased to a certain extent. This is the more desirable in special houses built for small families, which might not otherwise be readily adapted for normal requirements.

Although it is usual and generally convenient to place the bedrooms on an upper floor, where the conditions of planning suggest the desirability of one or more bedrooms on the ground floor, it will be wise not to let custom stand in the way of convenience. Bedrooms on the ground floor are specially adapted for partial use as sitting-rooms, and where the bed is placed in an alcove or recess, and screened during the day by a curtain, the room itself may open with folding-doors on to the hall and add to the general floor space. The furniture of the bedroom in this case would be of a special type – the dressing-table and washstand being enclosed with doors on the recessed portion, for the bed may be made large enough to include the appointments of the toilet.

CHAPTER TEN

THE BATHROOM

THE old country-houses of England can generally be adapted, without doing violence to their structure, to the requirements of modern life; and, with a few slight sacrifices of material comfort, it would be possible for a modern family to live in comparative ease in an old-world manor-house. In only one respect would it be wanting. It would contain no bathroom, and none of those sanitary appliances which the smallest modern villa can boast. It has been said that cleanliness is next to godliness, but historic evidence would seem to show that cleanliness has hitherto been the mark of the ungodly, and that it is only when man has ceased to concern himself with the things of the soul that he turns his attention to the care of the body.

In the development of the modern bathroom there is therefore no precedent in the tradition of the house, and in the average modern dwelling it will be well that the suggestion of spotless cleanliness and practical efficiency should be its salient characteristics. The floor and lower part of the walls of tiles, the bath and basin of white enamel with no pipes enclosed, with no dark corners to harbour dust and dirt, and the art of the bathroom as expressed in useless and dirt-concealing patterns rigorously excluded – such a scheme will, perhaps, represent the best that is possible for the average household. Under stricter economic conditions the floor will perhaps be covered with a plain linoleum, a cork carpet, and whitewash take the place of the tiled surface of the wall. The bathroom should be so placed that the plumbing is reduced to a minimum, and the whole system is as simple and compact as possible, free from possible damage by frost, and capable of repair in all its parts without interference with the structure of the house. The quality of mystery has its artistic value in the house, but in the matter of plumbing it will probably only be appreciated by the plumber. In connection with the bathroom in the small house it is generally possible to arrange a linen closet, which contains the hot-water cylinder, which serves the double purpose of keeping the linen dry and the bathroom warm. In a slightly larger house in addition to this general bathroom there may be a bath and basin fitted up in the master's dressing-room, and fitted washstands with hot and cold water in the bedrooms help materially to reduce the labour of the house. The housemaid's closet with its slop sink and space for pails and brooms, is also an important feature in the house. In larger houses each bedroom or suite of bedrooms will be provided with its separate bathroom, and here it will often be admissible to indulge in a bathroom which may possess some of the beauties of the classic baths. In the "House for an Art Lover" a scheme for a bathroom is shown in which a circular central bath lined with mosaic is surrounded by a marble pavement. The bathroom itself is octagonal in form, each angle being formed by a column, between which niches in the walls give spaces for special baths. The roof of blue mosaic represents a mimic firmament, from the centre of which showers descend at will. The whole of this interior represents an arrangement of broad slabs of marble, of which the most prominent is the green Irish Connemara, which, with its deep tones of varied green, seems to suggest the still depths of some mountain pool. To complete the colour scheme one must imagine the deep green tones of this marble relieved by the brightness of the silver fittings and the opalescent tints of the Norwegian midnight sun marble which appears to contain all the hues of a sunset.

The swimming-bath is a luxury which might well form a feature in the large modern house, and, if circumstances allow of the use of marble, mosaic and stained glass arranged in a definite colour scheme it would be possible to realise a dream of the enchanted palaces of fairy land. The bath itself, lined with mosaic of green, blue, purple, and gold, would appear as a little inland sea shimmering with colour. Around it would stand the white columns which support the blue dome, in which golden stars lean over the water.

Broad spaces of white marble would cover the surrounding walls, warmed to an opalescent beauty by the coloured lights from the stained-glass windows, and set with coloured marbles, used as jewels are in the white setting. In the effects of artificial light one may imagine a dim yellow moon reflected in the purple water, which would appear as that sea over which Goorelka sailed in her cockle-shell "enchanted even to the very bed."

CHAPTER ELEVEN

THE MUSIC ROOM

THE principles of acoustics are so little understood that it is difficult to advance any definite suggestion as to the best size or shape for a music-room. In most houses it is the drawing-room which usually fulfils this function; and, when crowded with furniture and draperies, the result is not usually satisfactory, as the sound becomes muffled and choked. Amongst other advantages of sparse furnishing and uncarpeted floors may be included the appropriateness of such surroundings in a room which is used for music. A room specially designed for music should have few draperies and rugs and no carpet. Panelling is the best covering for its walls, and the best position for the room is probably one where it is surrounded by other rooms. Thus, if it is on the ground floor it would be improved if placed over a cellar. In a large music-room a stage may be introduced with good effect, and this isolated floor for the piano will often improve the sound.

In some cases a gallery to a hall may be used for music, and this traditional feature may meet modern requirements in the most satisfactory way. It will be especially appropriate on festive occasions, and the position of the performers will help to give a quality of mystery to the music, which may add greatly to its effect.

MUSIC ROOM

CHAPTER TWELVE

THE BILLIARD-ROOM

IN houses which do not possess a separate billiard-room one may sometimes find the billiard table placed in the hall. This arrangement, unless the hall is of considerable size, can hardly be recommended, because not only is the floor space much restricted where an impression of ample space is much needed, but the central and dominant position of the billiard table in the plan suggests that the practice of the game is the essential domestic function. Such an arrangement would be suitable only for a professional billiard player, and the effect might then be emphasised by the modern Jacobean mantelpiece ingeniously adapted to serve as a billiard marker.

Much may be urged, on the contrary, in favour of an arrangement of plan which enables a recess in the hall to be treated as a billiard-room. Here a game of billiards may be indulged in by visitors, or members of the family, without sequestration in a separate compartment of the house, and the dislocation of the social circle thus involved.

The space devoted for the billiard table becomes added to the hall; and thus, without detriment to the general character of the hall, it becomes more spacious than if the billiard-room were planned as a separate apartment, and the players enjoy the advantage of the central fireplace. Where a full-sized table is used, this arrangement will only be entirely successful when the hall is sufficiently large to admit of the billiard recess taking a secondary place. Such an arrangement is shown in the plan and photographs of the house "Blackwell."

In the house described as "Trecourt" the billiard-room is shown as a secondary hall, large enough to admit of ample floor space apart from that required by the table and the players, and with a wide ingle fireplace under the gallery, which forms one end of the open timber roof.

In a more economic scheme it will often be possible to arrange a billiard-room either in the basement or roof space. In the former case the billiard-room will be more accessible, but not well lighted, unless, as in the plan illustrated of "A House and Garden in Switzerland", the fall of the ground admits of window space. This, however, will not be a great objection where billiard playing is an evening pastime. In the roof there will, on the contrary, be ample opportunity for top light, but in the average house of two storeys or more the use of the room will involve considerable climbing.

In these remarks on the billiard-room it is assumed that billiards is a game merely, and not a serious pursuit. The man who takes his billiards seriously will demand probably an isolated apartment for the billiard table. Inasmuch as he will not be content to play only in the evening or amidst the disturbing shadows cast by the side light from windows, it will be necessary that the room should be so planned that it is possible to light it entirely from the roof by means of a skylight, which should be the full size of the billiard table, and immediately over it; and the floor will be so constructed that the table is incapable of the least degree of vibration. But in the average household it will be enough if the billiard-room meets the not too stringent demands of the casual player, and in this case it will not require that special treatment which makes it unsuited for other uses. In its general treatment it is suggested that a certain informal and easy going character is more suitable than formality, and in its decoration the green of the cloth must be considered as the starting point of the colour scheme. The treatment of the shades to the light over the table gives opportunities of design in metal work, and the table itself is capable of great variety of design.

CHAPTER THIRTEEN

THE GARDEN ROOM

THE success which has followed the open-air treatment of consumption has led the modern world to realise the beneficial effects of an outdoor life; for if it can strengthen the body, and so enable it to throw off a disease apparently curable by no other means, it must surely help to prevent the healthy from contracting ailments. Human life, like plant life, flourishes in sun and air and grows pale and anaemic when it is deprived of these.

And so the garden is conceived as an outdoor extension of the house, with its sheltered apartments for sunshine or for shade.

But in our own inconstant climate it is not always possible to use the garden entirely. It is desirable, for instance, that meals should be taken in summer weather out of doors. But the constant removal of furniture alone would make this difficult for the average household, and so the need of a wide verandah or garden-room is increasingly felt. Here the necessary chairs and table can be left out without damage from a passing shower, and a certain degree of shelter be secured. On summer mornings breakfast in such a room will have much of the charm of breakfast in the garden without its disadvantages, and in the evening it will be pleasant to sit there and enjoy the prospect of the garden after a day perhaps spent perforce indoors. Such a room should be planned to be free from draughts, and should face south if possible. It should be wider than the ordinary type of verandah, so that it can be used as a room. The garden adjoining it should be arranged so that its most attractive vistas are commanded from the garden-room. It may often be formed by an extension of the roof supported by posts, or it may be included in the house plan and enclosed with arches. A room so arranged will often be welcome even in wet weather, and nothing but cold will make it untenable. It can be adapted for winter use by the introduction of movable glass screens, and thus become a miniature winter garden.

In some cases a similar feature may be included as an appendage to a bedroom, and such an arrangement is specially desirable in a sick room.

CHAPTER FOURTEEN

THE STAIRCASE

IN the planning of the staircase it is well that it should be in scale with the rest of the house. In a small house it should not be too extensive, but should represent the simplest and easiest way of getting up stairs, and not necessarily a feature in the effect of the interior.

It is not generally advisable to include an open staircase in a hall which is used as a sitting-room as it will often be a source of draughts, as well as somewhat detracting from the privacy of the room. The staircase is really part of the passage scheme of the house, and especially in cases where there is no second stair it should be so placed that its use will not interfere with privacy of the sitting-rooms. When placed in such a position, for instance, as that shown in the house described as "Bexton Croft," it can be used by servants and family without detracting from the privacy of the hall.

One of the great advantages of low-ceiled rooms, an advantage which is not always recognised, is that it reduces and simplifies the staircase, and makes unnecessary that long precipitous flight which is usually such a painful feature in the loftily-ceiled villa. It is generally desirable that the staircase should be broken up into short flights of steps with intermediate landings. Not only does this improve the appearance of the stairs, but it also makes it easier of ascent and less dangerous. There are probably few who have escaped from a tumble down stairs at some early stage of their existence; and in view of the prevalence of this method of descent amongst children, the division of the staircase into short flights is desirable. Besides the main staircase, smaller special stairs may often be introduced for convenience of access to special rooms. In the house previously referred to, such a small stair starts on the ground floor, at the side of the drawing-room window-seat. Here a panel opens by touching a spring, and this little stair affords a means of reaching the little gallery overlooking the hall and the bedroom beyond, into which it opens through a door which in the room appears as part of a fitment wardrobe.

In the "House for an Art Lover," spiral staircases are introduced at the angles of the building, which, besides affording a means of communication between certain rooms, also give access to the garden. Apart from their practical uses, these little staircases help to give to a house a certain romantic quality. Mere utility alone will never completely satisfy human demands in the home. It is well that a house should be nicely adapted to its uses, but, beyond such practical considerations, it should contain features which add to its mystery and charm.

Something may here be noted as to the general significance of steps and changes of level in the house. It may generally be stated that steps up to a room, or to any feature in the house, conveys at once an impression of dignity and importance. In the church such an impression is suggested by the steps to the altar, and the front entrance of a building always gains in dignity if approached in this way. On the other hand, what is gained in dignity is lost in homeliness, a quality which is accentuated by downward steps. Those old country cottages which one enters from a roadside, which is slightly above the level of the floor, owe much of their charm to this slight change of level.

Much of the artistic effect of changes of level in a house is due to the corresponding changes it affords in the point of view; and in stepping down into a room from a higher level, from which one looks down on the interior, an impression is gained which differs materially from the normal, and whatever quality of homely comforts an interior may possess will be much accentuated when approached from a higher level.

CHAPTER FIFTEEN

ACCOMMODATION FOR FAMILY PETS

I AM not aware that any special modifications of plan have yet been made to meet the demands of the family pets. I do not suggest that the fitting of the ingle should include a special niche for a dog or cat, for such is the contrary nature of these animals that it is doubtful whether such accommodation would be appreciated or used. It is the same spirit which makes them whine or scratch at a closed door which has been open five minutes before and which must often be opened again in deference to a change of plan in the movement of the cat or dog. In view of this erratic disposition in these animals it might be reasonably suggested that a little passage made in the thickness of a wall or chimney breast might be introduced, provided with self-closing valves or doors hung from the upper edge.

This would allow free ingress and egress without draughts, and the animals would soon learn how to push open these little doors.

Such an arrangement in connection with a chimney stack might even be made large enough to afford a sleeping place for a cat or dog, and its position near the fire would make it warm and dry.

Such arrangements would probably appeal only to lovers of animals, but I feel sure would be appreciated by those who are in the habit of keeping family pets.

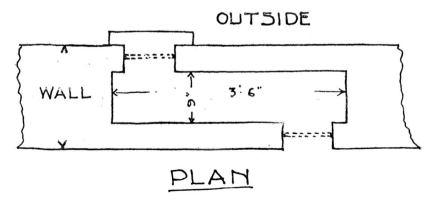

OUTSIDE

WALL 3' 6"

PLAN

CHAPTER SIXTEEN

SOCIAL FUNCTIONS AND THEIR INFLUENCE
ON PLANNING

T HE suitability of a house to the entertainment of guests according to traditional methods seems to be the ruling idea in modern planning, and the comfort of the family is often sacrificed to this idea. While I quite recognise the importance of this consideration in planning, for the average house at any rate, the primary consideration should be the suitability of the plan to meet the requirement of the daily routine of its occupants, and its adaptability to social functions must be considered as a secondary matter.

The three traditional forms of social functions to be considered are, firstly, the afternoon "At home," secondly, the dinner party, and, thirdly, the dance.

The first is a one-room function, demanding for its proper performance, according to conventional usage, a good-sized drawing-room; the second is a two-room function, requiring a good-sized dining-room and drawing-room; and the third, while it also requires two rooms at least for its proper performance, also demands that one of these shall be of considerable size.

The difficulties of meeting the problem of making the house fulfil these functions is not so great as at first appears, because the restricted income which necessitates the small house also prevents the entertainment of visitors on an extensive scale. While the drawing-room in its embryonic condition as a recess in the hall may accommodate a few visitors to afternoon tea, the hall might be used for this function on special occasions. While the dining recess would only accommodate a few guests on a special occasion the hall would become a dining-hall with the table in its centre. The ladies withdrawing to the bower, and the men to the study, to meet again in the hall after the table and its contents have been removed.

For the dance, the hall, with its gallery for the musicians, is specially adapted – the supper being served in one of its recesses. It will thus be seen that the type of plan suggested by the daily requirements of the family is not ill-adapted for occasional festivities, and the possession of one large central apartment will more than compensate for any failure to meet the arbitrary conditions of conventional usage.

In less formal gatherings, such as family reunions at Christmas for instance, the central hall with its great open fireplace will meet the occasion much better than the house designed as a row of boxes connected by a passage. In the average house the accommodation required for the resident governess, or for that singular anomaly, the paying guest, known in circles less polite as the lodger, or for the occasional visitor staying in the house, will not suggest any further modification of the plan than the inclusion of a bed-sitting-room.

It is only in the larger houses where entertainment is practised on a large scale that it necessarily modifies the plan. The central hall becomes then the focus of a series of common rooms – the guests may be accommodated in separate suites containing bedrooms, sitting-rooms, bathrooms, &c.

In some cases, the family may give up the whole house to the guests, and so there may also be a private family suite.

CHAPTER SEVENTEEN

THE SOUL OF THE HOUSE

Malvolio. I think nobly of the soul, and no way approve his opinion.
"Twelfth Night."

THE greater part of the arguments used in support of the reforms in house planning here suggested are designedly of a somewhat utilitarian and practical nature. It is indeed doubtful whether any other basis for an argument would be understood in an age when the average man is radically though perhaps unconsciously essentially utilitarian. But although it is held that the house should be convenient and aptly fitted to its material functions, it is but a mean thing if it does not express something of the aspirations of the spirit of its builders, and indeed possess, as it were, a soul of its own. It is a strange but incontrovertible fact that houses do so acquire a personality. Some are so mean and sordid that while possessing all the conveniences of modern life they seem to cast a blight over all around them. To pass them unharmed it would seem necessary to "cut a pious cross in the air;" to live in them would be to one sensitive in such matters worse than confinement in a prison cell. Others again are like mere husks, shallow and empty, while some, and these chiefly old houses, survivals of the great ages of building, thrill one at the first glance with a sense of their personal charm. And as one enters and passes from room to room their deep and intense stillness seems eloquent with messages and blessings. What magic is there in the mere putting

73

together of wood and stone to so impress the soul, and is it a small thing that we have lost that seeming miraculous gift? Let us never fall into the blindness of thinking of the modern house as a mere matter of hot-water taps and patent kitchen ranges, or think we do wisely to utterly disregard the possibilities of greatness that lies in mere building.

For houses and cottages once created are not merely arrangements of materials to secure certain practical ends. They each and all develop, we know not how, a personality which is either base or noble, and those who realise the possibilities of expression in the building of a house will never approach the matter lightly or irreverently. To him who creates a house is given a godlike function which it should be his endeavour not to abuse. And how great his triumph if as the reward of all his anxious labour it should be vouchsafed him to achieve a dwelling which should prove to possess a soul worthy to be ranked with the noble houses of the past!

A house too may possess that strange inscrutable quality of the True Romance. Not shallow, showy, and pretentious as most modern mansions are, but full of a still, quiet earnestness which seems to lull and soothe the spirit with promises of peace. Such a house is the greatest achievement possible to the art of man better than the greatest picture, because it is not a dream alone, but the dream come true – a constant daily influence and delight.

To illustrate this magical quality of spirit which buildings have the power of retaining, one has only to consider the houses of the past. To understand the true inwardness of the history of any period no written word can convey such an intimate and convincing message as may be read from ancient buildings by those who know their language. I do not refer here to archaeological lore, the mere cataloguing of mouldings and assignments of dates, though this has its uses in so far as it brings the mind into constant and continuous contact with the object of its attention, and so induces an attitude favourable to a deeper kind of knowledge than can be expressed in words. For the ancient building guards the heart of its mystery jealously, and reveals itself only to those who approach it with due sympathy. And so the unbeliever is apt to scoff at an experience he does not share, and may consider impressions of the past gained in this way misleading illusions.

And /this view is apparently justified by the fact that such impressions lead one in many cases to see the past through rose-coloured glasses – to idealise it in comparison with modern vulgar life. Just as when death has severed a friendship petty faults are forgotten, and we see in a true perspective the essential spirit unobscured by baffling clouds, so it is with buildings which retain no record of the superficial doings of their time, but only congeal in their structure the deep music of the soul.

And so we may well conclude that in building a people is writing its deepest history on the earth. Do you wish to estimate the sublimity and depth of the Gothic devotional spirit? You may find it writ large in our cathedrals, or set forth in lesser but no less truthful characters in our village churches. I say you may read it – it would perhaps be safer to affirm that you *might,* for the modern Churchman, with no faculty for deciphering the language of the building committed to his care, defaces its ancient glories under the excuse of restoration. With just the same kind of innocent indifference as the child who burns a precious manuscript in the fire and claps its hands at the blaze, the unsuspecting vicar expands with pleasurable delight over these devastating restorations of his.

Or again, it you wish to understand the romantic spirit of ancient chivalry, where will you find it so well inscribed as in the ancient Norman and Edwardian castles? And so on to our own times, each subtle change in the time spirit is duly recorded in terms of bricks and mortar. The mellowing and broadening of the somewhat narrow and intense Gothic spirit which took place with that sudden influx of classic lore which gave England her golden age – how well we find it inscribed in many an old manor and farm of the period! And then one may trace the gradual fading of that light till the chill frosts of commerce and the machine made building such as we find it today.

Few things are indeed so strange as this thaumaturgic art of the builder. He places stones in certain positions – cuts them in certain ways, and behold they begin to speak with tongues – a language of their own, with meanings too deep for words.

CHAPTER EIGHTEEN

FURNISHING

HAVING built a small house on the principles which have been advocated, it would seem a relatively simple matter to obtain the necessary movable furniture to complete its interior. Already the house with its cupboards and seats will be partially furnished, and the additional furniture required, being not essential for effect but merely for use, will not include those unnecessary articles, which are merely so many stumbling-blocks for the occupants. Such furniture cannot be bought in shops any more than the kind of house I have endeavoured to describe can be found ready built. The shops will merely offer a choice between the ugly furniture made to meet the demands of those as yet innocent of artistic cravings, and the "Art" furniture made for those who are presumed to be better informed.

But the New Art as interpreted by the shops is more to be avoided than the old ugliness. Whatever Art may be admitted to the house it must be genuine Art and not Trade Art. The best way to secure a satisfactory result in furnishing is to have the furniture made specially for its position – a few things soundly and simply constructed which shall seem a part of the whole scheme.

In many parts of the country old furniture of a simple type – gate tables, rush-bottomed chairs, bureaus, &c. – may be obtained at a very reasonable cost; and such things, with a few special made furnishings which cannot be obtained in this way, will always be at home in a house such as I have described. This old furniture has a sort of human character about it; and the varied planes of its surfaces, with its strong construction and evidences of careful leisurely work, make it inviting and homely. The modern "Art" furniture bears testimony, on the contrary, that it is the work of a drilled automaton. Its pretence to finish is a mere superficial deceptive smartness. No human being ever loved or lingered over its completion, and its Art is the bait held out to the purchaser as a substitute for real excellence of design or manufacture.

In modern furniture all the charm which belongs to the imperfect efforts of the hand of man, all the sympathy with material and carefulness of finish, are replaced by this superficial mechanical perfection. The old furniture stands against the wall at its ease. It is affable, generous and comely, but the modern work is stiff and repellant. There is nothing personal or human about it, and while its shallow smartness may be well enough for a room kept for show, it will never seem quite at home in the rooms we live in.

To the man about to furnish perhaps the best advice is that contained in the single word "Don't." Or at least he may be invited to pause and consider. Furniture making and furniture selling, as now practised, is a trade rather than an art, and the only artistic skill apparent is that evinced by the salesman in inducing the public to believe that they must have things which they can very well do without. The art of furnishing is perhaps best understood by the Japanese, who have no furniture at all in their houses. But in the Western World we have acquired the habit of sitting on chairs and at tables, and a certain degree of furnishing is essential. The great fault of nearly all modern rooms is that they are over-furnished, and the first step in their reform would consist in removing all the unnecessary and cumbrous furnishings which crowd floors and walls. There would then be sufficient floor space for the use of the occupants, and the few furnishings carefully disposed could be seen to the best advantage, while the domestic evolutions – the turning out of rooms and the daily dustings and cleanings of furniture – would be a simple matter.

The modern lady who wishes to achieve in her drawing-room an effect which is "quite Japanese" fondly imagines she is doing so by accumulating the greatest possible number of vases, fans and bamboo furniture, In the real Japanese room how different is the aim of its occupant! The walls and the floor are alike bare, and there is nothing to distract the attention from the single flower arrangement or picture which adorns the room. Or again, the collector of the antique surrounds himself with a host of cabinets, tables and chairs, and other pieces, and thinks in this way to recall the beauty of the Old English apartments. But here again it is not realised that the furnishing of these was really of the simplest, and the single contents of one modern house would furnish a dozen houses in the old way. While, however, this custom of over-furnishing may be tolerated in the mansion, in the contracted space of the smaller houses, where space and means are alike limited, there is nothing to be urged in its defence. The custom has its origin in unchecked acquisitiveness – the desire to possess merely for the sake of possessing things which take our fancy and will help to furnish our rooms. Such a desire it is the part of the salesman to foster and encourage; and just as we find the speculative builder pandering to the public demand for pretentious and comfortless buildings, so the furnishing firm strives to get them filled to over-flowing with pretentious and comfortless furniture.

In the much-abused Early Victorian era, the furniture of the shops was frankly and consistently ugly, and however repellent it was there was at least no spurious art about it. Art as a modern trade term was happily not invented. But just as the corruption of the best is always the basest, so the modern art show-room has reached a depth unplumbed by the work which preceded it. This spurious Trade Art with its canting catchwords follows sedulously every step of the small band of serious workers in the Arts and Crafts, with caricatures adapted and exaggerated to suit the public taste. If occasionally it enrols amongst its designers an artist who produces really good work it cannot refrain from producing a "line" of goods which are nearly enough allied to his to deceive an easily gulled public, and so the last state is worse than the first.

Real beauty of work, it cannot be too often insisted, can only be produced by designers and workmen who are engaged primarily in their work for its own sake. If it is done with money-making as a leading motive it must necessarily become debased. In order to attract the public it is necessary that furniture should aggressively intrude its claims to Art on the passer by, and in the specimen rooms of the modern firm the art must all be underlined. In such surroundings there is indeed no escape from this persistent appeal. Everything seems to pose and smirk, and Art is shrieked from every corner.

To turn from such surroundings to the showroom of real antique furniture is to experience an intense sensation of relief. There is no superficial smartness of trade finish here, but a welcome sense of leisured workmanship. The measured tick of the grandfather's clock seems to set the key to the whole effect, and the excellence of the furniture is of a reticent kind which does not insist on recognition. It possesses in short that quality of repose which should be the essential attribute of the home.

But it does not necessarily follow from this recognition of the superiority of old work to the New Art of the shops, that modern furniture should consist of copies of old, or that all new designs are necessarily blatant and vulgar. But the better class of modern work cannot be produced under the conditions which obtain in the modern factory, but must be the result of careful design and workmanship which shows a sympathetic treatment of material. It must be the expression of convictions instead of mere interests, and the questions "will it pay?" or "will it sell?" must be subordinated to the inquiry as to whether it is good work or bad.

To the man who wishes to furnish nowadays, it is a little difficult to know how to proceed, and more than a little difficult to avoid the various baits held out to him by the enterprising manufacturer, and the result is often injudicious purchases afterwards repented of. It must be remembered that what happens to take the fancy in the showroom is not necessarily the thing which will maintain its charm in daily life, and the very insistence of its appeal gives a fair indication of its transient nature. The beauty of furniture is to a great extent a relative matter, and its fitness for a special place in a room will often be a more important point than its intrinsic merits, which may be quite at variance with its surroundings. And so it will be most desirable to have furniture specially made to suit particular rooms, and so to form the finishing touches of the scheme which begins with the structure of the house. There should be no hiatus between house and furniture. Wherever the conditions make it reasonable, the furniture should in the form of fitments constitute a part of the building, and the movable furniture should seem a part of the house, and not an alien importation.

Furniture, like everything else in the house, should be the best of its kind, and it is better to have a first-class article of an inferior kind than a second-class one of what claims to be a higher order, just as in building it is better to have the best possible kind of cottage instead of the worst kind of mansion.

The furniture of the shops often fails, because while it poses as artistic and pretends to features and qualities which can only be obtained by the single desire of the designer and workmen to achieve beauty, it is really at heart entirely commercial, and produced under factory conditions which make the Art of the workman impossible.

But there is a kind of furniture to be had which, frankly factory made, is excellent of its kind. The kind of chair used for churches is an example of this. There is no pretence here of "Art" finish. It bears evidence that it is put together quickly and simply, and turned out in the least possible time.

To French polish it, to put a little bit of carving or inlay on the back, to add what is popularly supposed to be Art to it, would be to hopelessly vulgarise it. It would become good enough for the suburban drawing-room perhaps, but would be no longer good enough for the church. There are several types of chair of this kind which are all excellent in their way. They are made chiefly of ash, but often a piece of beech or other wood is used, and this casual combination of material is quite in character with its simple and direct appeal of the whole. If furniture is to be turned out in factories, this is how it should be made, with no affectation of arts and crafts.

In making special furniture for a house it must be recognised that it is necessarily more expensive than furniture made by the dozen – and in furnishing under economic restrictions it is desirable to include as much as possible the cottage antique, and the factory furniture described above. But if furnishing is undertaken on the principle of omitting everything that is not actually required, it will be possible to have a few things specially made, instead of a multitude of articles not really required, and which cannot be said to be cheap at any price.

In the making of furniture there are two principal methods of construction in the joining of its woodwork. The simplest is that now used in making packing-cases, the wood being joined by means of nails. The more complicated is that in which the wood is joined by letting one piece into another by the use of what are called mortices and tenons.

It is a foregone conclusion nowadays that the simplest way of doing a thing is necessarily the worst way, and the nail in modern woodwork has been considered a thing to be hidden. While in all other details of construction a virtue has been made of frankness, and while the pegs of the tenon are displayed to view, the nail is sedulously concealed by all kinds of artifices. In the making of the simple kinds of furniture in which the wood is joined by nails of the kind known as clout-headed, made by a blacksmith, these might be shown without shame, and form a feature in the design, and nothing could be reasonably urged against this simple and direct "packing-case" construction for a chest or cabinet.

As to how far it is justifiable to attempt to reproduce ancient styles of furnishing in modern rooms will depend on many circumstances. It must necessarily always be absurd to aim at reproducing the styles of the Gothic period, or those which were in the Renaissance time coloured by its influence. The modern Jacobean room, if it include all the carving and ornaments of the period, must necessarily be a failure, simply because Jacobean art was a workman's art to a great extent, and we have no workman now who would be able to re-create the spirit of the Jacobean age. It would be as reasonable to ask of the modern workman to write you a Shakespearean sonnet as to carve you a Jacobean panel. A judicious selection of those features and principles which are suitable for reproduction under modern conditions would lead to a room which in its traditionalism would bear the stamp of reasonableness. And this thoughtful modified version of old work must not be confounded with the Wardour Street tradition of artificiality, worm-eaten carving, and other deceptions.

The later and more histrionic styles of furnishing in which ethical standards are given up for superficial refinements, and which were the setting for a life divorced from realities, and which seem a kind of elaborate play acting, are more easily reproduced under modern conditions. Your modern workman may copy a Louis XV chair, though he cannot a Jacobean one. In the modern school of furniture that is generally the most satisfactory which is based on the principles of old work. In its aim to achieve a rational quality of simplicity it sometimes tends to become somewhat unsympathetic and severe, and the recognition of the materials is not so much considered as qualities of lines and surfaces. A straining after effect and over-accentuated ornament is often found, which destroys all sense of repose. The true course seems here a middle one, between the extreme of archaic revivals on the one hand, and aggressive originality on the other, and in reaching forward to the unborn beauty of the future still to hold fast that which is good in the work of the past.

The enthusiasm with which the designer of the revival period set himself to copy exactly medieval work may have been ill-judged; but it seems no less fatal to deliberately ignore traditional work, and to set up a personal and isolated effort against the accumulated knowledge of centuries.

The extent to which tradition may thus be admitted will depend on the fitness of the style which has inspired the work to modern conditions of workmanship and to modern life. A house, it may be urged, should be homogeneous, and to design a Jacobean dining-room and a Louis XV drawing-room in a building of the Georgian period can be hardly defended. The building and its furnishing should present an all pervading unity, and not a heterogeneous collection of samples of historical periods; and while the general scheme may become more dainty and elegant in the drawing-room, and more homely and masculine in the hall, there should be no definite break in the continuity of the whole, while the structure itself should bear a definite relation to the furnishing and decoration.

And this necessity for unity of effect which has been urged in the planning of the house – this necessity to break away from the conception of a house as a series of unrelated compartments – suggests at once the advisability of not seeking to reproduce historical styles, but to treat the whole scheme broadly, introducing, it may be, much that has been used in the past, and combining and arranging the new to form a completely harmonious result.

CHAPTER NINETEEN

DECORATION

IN turning now to consider the matter of decoration, one is conscious of crossing a definite boundary-line and entering a new land where practical realities are exchanged for dreams. So far in the building of the house, and in its furnishing, everything that has been done has had a practical purpose at the root of whatever beauty it may have achieved – a purpose which one could fall back on, as it were, so that at the worst the house might claim to be a shelter from the elements, and its furniture to minister to material needs. But in the decoration of the house no such excuse can be urged for the failure to achieve beauty. If it has no beauty it is useless, and worse than useless – and before covering our walls with sprawling patterns it will be well to consider this carefully. There are no laws which compel a man to decorate his house, and unless there is a real desire for beauty in the house there seems little excuse for its decoration. In the days when heraldry flourished, decoration had a definite purpose. It was a kind of graphic writing, which, besides being eminently decorative, conveyed definite facts. This heraldic system still survives in a kind of fossilised form as a pedantic dilettantism which has quite lost its former significance. If, however, heraldic decoration is used in the decorative rather than the archaeological spirit, it affords an extremely effective means of adornment for the house.

It constitutes a complete science of decoration, and in its symbolic birds and beasts, and its simple checkers of primary colours, one finds the elements of a kind of decorative language.

Among the objections which may be raised to the use of heraldry in the decoration of the modern house, one may first consider the suggestion it may be held to convey of family pride. But heraldic work need not be confined nor need it even include the bearings of the family. The arms of a college or school at which the members of the family have been educated, or those of the neighbouring town, the diocese or other local bearings, may all be included in a heraldic scheme of decoration, and the family arms in such a comprehensive company will perhaps lose that note of personal egotism which they might otherwise be thought to convey.

Again, it may be urged against the use of heraldic decoration that it is a part of those trappings of the mediaeval world with which we moderns have little to do. In these days of mauser bullets and khaki uniforms these blazoned shields appear, perhaps, something of an anachronism, while the somewhat blatant and brutal mottoes are also reminiscent of a less gentle age than our own.

The historic significance of heraldry may be, perhaps, held sufficiently to outweigh such objections. It connects the house with the past and records something of the history of its surroundings and its owner, and while it affords patterns of colour of great decorative value it also has a definite story to tell to those who can read its message.

In the modern house what is usually understood as decoration consists chiefly in the painting of woodwork and the covering of walls and ceilings with wallpapers. It is entirely a matter of painting and papering the surfaces of so many plastered boxes or rooms. Decoration properly considered may rather be taken to represent the clothing of architecture with pattern and colour. The building without its aid should possess real beauty of the structural kind, to which decoration provides the finishing touches. The house should not be made for the decoration, but the decoration for the house.

It may be doubted whether the house which is built under economic conditions should be decorated at all. The natural texture of plaster colourwashed some plain tint will generally be far more satisfactory than a cheap wallpaper. Here, as elsewhere, one may decide that if means will not allow of the introduction of good thoughtful work, it is better to do without pattern altogether. If a house is properly built it does not demand decoration to make it "possible," and so, whatever is done towards its further adornment in the way of wall-coverings may well be postponed for a little and introduced at last with due circumspection and deliberation. The possibilities of heraldic decorative schemes have already been alluded to, and the historic significance of this method constitutes an added charm to decorative qualities. But apart from heraldry one may take some flower or tree as the symbol for a room, and evolve a scheme which is based on that. The rose, the lily, or the daffodil may thus be taken as the motif for special schemes; or some woodland tree, perhaps, such as the mountain-ash, with its orange berries and white flowers, may form the basis for the decoration of the walls. In the choice of such subjects a certain appropriateness is desirable, and thus a dining-room might well be adorned with the grey leaves and purple clusters of the grape, or a bedroom with the drowsy poppy. The cottage character of a small house may be enforced by decoration with the simpler woodland flowers, such as the daisy or buttercup, and wherever these are used they should vary in their treatment according to the special conditions and limitations of a material or craft; and while embroidery or painting might admit of an approximation to realism, such processes as stencilling, metal work or wood-carving would each demand a special convention. For the conventional treatment of natural forms should mainly consist of a modification of actual forms to suit the possibilities of particular materials and methods of work, and such considerations will often make it desirable to depart from actualities and to give but a more simplified symbolic rendering of the natural form. The success of the work will depend not so much on the accuracy with which a given flower is copied as in the sympathetic knowledge displayed of the limitations and possibilities of materials and tools.

DESIGN FOR STENCILLING

CHAPTER TWENTY

MOTTOES FOR THE HOUSE

IT has been said that a room should express in its decoration and furnishing something of the individuality and characteristics of its occupants, and that its general aspect should inform us in an inarticulate way of the kind of person who lives there.

It must be confessed, however, that the expression of personality which a room is capable of conveying in this way is not very explicit and may be misleading, but when decoration becomes articulate in the writing on the wall it affords a more definite revelation of the character and tastes of its owner.

In an age when conversation is often limited to trivial and insignificant subjects, such a form of expression is not without its uses, helping us to understand something of the ideas and conceptions of life which a man is prepared to subscribe to.

But the instinctive reticence which makes us unwilling to blurt out our thoughts to every acquaintance may suggest the advisability of making these writings somewhat cryptic in their character, and to still further conceal the heart of our mystery it may be well that they should not only be written somewhat illegibly but also in a foreign tongue. Mottoes should then be disposed with the idea of decorating a space with a compact and definite form, and only on closer inspection should they be decipherable. The blatant use of mottoes will only remind one of the advertisement at the railway stations; and however much we admire or believe in some ancient proverb or modern epigram, it will soon be transformed into an insipid platitude if it forces itself upon our attention day after day.

In giving a few examples of mottoes here I do not suggest that they would be appropriate to a special individual. The choice of mottoes is such a personal matter that every one who wishes to include them in a decorative scheme should choose their own.

In the studio, for instance, a helpful idea may be expressed in the phrase "Il n'y a rien plus." Few would recognise the force and application of such a phrase, for it would be necessary to remember the anecdote of the famous French painter whose reply it was to the friend who asked why he was still at work. However much beside there may be in the outside world it will be well to remember, in the studio at any rate, that there is nothing else but the work in hand.

Or, again, the spirit of the artist may find expression in Kipling's verse:

> The depth and dream of my desire,
> The bitter paths wherein I stray,
> Thou knowest who has made the fire,
> Thou knowest who has made the clay.

Or perhaps the student may turn to the Proverbs of Solomon and find a stimulus in the following:

> In all labour there is profit,
> But the folding of the hands leadeth only to penury,

with perhaps a cynical afterthought to the modern application of this saying to cases where the profit or the labour is indeed forthcoming but is not enjoyed by the labourer. Or, perhaps, in view of those menacing difficulties which vanish when the task is once begun, another proverb might be pictorially represented:

> The slothful man has said,
> There is a lion in the path.

In the dining-room the mottoes may be in a less heroic strain, such as:

> Stay me with flagons,
> Comfort me with apples,

from the Song of Songs: or from Omar Khayyam :

> Ah! fill the cup, what boots it to repeat
> How Time is slipping underneath our feet?
> Unborn to-morrow and dead yesterday,
> Why fret about them if to-day be sweet?

which might perhaps be inscribed in the original decorative Arabic.

In the bedroom sleep may be invited in many a classic and poetic phrase:

> To Mary Queen the praise be given,
> She sent the gentle sleep from Heav'n
> That slid into my soul.

And

> Sleep that knitteth up the ravell'd sleeve of care

may be quoted as examples from Coleridge and Shakespeare. For a picture-gallery

> dost thou love pictures ?

But so many examples of mottoes suggest themselves for the apartments of the house that it would not be difficult to fill a book with appropriate quotations, and the space at my disposal only enables me here to suggest a few.

In their application an excellent idea is suggested by R.L. Stevenson, who wished to procure a set of gilded letters in metal which might be fixed easily to woodwork, and by means of which special mottoes might be arranged for special occasions, and this temporary use of mottoes would admit of a much larger range of sayings grave and gay.

CHAPTER TWENTY ONE

COLOUR

IN the use of colour in the house, perhaps the most important question to consider is, Will it fade? It may be noted that those colours which at once captivate and attract the eye are generally the most evanescent.

As in the world of letters there is a kind of book which has a brief passion of life succeeded by total neglect, so in the decorative world there are brilliant colours, the stimulating effects of which soon pall. In the natural world these intense colours are found in the passing pageant of the flowers, while the constant tints are those sober, quiet tones which one may love little, but which one can love long; and inasmuch as these vivid colours are those which fade, one may perhaps take the hint which nature thus conveys, and in the permanent dyes for the adornment of the house keep to quiet colour as a setting for the transient brightness of flowers, or the concentrated brilliance of a decorative picture in stained glass.

The use of aniline dyes instead of the old vegetable ones has been the chief cause of the prevalence of unreliable colours in modern materials. William Morris made a careful study of dyeing, and revived the use of most of the old vegetable dyes, so that the great merit of the Morris fabrics apart from their beauty of design is the permanence of their colouring. The most reliable colours generally are yellow and reds, but blue and mauve should be used with caution. Some colours, while they fade, may end by becoming pleasant tints, and a vivid green may thus become eventually a uniform grey green tone. And such materials may often be used when experience has shown to what extent they will change in time. For curtains or other materials which are exposed to direct sunlight, the use of undyed materials may be recommended as a safe course.

If the spectrum of sunlight is examined, it will be found to range from purple at one end, merging into blue, and a central zone of green, which passes through shades of yellow and orange into red, at the opposite end. The central green zone may be said to represent in the decorative world a normal colour – "work-a-day" green, as Morris called it. The blue and purple end represents the more "spirituelle" tints, while the yellow and red appeal to the animal instincts and merge into the heat rays. The cultivation of the colour sense leads to the extension of the spectrum and the inclusion of many gradations of exquisite subtlety. The central green invariably satisfies the normal eye, while the pleasure conveyed by the extreme tints of the spectrum varies according to the predominance of the spiritual or animal in the mood of the observer.

The terms "spiritual" and "animal" convey the idea I wish to suggest somewhat inadequately, and I do not wish it to be inferred that the heart-warming pleasure conveyed by red is necessarily base, or the refined appreciation of mauves and blues an indication of superiority. In the complete human consciousness each pleasure has its appointed place, and to be uncheered by a red colour is a sign of an incomplete rather than a superior mind.

A room decorated in tones of blue and mauve may be dainty and refined, but it is somewhat lacking in virility, and it may very well be complemented by a scheme derived from the opposite end of the spectrum, but generally the central green tone of the spectrum is most satisfactory with the introduction of its adjacent tints of either blue or yellow. The decorative use of colour implies the cultivation of the faculty of thinking in colour, as the musician thinks in sounds – and this process does not involve the indication of natural forms as a medium for expression of an arrangement of tints which may be disposed in a purely conventional way. As an example of this thinking in colour, one may instance the Japanese prints, which judged on their merits as imitations of nature may seem somewhat crude, while considered as scheme of colour arrangement they are wonderfully beautiful and full of suggestions for decorative schemes, which those who regard painting as merely an imitative art will perhaps hardly appreciate.

Passages of colour occur just as passages of sound in a musical composition having no relation to any natural objects, and these are charged with a mysterious and inexplicable beauty which is elusive and unsubstantial. But while this kind of beauty is recognised and expected in the musical composition, it is considered, when it is considered at all, only as secondary to imitative art in the picture. The highest form of picture making is often held to be that which creates the most convincing illusion of reality; and the artist who, giving up the impossible ideal involved in competing with Nature uses his subject as a field for an arrangement of colour, is generally misunderstood and often condemned. For those who can refrain from abusing what they do not understand are unfortunately represented by a very small minority.

CHAPTER TWENTY TWO

PICTURES

IT would be interesting to inquire how far the art of picture painting is coincident with the decline of Art in its widest interpretation, representing the last stronghold of the artist driven from the service of life behind the gilded pale of the picture frame, where he dreams in a little shadow world all his own. It is curious to note in the daily newspaper that the concerns of art are dealt with in a separate column applied to the discussion of pictures. And these "Art Notes" seem to bear such an insignificant place in the record of life which the newspaper presents. In the ages when art was a vital part of the national existence, how inadequate such a classification would have appeared Then there was hardly a thing which the hand of man could do or his brain conceive which was not an expression of unconscious art. It is true we have now the art of the shops, but it is a spurious art, crushed under the iron heel of commercialism.

If art is then to become again an all-pervading influence instead of the concern of a few dilettante connoisseurs, it must reconstruct the old conception of its scope. Primarily it will be concerned with buildings and their adornment, and here the picture falls into its proper place as the decoration of the wall. As such it can no longer be an isolated product. The picture painter will be the first to admit that the beauty of the picture as a whole depends on the relation of its parts; but if the relation of one colour to another is so important, the logical inference is that the picture itself must depend for its beauty on its place in the scheme of things. And so one finds in the earlier ages of painting the painter at his best was a wall decorator. As

HOUSES AND GARDENS

Ruskin has said, "There is no existing highest order Art but is decoration. The best sculpture yet produced has been the decoration of a temple front – the best painting, the decoration of a room. Raphael's best doing is merely the wallcolouring of a suite of apartments in the Vatican, and his cartoons were made for tapestries. Correggio's best doing is the decoration of two small church cupolas at Parma. Tintoret's of a ceiling and a side wall belonging to a charitable society in Venice; while Titian and Veronese threw out their noblest thoughts, not even on the inside, but on the outside of the common brick and plaster walls of Venice. Get rid, then, at once of any idea of decorative art being a degraded or separate kind of art. Its nature or essence is simply its being fitted for a definite place, and in that place forming part of a great and harmonious whole, in companionship with other art; and so far from thus being a degradation of it – so far from decorative art being inferior to other art because it is fixed to a spot – on the whole it may be considered as rather a piece of degradation that it should be portable. Portable art – independent of all place – is for the most part ignoble art!"

An unkind critic might be tempted to wonder why a writer who thus dispraises portable art should have written so eloquently in praise of portable art as displayed in the pictures of Turner. But this is to judge by the letter instead of the spirit.

However beautiful a picture may be, it is an isolated and unrelated beauty. It is not a member of that great fraternity of the arts where each has not alone its individual qualities, but its definite and calculated relation to its fellows.

But this portable art in the form of pictures painted for no place in particular is a thing to be reckoned with in the making of a modern house – and as the pictures we possess have not been made to fit the house, we must needs pocket the pride which claims that architecture is the essential and ruling art, and try to make the house to fit the pictures. If Mahomed will not come to the mountain, it is the mountain which must go to Mahomed. It has already been suggested how, in the decoration of the wall, a gilded canvas may help to connect the picture with its surroundings. What is required is not so much what is called a good background for pictures in the treatment of the wall on which they are to be hung, for this, in relieving the picture and its frame unduly, still makes it appear an alien there. Rather it must be our aim to make the picture merge into the wall surface and appear a part of it. The frame thus becomes the connecting link between it. On a wall panelled in dark oak, for instance, dark oak becomes the best material for the picture frame in most cases. Pictures should not be dotted over a wall, but definitely arranged to emphasise certain focal points framed in panelling over a mantelpiece, perhaps, or placed over some important piece of furniture. They need not always be hung, but may stand on shelves flanked by ornaments. If they are few and choice, and possess a decorative quality, they will thus become really helpful in accentuating centres of interest in the decorative scheme.

In a large house a collection of pictures should be displayed in a private picture-gallery. It has already been urged that the house should not be a museum. Still less should it be a picture-gallery. Many of the historic houses of England, where the walls of the apartments are lined with pictures, are, indeed, full of artistic and antiquarian interest. But they are no longer homes in the best sense, and convey little idea of that early beauty they possessed when their furnishing consisted of a few essential things, and their walls were covered with real decoration in the form of panelling and tapestry.

An excellent example of this kind is the old Elizabethan house, "Plas Maur," in North Wales, which has recently been made into a picture-gallery, and where the dignity and reality of the ancient art of building seems to make the best of the modern pictures on its walls appear frivolous and vulgar. From the decorative point of view, a picture is merely a pattern of certain colours and tones. That it should be more than this I do not wish to deny, but whatever interest it possesses in its subject and its associations is not a matter of decoration. As decoration, it would probably look as well hung upside down. And it is the decorative qualities of the picture which really count. To the occupants of a room the pictures normally exist merely as patches of colour with gilded outlines. It is only by a definite and conscious effort that one perceives at intervals beauties of subject or composition. The decorative quality is a constant factor. If we imagine, for instance, the tired man of business returning to his suburban home in the evening, it can hardly be supposed that he will be prepared to make the special mental effort involved in an inspection of his pictures; but whatever decorative quality they express in conjunction with their surroundings will at once enfold him as in an atmosphere which soothes and charms like harmonious music.

A man may leave a room so adorned without being able to render an intelligible account of anything in it, and yet have felt its beauty to the full.

Pictures, then, in the house, it may be said, should possess a decorative quality which should be brought into harmony with the whole scheme of which they form a part.

CHAPTER TWENTY THREE

THE FIREPLACE AND ITS TREATMENT

But they've a wall'd up now wi' bricks
The vier pleace vor dogs an' sticks
An' only left a little hole
To teake a little greate o' coal,
So small that only twos or drees
Can jist push in an' warm their knees.
And then the carpets they do use
Ben't fit to tread wi' ouer shoes;
An' chairs an' couches be so neat
You mussen teake em vor a seat:
They be so fine, that vo'k mus' pleace
All over em an' outer cease,
And then the cover when 'tis on,
Is still too fine to loll upon.
Ah! gie me, if I wer' a squier,
The settle an' the girt wood vier.

William Barnes

FROM the modern utilitarian point of view I suppose it must be conceded that the open fire is an extremely unscientific and unsatisfactory arrangement. But the modern scientist satisfies himself with putting the matter to the test of the thermometer, and the value of the system is judged by its effects on mercury, rather than on the complex human, whose attitude in the matter is not altogether a question of degrees Fahrenheit.

In the house the fire is practically a substitute for the sun, and it bears the same relation to the household as the sun does to the landscape. It is one of the fairy-tale facts of science that the heat and brightness from the burning coal is the same that was emitted from the sun on the primeval forests; and so the open fire enables us to enjoy today the brightness and warmth of yesterday's sunshine, and the cheerfulness we experience from the fire is akin to the delight which sunlight brings. To live in a scientifically adjusted temperature with the fire relegated to the basement is to live in a grey and cheerless world; and so the house, however warm, without a fire may very reasonably be compared to a summer day without the sun. It is, therefore, no mere archaic affectation which leads us to cling to the open hearth and the blazing fire; and although, especially in large houses, it may be desirable to introduce more effectual means of heating, this should never replace but only supplement the open fire.

In glancing back at the evolution of the house one of the most interesting features is the treatment of the fireplaces. The earliest arrangement was to place the fire in the centre of the room, the smoke finding its way out through the roof; and were it not for this difficulty of disposing of the smoke this central position seems to possess many advantages, and the family gathered round such a fire forms a complete circle.

When, however, the fireplace became to be placed against the wall the fireside became more restricted and the family circle was reduced to a semicircle. Still the fire was not enclosed in a recess, but covered merely by a projecting hood to take the smoke, or perhaps by an ingle recess which still left the sides as well as the front of the fire accessible. This arrangement, however, did not entirely dispose of the smoke problem, as such a fire was subject to cross draughts. Next may be noted a transition stage, in which the fire was partly covered by a hood and partly enclosed by a recess, until at last the fire was placed entirely in a recess in the wall. Gradually this recess became contracted into the modern grate, so that the whole evolution of the position of the fireplace seems to be first the pushing of the fire to the wall, and then its gradual absorption into the wall, followed by the reduction of its size. It is not implied that such a process was chronological, and its later developments were much hastened by the use of coal instead of wood as fuel. With a wood fire a certain amount of smoke is not entirely objectionable, for the aromatic odours of burning wood are too pleasant to be entirely lost. With coal, however, the case is different, and the least smoke is objectionable, and so in the modern grate where coal is burnt this question of the elimination of the smoke becomes a most important one, and the whole problem of the position and treatment of the modern fireplace resolves itself into the getting rid of the smoke without unduly cramping or enclosing the fire itself, and to secure the charm and beauty of the open hearth without its drawbacks.

In passing to the consideration of the materials used in the construction of the fireplace we find these naturally divide themselves into three classes. Firstly, such material as will bear actual contact with the fire, such as iron and other metals, firebrick, &c.; secondly, those materials which are incombustible, but will not stand contact with the fire, such as stone, glazed tiles, &c.; and thirdly, materials which are inflammable, and which must not be placed too close to the fire.

In the ordinary fireplace we shall find all these three classes of materials represented in the iron grate, with its surroundings of glazed tiles and wooden mantelpieces.

To secure simplicity and breadth of effect it is often desirable to simplify this formula, and the fireplace will afford the best opportunity for displaying the actual structure of the house itself – the brickwork or stonework of its walls. The reality and sincerity of the structure so displayed will outweigh the claims here of superficial materials, especially in view of the desirability of surrounding the fire with a space of material which is not inflammable. Moreover, the fire itself and its fuel are necessarily rather rough and homely in their character, and look still more so if brought into too close contact with over-refined materials. The mark of the smoke on the rough surface of the brickwork will but add new notes in the scale of its varied colour, and if the whole appointment of the fireside have a like homely character, the fire will seem at home there, instead of an alien amidst its superfine surroundings too dainty for the blackness of its smoke. And so the rugged virile spirit of the fire should dictate the proper character for its setting, and however delicate the rest of the room may be, this character as it approaches the fire should merge into a more serviceable quality. It has already been urged that the house should contain at least one good-sized central room, and it is no less important that this room should have a fireplace broadly designed to dominate the scheme, and form, as it were, the centre of a solar system to which the lesser fires are duly subordinated.

The whole question of the occupation of rooms is largely a question of fires. In the cottage the front parlour is not used, mainly because the household is a "one-fire" household, and that one fire must necessarily be in the kitchen. Its logical expression in a plan would show a large kitchen as the house plan, with a parlour reduced to the small dimensions its limited functions suggest. Again, a two-fire household implies fires in the kitchen and in the dining-room, and should be expressed in a large dining-hall as the central feature, or at least the dining-room should form a recess in the house place. In larger houses these limitations do not occur, but even here it is desirable that the focus and centre of the house should be expressed by the large fireplace in the large hall. In considering the house thus as a winter dwelling, I am assuming those conditions which test its real qualities. The main function of a house is that it affords a retreat from the cold or a shelter from the rain. In fine warm weather its occupation is gone, and its tenants should chiefly live, if not in the garden, at least in an open verandah. In the English climate the apartments of the house can be quite adequately heated by means of open fires alone in houses of average size; but in America, and on the continent, some more effectual means of heating is required. In America, the English tradition of the open fire is still maintained in connection with artificial heating; but on the continent the fire is usually interred in a porcelain tomb, and the house is robbed of one of its greatest charms – the ruddy glow of the open fire.

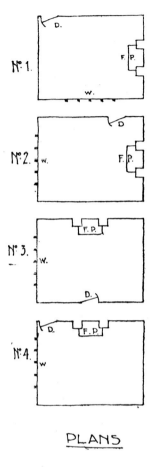

PLANS

While, however, the central house place should have its large fireplace, in a house which is also artificially heated, where the remaining rooms are small, it is not always necessary to follow the English tradition of a fireplace to each room, and apartments used for writing or sleeping may be heated merely by artificial means. This is largely a matter of individual taste, but in a house of small size, containing only the kitchen and hall flues in one chimney stack, the cost of building extra chimneys to its smaller rooms might be devoted to artificial heating.

Some such compromise would form a reasonable basis for a modern plan, and would save a certain amount of lighting fires and cleaning grates. Where fireplaces are introduced in the various specialised rooms their position and treatment should be modified accordingly, and in the bedroom the fireplace may be of modest dimensions and simple treatment.

In selecting the position for a fireplace in the room, it is important that it should be placed in relation to doors so that it is not subjected to cross draughts, and in relation to windows so that it is well lighted.

In the four small sketches shown here, the arrangement shown in No. 1 is the best, as the fireplace is free from draughts and lighted from the side. If, however, the door is moved down the side wall to the position shown in No. 2, the comfort of the fireside is destroyed, while the window at the opposite end of the room is also in a bad position for giving light at the fireplace, and cannot be opened without a direct draught.

The arrangement No. 3 is also defective, owing to the direct draught from door to fireplace; while No. 4 is good, though not so entirely satisfactory as No. 1.

These remarks, of course, presuppose that the room is one where the custom of gathering round the fire may be reasonably implied, and in other apartments the position of the fireplace may be governed to some extent by other considerations. In the specialised dining-room, for instance, the position of the fireplace should allow for ample space between it and the dining-table; and in the bedroom, while it is desirable that the fire should be visible from the bed, it is not necessary that it should bear any special relation to door or window. As, however, the future uses of a room cannot be foreseen, it is well that wherever possible the fireplace should meet the demands of the sitting-room.

The construction of the ingle-nook must take us back to that point in the evolution of the fireplace when the fire had been placed in a recess in the wall, but when that recess was large enough to accommodate not only the fire but those who gathered round it. On the great hearth of stone or brick the burning logs rested, partially supported by the fire-dogs, with their primitive arrangements for cooking, the toothed rack for the spit and the rings for holding pots and pans and the wide oven built in the wall. Cooking in those days had a fine romantic quality, and the hissing of the birds on the spit and the bubbling of the steaming pots added to the homeliness and cheerfulness of the ingle. Those who sat in the wide chimney-corner could, by glancing upwards, see through the swirling smoke a patch of the dark sky, with, perhaps, a star or two. At times, it must be confessed, the wind which howled in the chimney must have driven the smoke into the room, and hail and rain would sometimes fall in miniature fusilades on the fire; and on a cold and stormy night this constant reminder of the external warfare, these occasional glimpses of the moon, pursued by flying clouds, and the expiring kisses of rain upon the fire, kept the occupant of the ingle-nook constantly in touch with the outside world and constantly conscious of the warmth and comfort of his surroundings. Perhaps the sympathetic reader will realise the spirit of romance which belongs to such a picture of "fire and sleet and candle light," a romance which, now banished from the modern house, we are driven to find in printed books, but which is not so incompatible with the conditions of the modern house as may be supposed.

Science starting out at a tangent, after many improvements and complications, comes back at last to some slight modification of the simplest and earliest methods, and the most recent developments in the modern grate on scientific lines show a return to the ancient custom of the fire on the hearth.

In the planning of the modern ingle-nook it is well to consider it not so much a recess in the room in which is another recess for the fire, but rather as an enlargement of the fire recess itself. Modern requirements will insist on a more satisfactory disposal of the smoke than the old type of ingle allowed of, and so there must be a hood over the fire of metal or masonry; and if the fire in the ingle is placed in an inner recess, this should be shallow and wide, and not be too sharply defined in structure or materials from the whole treatment. The spirit of the fire should govern the design of the whole.

It is not desirable that the modern ingle-nook should be very deeply recessed, or the room itself is not satisfactorily heated, and yet the best position for a settle or couch in the room is often at the side of the fire. These conditions suggest that the ingle-nook should not be in the centre of one side of the room, but placed in the corner with a long seat against the wall on one side, and the other side of the fire left open for movable chairs. Modern ideas of comfort are apt to place the arm-chair before the couch, except for actual reclining, as the former encloses its occupant at the sides, and gives support to the arms. And so the fitting of an ingle, with fixed seats on each side, is not always desirable. Here, as elsewhere in the

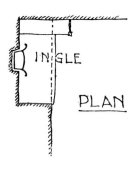

PLAN

house, the fixing of furniture to the structure is readily capable of abuse. Where the form of the room and the special conditions suggest fixtures, this principle may well be followed, but pushed to excess it constitutes a tyranny of the designer which may justly annoy the average man who may wish to use his own judgment as to where he shall sit or write.

A necessary qualification of the designer of interiors is a saving sense of humour, which, after all, to a large extent, consists in a fine sense of the fitness of things, and few could occupy one of these little polished and upholstered seats which flank so many modern ingles without being conscious of the absurdity of the situation. As a matter of fact, the average person who indulges in the art ingle does not occupy the seats, and so reserves for them that admiration which is only awarded to those features of the house which claim to be merely ornamental.

In the treatment of the fireplace generally what is mainly required is a greater breadth and simplicity. The little grate surrounded by its scrap of tiling, and wooden mantel, full of niches and shelves, is a formula which may well be discarded for something simpler. The grate may be surrounded by a broad space of tiles only, or the brickwork of the chimney breast may be surmounted by a single shelf.

Above all, the fireplace should connect itself with the general treatment of the room, and the wood mantelpiece is at its best when it constitutes an enriched and accentuated portion of the panelling which covers the remaining walls.

Of all the defects in a house, smoky chimneys are, perhaps, the most trying and the most common. In the new house they are most apt to be caused by the coldness and dampness of the flues, and represent a painful initial experience which does much to obliterate the pleasure and comfort of existence in surroundings otherwise harmonious. With a modern contracted grate, designed on scientific principles, the danger of smoke is minimised, but the large, hospitable open fire, however carefully designed, is apt to give trouble at first.

So essential, however, is this type of fireplace to the homeliness and beauty of at least the central hall or house place, that it is well worth facing a possibility of some difficulty in this respect, instead of resorting to the inglorious safety of the mean and paltry-looking modern fireplace. Such precaution as circumstances will allow are, of course, taken by contracting the orifice of the flue and by introducing no flat surfaces for the smoke to strike against, and by gathering and curving the flue to prevent down draught; but in some cases where every precaution is taken until the flue becomes thoroughly dried by use there is a tendency to smoke. It is important, in view of this, that fires should be lighted and kept burning during the later stages of the building, so that the flues can be dried and tested before the house is inhabited, and any slight modification that may be required can then be made beforehand. It will often be noticed, for instance, in modern open fires, that a piece of thick glass is fixed across the upper portion of the opening. It is better to fix a piece of metal – brass or copper – in this position, and after a time it will probably be found that this can be removed. The object aimed at is to get the fire as unconfined as possible without smoke. To shut the fire in a small and low recess is to lose that liberal aspect which is so important and to shirk the difficulty of the problem, and the important point is to get whatever nice experimental adjustment done before the house is inhabited, and for this purpose the metal placed across the upper part of the fire is an expedient which does not spoil the appearance and can easily be either removed altogether or raised to the maximum height which the completely aired flue will allow. In special cases where down draught is caused by special winds or local features, a special form of chimney-pot may be required, and of these the Boyle extractors are the most satisfactory.

CHAPTER TWENTY FOUR

DOORS

IN considering the individual features which go to make up a house, it must be remembered that they form part of a structure which should be homogeneous, and as a learned professor may build up the structure of an extinct animal from a few bones, so, in the house, a single door for instance, should express in its design much of the general character of the building to which it belongs. Eclecticism is a principle which may be followed in the designing of a house only under severe restrictions. We may choose, indeed, from all the Ages, but in choosing we must change till all is in harmony.

The simplest kind of door is one composed of vertical planks, secured to horizontal cross-ledges. The candid construction of such a door finds itself peculiarly at home in a house where the direct and simple use of materials is the keynote of the design. In the average modern house it has been relegated to back premises, in favour of elaborate arrangements of mouldings and panels, but in many respects it is more appropriate and more interesting than the panelled door.

In the first place, its two sides are quite distinct in character, one with its unbroken surface forming a field for the decorative use of ironwork in hinges and latch, and the other with its ledges barring the surface of the door with horizontal lines.

This type of door may be most consistently used in a solid frame of wood, or hung on gudgeons set in stonework, or brickwork of the doorway. It is less desirable when the internal finishings of the house are entirely superficial, and in carrying the principle of direct expression of constructive decoration which such a door exemplifies to its logical conclusion in the house, the universal use of plaster as an internal finish for the walls is not always desirable, for plaster entails the use of superficial woodwork in the form of fascias and skirtings, which are not quite in harmony with the ledged type of door. A compromise may, however, be effected in this matter by reducing such fascias to their smallest dimensions, and thus keeping them quite distinct from the structural woodwork, to make them appear rather part of the plaster than part of the door frame.

Or if the actual brickwork or stonework of the wall or the woodwork of the framed partition is left exposed, this will form the most satisfactory setting for a door of this description.

The consideration of the old Scandinavian door frames which were so intricately carved, suggests the use of the plain surface of the ledged door as a foil to the carving of the frame which embowers it with branches, leaves and fruit.

The next type of door to be considered is the panelled door, which presents many possibilities for design in the number and proportion of the panels, and the moulding of the rails and styles.

In the simpler types of door the mouldings may be omitted altogether, and wherever mouldings are introduced, they should justify their existence by the refinement and beauty of their lines. Inasmuch as they serve no practical purpose, and rest their claims to our regard solely on æsthetic qualities, there seems little excuse for the existence of the coarse and ugly mouldings which disfigure the doors of the average house.

In a panelled room it is generally desirable to make the doors a part of the panelling, so that the continuity of the wall treatment is unbroken. In this way the door becomes almost a secret one, and does not assert itself as a feature in the room.

In the same way a door may be effaced by covering it with arras cloth or canvas in a room which is hung with this material, and this leads us to the consideration of the door which is made specially to cut off sound, and which tradition has decreed shall be covered with red or green baize. This type of door may be covered with canvas and decorated with embroidery or stencilling.

Doors may also be covered with metal work of various kinds – with brass, copper or lead, and ornamented with repoussé work, or with leather which may be embossed and tooled.

The use of metal is particularly suitable for an exterior door, where it suggests permanence and strength.

In the number and arrangements of the doors in a house, it will be found generally desirable to have but one to each room, and that so placed as to avoid draughts at the fireside.

The multiplication of doors in a room may seem desirable if convenience of access only is considered, but they do not make for comfort of habitation, and in most cases every additional door means a possible draught, and a corresponding decrease in the comfort of the room.

In the hanging of the doors it should be arranged that they screen the room as far as possible when open.

CHAPTER TWENTY FIVE

CEILINGS

ONE of the most widespread of the popular delusions about houses is expressed in the demand for a high ceiling, quite irrespective of the scale of the house or the size of its apartments. The mansion, with its numerous apartments and lofty rooms, is still the model for the small house. Under the inexorable pressure of the limited site and limited means the rooms are reduced till each is too small for human habitation, but still the lofty ceiling is retained, partly because it is an attribute of the ideal mansion, and partly because of the baseless superstition that it is healthy.

This "hygienic falsehood," as Mr. Voysey justly describes it, has been sufficiently exposed, but apparently to little purpose. Conditions of perfect ventilation are quite independent of the cubic capacity of a room. A man enclosed in a box sufficient only to accommodate his person may enjoy perfect hygienic conditions as regards ventilation. But the question is not one between a small cubic capacity and a large cubic capacity. We have, it may be assumed, a certain sum of money to expend in cubic feet of air in a room, and the question is, how are these cubic feet best arranged to secure the best results – to what extent shall they be disposed vertically, to what extent horizontally? Now it is obvious that, as man cannot fly but wants all the elbow-room he can get in a small house, it will be wise for him to extend his rooms as much as possible horizontally, and as little as possible vertically; and the first improvement which suggests itself in the small house will be to make it lower and broader, so that all the wasted space overhead may be exchanged for extension of the floor area. Such a change, it must be borne in mind, will not decrease the cubic capacity or increase the cost. Not only will it increase the actual size, it will also add to the apparent size of the rooms. They will become at once large rooms of a small kind instead of small rooms of a large kind. We shall so far achieve the roomy cottage instead of the cramped mansion. It is unfortunate that the by-laws in many districts reflect the popular superstition in this matter, and minimum heights of ceilings are often fixed which make it impossible to build a small house on rational lines.

For the height of the ceiling is not an isolated and independent feature in the plan, which may be modified at will. It is one of the ruling factors in the design of a house, and governs the whole structure. The long, low window of the horizontal type, which has so many practical advantages, follows as a necessary result of the long, low room. The staircase becomes easy of ascent and occupies little space. The house itself becomes broad and low and snug, and in its rooms this breadth and spaciousness is exchanged for the cramped floor-spaces of the vertically extended house. The ceiling, too, comes into the picture of the room and completes it, and the whole effect is comfortable and homely.

The fixing of the ceiling height of rooms, which is often so thoughtlessly and lightly decided, will influence its final effect inside and outside far more than any subsequent decorations, and the initial mistake made of a badly proportioned room will consume the abilities of the decorator in trying to palliate it with all kinds of divisions of the wall-space.

The test of good proportion in a room, as in a house, is that the structure can be left alone if desired, and while its wall-spaces may be subdivided horizontally for decorative purposes, this is not essential to palliate bad proportions or to disguise the defects of the original structure.

One of the most important functions of the ceiling is to act as a reflector for light, and for this purpose it is generally advisable that it should be white.

In cases where the joists of the floor above are shown in the ceiling, the most important consideration will be the proper "deafening" of the floor. This may be done as shown in Fig. 1, where two thicknesses of boards are used for the floor, with a layer of felt between. It will be noticed that the joists are here flatter in proportion than those generally used, and they should also be somewhat wider apart than modern usage demands.

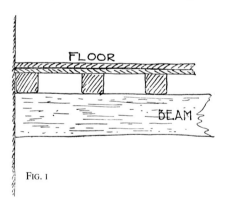

FIG. 1

The under side of the flooring-boards and the joists and beam may all be left roughly finished from the saw, with the edges merely taken off them, and then the whole may be whitewashed.

In the spacing, as well as the actual sizes of the joists, it is not desirable that mechanical accuracy should be insisted on. They may be placed with such regularity in their distance apart as the eye may be able to judge, and it would be well also if they slightly varied in size, and all these slight variations in the size, direction, and spacing of the timbers will give a vitality to the whole effect, and the eye will not be repelled and chilled by that monotonous and cast-iron regularity which is the ideal of modern work. It is the eye of the observer which is to be satisfied with such work, and to the intelligent there will be no pleasure in an inhuman precision which is obviously obtained by mechanical means.

There are occasions and places in the building where an extreme accuracy is necessary, but in this, as in many other cases, a certain variety is essential. It is just such little points as these which make the difference between the vital beauty of old buildings and the lifeless uniformity of modern ones.

Other and more elaborate ceilings may be divided into panels with wooden ribs. In such cases there is an obvious departure from the floor structure of the room above, and such panellings should therefore not be too structural in their character, but of such sizes as will lead to the recognition of their superficial character. They may most reasonably be used in passages where it may be desirable to form the ceiling at a lower level than the upper floor, and the narrower the passage the lower its ceiling should be. Nothing is so fatal as the Procrustean method of making every department of the house of the same height irrespective of the size of each, and nothing makes a narrow passage look so narrow as a disproportionately high ceiling.

In the treatment or the plaster ceiling it will be well to consider first whether the plaster cornice is really necessary. It does not in its usual forms represent a reasonable use of the material, because plaster is necessarily a superficial substance, and should as far as possible clothe the structure like a close-fitting garment. The cornice has no structural significance whatever, and is merely an expedient to get round the corner between wall and ceiling. A much better way in most cases is to omit the cornice altogether, and whitewash the whole of frieze and ceiling. In this way, the angle between ceiling and wall will practically disappear in the universal whiteness. The plaster ceiling should not, moreover, be made absolutely and mechanically level, except as a basis for superficial decoration. The plasterer should not be allowed to use a long "float," but it should only be permissible for him to gain such regularity as may be possible in the use of a short "float" with the assistance of the eye. I do not suggest that the ceiling should be obviously irregular. It should appear to the casual observer to be quite level, but it should present a subtle variety and change of plane in its surface. Why, too, it may be asked, should the plaster ceiling be necessarily finished with what is called "fine stuff"? Plaster has a characteristic texture, which is far more interesting than the smoothness of finish invariably insisted on. Such subtle modifications in the plastering of a ceiling will all tend towards vitality in the appearance of the work.

Perhaps the most reasonable and effective way of decorating a plaster ceiling is by means of the use of modelled plaster work, which Mr. Bankart has so bravely rescued from mechanical ineptitude. Here the modelling should be vague and suggestive rather than sharp and incisive, and flowers and fruit should seem to have floated, as it were, to the surface – to have been coaxed from their white bed instead of stuck on to a surface from which they are clearly detached.

Much of the old plaster work has obtained an excellent quality by repeated coats of whitewash, and if any of the mechanical embossed materials are used, their undesirable sharpness can be removed by the same means.

It is not necessary, if modelled plaster is used, to have an elaborate scheme of decoration for the ceiling. Much may be done by stamps, such as those used for pats of butter.

In upper rooms it is often possible to obtain an excellent effect by means of a curved segmented ceiling, which affords an excellent field for decoration in many ways, and in a room where the walls are covered with leafage with glimpses of blue sky, this ceiling may develop into a blue sky without a cloud and set with circling swallows.

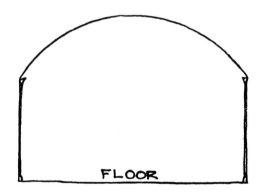

The consideration of vaulted ceilings hardly comes within the scope of my present subject, and can but be barely touched on here. A small example of this form of ceiling occurs in the little staircase to the room over the fireplace in the hall, illustrated in the description of "Blackwell."

Simple types of vaulting may often be used in corridors with excellent effect, but this method of ceiling is hardly appropriate for the average room.

CHAPTER TWENTY SIX

WINDOWS

When Pentridge House wer' still the nest
Of souls that now ha' better rest,
Avore the vier burnt to ground
His beams an' walls that then wer' sound—
'Ithin a nail-bestudded door,
An' passage an' a stwonen vloor,
There spread the hall, where zanlight shone.
In drough a window fream'd wi' stwone.

William Barnes

THE primary object of the introduction of windows into a house is to let light into its rooms. They also afford a means of looking at the outside world, and in their modern development also afford the outside world a means of looking in. While apart from these uses they also serve for the ventilation of the house.

In the modern house, windows are almost invariably too large, and this excessive size is fatal both to the comfort and beauty of the rooms. If we enter an old house on a hot summer's day, one of the most pleasant qualities we notice is its coolness, and though it is amply lighted there is a sensation of remoteness from the outside world. We feel at once really an inhabitant of an indoor world, where the blazing sun, or the pouring rain, may be almost forgotten. It is a shelter and retreat – a pleasant haven, and this quality about it goes far to give us the feeling of rest associated with the idea of home.

And all this is greatly due to the small windows. But on entering the modern villa no such pleasant impression meets us. Already from the outside we have been made aware of these gashes in the structure, which reveal the window arranged, like a shop is, for outside effect. There is the table with its vase, the lace curtains, and the rest. Inside, we are met by a glaring and pitiless light which destroys all sense of repose or shelter. The rain beats in torrents against the glass, and the sun blazes unchecked into the room. The window is indeed furnished with all kinds of expensive dust collecting upholstery, but even this cannot cloak the glaring light. The window has also made the room susceptible to every change of temperature outside. It is impossible to cool it in summer, or heat it in winter.

So much for its practical effect. To say that large windows make architecture all but impossible is to touch an aspect of the case which will interest few, but I can recall no example of building where the windows are formed with large sheets of glass which have survived their disastrous effect. The beauty of glass depends entirely on its use in small pieces, in a setting which, allowing of a slight variation in their planes, will make them sparkle and twinkle. The large sheet, with its blank and vacant stare, should never be used unless under stress of circumstances.

One of the most essential reforms in the modern house is the reduction of its windows to a reasonable size, and their careful placing to amply light the interior without destroying its repose, or making it unduly subject to the changes of the external temperature. With the large window will also be banished all its trappings and the venetian blind, and the rest of the upholstery with the cumbrous poles and rings will be replaced by a simple curtain blind, on a light rod of brass or iron.

Many people who regard the window mainly as a means of prospect demand the large sheet of glass. Such a demand can, however, be generally met by concessions introducing a larger pane of plate-glass to command a particular view. Windows can be made large enough to meet such requirements without any serious drawbacks, but there are those who find a peculiar pleasure in the prospect afforded by the smaller pane. The leaded line becomes a bar of shade which seems to enhance the beauty of the landscape it conceals, and yet reveals. Imagination, which is foiled by the bald complete revelation of the plate-glass window, has here a chance to play its part, and to weave a beauty of its own out of the actual facts partially displayed, and the window becomes a picture gallery of separate scenes, each with its own little frame. The type of window most suitable, at any rate in the country and suburbs, is the casement opening outwards like a door. It is the simplest to construct, and least likely to get out of order. As it enlarges it increases horizontally in the low room, and in higher apartments it increases vertically by one or more rows of lights separated by horizontal bars. The long low type of window has a practical advantage which is not always recognised. On a south aspect it may be left uncurtained without fear of the direct rays of the sun raking the whole room. The sash window is more suitable in the town than in the country, though it is a necessary part of the house which is based on Georgian traditions. It is better adapted for lofty rooms than low ones, and is not suited for the horizontal type of window which is advocated for the average house. In its modern form it has been much debased by the thinness of its

106

cross-bars, but when these are of reasonable thickness, and well moulded as in its earlier forms, it is more acceptable, but it never achieves the simple constructional appearance of the casement.

In the small house the casement window will, on economical grounds, be constructed in wood, but in larger houses stone will be admissible, and this building of the window-frame with the leaded glass let into the stone, reduces the openings to their simplest structural form. There is no external woodwork to require painting, and the whole exterior of the house will look capable of standing the weather. Stone window-frames are specially suitable in the stone house of a stone district, and especially in bleak exposed positions where woodwork often has a flimsy appearance. Casement window-frames of both wood or stone should be simple and solid in their construction, and should appear to be fully capable of carrying the wall over them without the addition of concealed lintels or arches. The wooden casement is most happily at home in the house framed in half timber, where its mullions appear part of the general framing.

In order to secure the feeling of enclosure from the outside world it is desirable that the window sill should not be too near the floor, and to make the best use of the window area for lighting it, is important that the window-head should be near the ceiling level.

In order to secure ideal artistic conditions, especially in low-toned rooms, it is desirable that all windows which are on the level of the eye should be toned by means of stained glass or other means. Any light in a room which has the effect of causing inhalation in a photograph of the room has also the effect of dazzling the eye and making it out of focus with the lower tones of the interior, which would be best seen if all the light came from above.

The function of muslin curtains to windows is to temper the crudeness of the light. For the same purpose the Japanese use oiled paper in their windows, and this suffused and tempered light helps to maintain that feeling of repose which is somewhat diminished by the glare of light from a window which is on the level of the eye. The objection may be much reduced by the placing of the windows so that the room may be viewed on entering it lighted from a side which is not facing the observer. In a hall, part of the lighting may be gained from windows at a high level, but it is impossible under ordinary conditions to quite get over this difficulty, and the best that can be effected is a more or less successful compromise. The objection is much reduced by the reduction in the size of the windows, which has been advocated; but as long as windows are considered necessary for outlook as well as inlets of light, they must necessarily involve a certain glare of light. It is best, therefore, to concentrate the window space so that the light comes from one side only, and that side being the one wherever possible which it is not necessary to face. This lighting from one point is also desirable for the general appearance of the room and its occupants. Cross-lights are always undesirable, and most things look best when lighted from one side only.

The function of the bay window is chiefly to enlarge the range of prospect and aspect in a room. By this means a window on an east or west front may admit the southern sun or display a view to north or south which might otherwise be lost. Their position and form should be to a great extent the outcome of local requirements in this respect. They also have their uses in extending the floor-space of the room. They may often be fitted with a window-seat, which, in helping to reduce the movable furniture, will tend towards the ideal of the unobstructed floor-space in the room.

Where means will allow it is desirable to glaze the leaded squares of the window with crown-glass. Instead of the absolutely flat surface of sheet-glass, this has subtle modulations which, while they do not detract from its uses, give it that characteristic quality which it should be one's aim to secure in all the materials for the house.

The casement window will give opportunities for some interesting blacksmiths' work in the form of casement stays and fasteners.

CHAPTER TWENTY SEVEN

WALL TREATMENT

I N the internal treatment of the walls of the house, before deciding on any superficial decoration which presupposes the usual formula of plaster and wallpaper, it will be well to consider what claims the structure itself has to be displayed internally and to what extent these claims should be admitted. At the fireplace, it has already been suggested that the stonework or brick-work of the wall itself is peculiarly appropriate as a setting for the fire. At the windows and doors the wall again may crop out in the form of arches, and in the upper part in some cases of the walls themselves. In order, however, to obtain a sense of comfort it is generally desirable that the lower parts of the walls should be finished with a material not too cold or rough to the touch.

It is in the stone house especially that the structure is most interesting, for brickwork is necessarily a little mechanical and monotonous in its effect, and the best stone for this purpose is that which is rather warm in tone.

Let us suppose the case of a hall for instance where the structure is completed with stone-mullioned windows, stone archways to the doors and fireplace, and the masonry left inside without plaster. Its effect would be a little cold, though it would possess that air of reality which the actualities of building have the power of conveying. In the modern phrase it would "palpitate with actuality," but it requires a certain amount of clothing to make it appear comfortable. Let us then fix to the walls, to a height of six or seven feet, some wide oak planks, and on a portion of the upper part of the walls hang a piece of tapestry. The room will now begin to look comfortable, though the superficial finishings will not destroy the sense of structure which they partially conceal. But a treatment of this kind would only be suggested where the stonework was good in colour – too good to hide with plaster unless the plaster is the basis for decoration which will compensate for the loss of the structural effect. In the room which thus becomes a decorated plaster box, the result is not an example of the art of building, of which architecture should be the supreme expression, but a purely decorative affair.

In a brick house the extent to which the wall is shown would be more limited – perhaps at the fireplace only, but in finishing the walls with plaster it is suggested that this should only be brought to an absolutely flat surface as a preparation for decorative work – in the same way that a piece of canvas is strained for painting a picture on. Plaster which is to be finished with a plain colour should have its characteristic surface and should be finished from the trowel.

In the use of woodwork on the walls, it is not by any means necessary to use expensive and elaborate panelling, and if ledged doors are used the most logical continuation of their construction will be expressed in the use of planks to the heights of the doors or forming a dado. These planks may be as wide as can be obtained, and of varying sizes, with a simple capping, which in some cases may develop into a shelf. The ordinary stained and varnished dado of V-jointed match-boarding of depressing regularity is an example of the most degraded use of good material. The V-joint represents a clumsy attempt to hide the opening of a joint, due to the shrinkage of the timber, which deceives nobody.

In the use of great planks of varying widths and somewhat roughly finished, the timber still suggests in a far-off way the beauty of the woodland, and still in the varied planes of its surface retains something of its individuality and tells of the workman and his tools; and all this interest should only be given up in the case of a material which, like mahogany for instance, demands a higher finish to bring out its beauty. The wall above this woodwork may either be the stone of the structure or perhaps brickwork whitewashed or finished with trowelled plaster, or if some more superficial treatment is adapted, the plaster may be modelled or stencil decoration may be introduced. All these should, however, possess a real beauty. They should be unique and individual, and few of the superficial decorative materials of commerce will have the same claim to our regard as the structural beauty they conceal.

Apart from economical considerations probably the best superficial material for the walls of a room is tapestry. A wall peopled with dim figures, with trees, with fruit, flowers, and flowing streams, illustrating, perhaps, some legend of "the supreme Caucasian mind," or of the Knights of King Arthur, or, better still, some story entirely local and peculiar, will be indeed well lost for such adornment, and on entering such a room one will become a member of its goodly company, wandering in imagination by stream and grove in a land where flowers always bloom and fruit hangs ripe on the bough.

Such surroundings are, however, only for those who having the means have also the wit to choose such company for their life, and these are few indeed.

A simple form of wall hanging, and one which will be within the means of the majority, is canvas unadorned. Specially suitable for a house by the sea is the ruddy brown of the sails of fishing-boats, with above, perhaps, a stencilled or modelled frieze of flying sea-gulls in white, grey and blue.

Canvas of its natural undyed colour is also an excellent basis for decoration, or if gilded it forms an excellent background for pictures merging into the gilt of the frames connecting the pictures with the wall, and absorbing them as it were into the decorative scheme, instead of emphasising that detachment from their surroundings which makes the picture too often appear an alien in the decorative community.

A warmer scheme may be inaugurated with canvas dyed a dull red and decorated with stencilling in dim gold, or green and blue canvas may form a basis for cooler arrangements of colour.

If wallpapers are adopted the quality of texture must be given up to some extent, though some of the plain ingrain papers with their rough surfaces are not entirely devoid of this quality. In pattern papers there are nowadays an overwhelming number of designs, many of which are excellent. Of these, one need only mention the famous Morris papers or those more recent designs by Mr. Voysey, Mr. Walter Crane, or others who are content to forego their claims to individual recognition in favour of the manufacturing firms. In the design of wallpapers it is universally considered essential to disguise the fact that the paper is pasted on in strips and it is suggested that papers might be designed which, repeating only vertically, do not attempt to disguise the joints formed by their edges, or the joints might be emphasised by dividing vertical strips of plain paper by narrow bands resembling in character ecclesiastical laces.

In choosing wallpapers as well as other decorative materials it should be borne in mind that their qualities are necessarily relative to their surroundings, and this relative suitability should always be considered in preference to intrinsic beauty.

Another material which has great decorative value on the wall is leather. It should retain its characteristic surface, and its qualities be suggested by lacing the skins together at the edges.

Whatever treatment is adopted for the walls it must never be forgotten that they are after all chiefly valuable as a background. A room is not entirely a thing to be looked at, but a place to be lived in, and its virtue will chiefly consist in forming a setting for the life of its occupants and the transient beauty of flowers. And it is here that so many modern artistic interiors fail. In the drawing-room with its multitude of insistent patterns you may fill every vase with flowers and they will seem to disappear; but in a room where the wall has not lost its quality as a background, a single rose will give one the impression that the whole room had been designed with no other object but to show off the curves of its petals. It is here that panelling is so valuable, and against a background of dark oak or mahogany everything will look its best. For woodwork has a quality of tone, a "timbre" which is unequalled. Full tones of green or greyish blue are also excellent background colours in canvases or paper.

One of the fundamental questions in wall decoration is whether the objects they relieve are to be dark on a light ground or light on a dark ground, and between these two classes are the middle tones.

As a general rule, and especially in informal rooms, a dark background is the best, because the objects displayed in the room merge into the background instead of being sharply defined against it. Against a wall of white woodwork, for instance, furniture in dark mahogany seems to demand a certain formality in its disposition, and the slightest disarrangement is at once perceptible. But place the same furniture against panelling of mahogany and its outlines are no longer salient, its exact disposition is no longer an essential matter. As, however, it is only the lower portions of the walls which form the background for furniture and people, the upper portions may reasonably be decorated in a less restricted way. A dark treatment of the background portion of the walls may tend to make the whole effect somewhat gloomy, and so it is desirable that the upper portion should be in a lighter key, and thus the old formula of dark oak panelling, with white plaster work above, forms a very reasonable solution of the problem. In the use of middle tones for the background portion of the wall it is important that they should keep their place and not compete with the furniture and ornaments. The use of patterns in this connection is chiefly valuable as a means of improving and enriching the quality of tone in the background.

I have insisted at some length on this subject of background because it is the point most readily lost sight of in modern work. The practice of exhibiting specimen rooms has led to a conception of an interior as something to be looked at and admired for its own sake – an arrangement of certain colours and patterns which is pleasing to the eye, whereas the final test of a successful room is that people look well in it. In the modern room the individual withers and becomes but an incident, and often a discordant incident, in a scheme which is complete and self-sufficing. The rooms of the past, the Elizabethan hall for instance, with its wall spaces of dark oak, appear incomplete without their inhabitants, and the individual seems to gain an importance and dignity in a setting so rich and yet so subordinated. Or again, in those French salons, which Orchardson paints, with their wall spaces of white, an elegant company is still more elegant, though here the white background in emphasising outlines demands a gracefulness of form and gesture which, with the more homely and less exacting dark background, is less essential.

Having decided to what extent structures shall form the decoration of the walls, and in considering the question of superficial decoration, it will be desirable to turn to Nature and think of the pleasantest natural surroundings one can conceive. Thus we may wish to surround ourselves with the green leafage of trees, where fruit gleams golden and blossoms white, where birds cling and flutter in the branches, from between which one catches glimpses of the blue sky. Here, where the greater part of the wall-surface is covered with leafage, the pattern becomes naturally a better background than if flowers are the motif, for, in conventionalising these, it may become necessary to tone down the brightness of their colouring if the pattern is used on the lower part of the walls, and they are, therefore, perhaps better adapted for the decoration of friezes.

But a certain reasonableness should govern the decorative scheme of the wall; and just as one should not be obliged to walk on flying birds and trees laid out flat on a carpet, so flowers in the frieze should not bloom over tree tops.

CHAPTER TWENTY EIGHT

THICKNESS OF WALLS AND INTERNAL PARTITIONS

I N small houses, where economy must be studied, it is not advisable to indulge in a thick wall in brickwork, for its advantages will hardly be justified by its cost, and the money so spent would probably be more wisely devoted to an increase of the floor space. In such cases a nine-inch brick wall covered with cement rough cast and strengthened where required with buttresses, will answer all practical purposes.

In stone districts, however, the thin wall is no longer an economic gain, and the exterior walls may be made two feet thick.

This has many artistic as well as practical advantages, giving deep jambs to windows and recesses, enabling one to get a broad window-sill or seat without projecting into the room, and giving the whole interior an effect of solidity and comfort. To enter such a house is to feel really indoors, sheltered and protected from external conditions. Practically, also, the thick wall helps to maintain in the house an even temperature uninfluenced by external heat and cold. In winter it is easily warmed, and in summer it remains cool. But these conditions do not apply to the average modern house, where the builder, having built a thick wall to retain the heat, makes a large window to let it out, and to reap the advantage of the thick wall the window openings must be small.

Another advantage of the thick wall is that, with a high-pitched roof especially, it enables one in many cases to get a lower eaves line with the same inside height.

Internal walls should vary in thickness according to their position and structural requirements. The kitchen premises should be divided from the rest of the house by a solid wall, and this may be made more impervious to

113

sound by the introduction of cupboards.

Between the family rooms generally, except those which require isolation, it will be noted that the principles advocated involve the breaking away of the usual partitions, and much of the beauty and interest of the house will depend on the extent to which this principle is judiciously applied. If, for instance, one imagines the corridor in the house called "Springcot," flanked with ordinary partitions, much of its character would disappear, and very much of its effect here depends on the suggestion conveyed by the glazed screen to the dining-room of something beyond half-concealed and half-revealed, and such effects as may be legitimately obtained by such means are very helpful in obtaining a successful interior. As in all Art this suggestive quality is more potent in its charm than a complete revelation. In old buildings the wood and plaster partitions were often constructed to display the framing, as in half timber work, and this displayed use of construction may be effectively used in the house. The practical objection to it is that the vibration caused by the doors is apt to shake the key of the plaster filling; and so in modern work it is usual to cover the joint between the plaster and the door frames with a piece called a fascia, and this gradually led to the elimination of the solid structural door frame, and the use of superficial exposed woodwork. By keeping the door posts solid and heavy as befits their structural nature, and by reducing superficial fascias to their smallest dimensions, the structural feeling of the whole can still be retained, or if the plaster is omitted and the timber framing built in with bricks and tiles the fascia will not be required.

Such a method of construction in internal partitions is especially suitable in a half-timbered house, where it represents the logical continuation of the external structure.

CHAPTER TWENTY NINE

THE FLOOR AND ITS TREATMENT

IT is difficult to over-estimate the importance of the floor in the house, and its successful treatment goes further to secure a satisfactory room than anything which may be done to walls and ceiling. And this importance of the floor increases in direct ratio with the size of the room, for while in a normal attitude we may not be conscious of the floor immediately beneath our feet, its distant portions come more fully into the picture. In a level landscape all that the eye can see up to the point where the sky begins may be considered as floor, but where a wall of trees encompasses the observer, the nearer it is the less important become the floor and the more insistent the wall, so that the relative value of wall and floor vary in direct ratio to the size of the room. But the floor has an additional claim in that, unlike the wall or ceiling, it is constantly subjected to the sensation of touch as well as sight. In considering the internal treatment of the house, it is suggested that the claims of the structure should be first recognised, and should only be set aside in favour of superficial decoration when such a treatment more than compensates for the loss of that sensation of reality and sincerity which the actual building alone can convey.

If we decide to obscure or partially obscure the structure by superficial treatment, it may be helpful to turn to Nature for inspiration, and to think of the best natural floors we know, and thus, for instance, one may evolve a conventional equivalent of a green meadow studded with flowers. But in the floor treatment there is a special reason for not too lightly setting aside the claims of the structure. It is the floor more than any other part of the house which is subjected to a constant wear and tear, and it is here that dirt and dust accumulate. It seems reasonable then that it should present a durable surface, and that it should be capable of being easily cleaned. All this points to the exclusion of carpets in favour of floors composed of stone, tile or timber. There is a special charm in the floor composed of large stone flags, not too regular in shape or too closely jointed. It conveys an impression of permanence and breadth combined with homely serviceableness, which it is difficult to gain in any other way, and with a few rugs giving warm notes of colour on its expanse of varied grey, it is not so cold in appearance as might be supposed. Red tiles or bricks also have, in a less degree, much the same qualities if they are not too highly finished and possess a characteristic surface and texture. Tiles used in patterns are less desirable unless designed with great skill, and mosaics of marble or glass, such as were so successfully used in Roman or Byzantine buildings, are hardly within the means of the average house-builder, and their beauty is hardly homely enough in its character for the modern English house. The uses of the room will to a large extent determine the treatment of its floor, and, while those apartments constantly used by the members of the family may have floors of timber with a few rugs, those only occasionally occupied may be carpeted, while the stone or tile floor is peculiarly adapted for bathrooms, lavatories and kitchen offices.

In the sitting-rooms of the average house there is one apparent extravagance which may prove wise, and that is the use of oak or some hard wood for the floor. It is lasting and durable, and will outlive a succession of carpets, and it meets both practical and æsthetic requirements. It need not be in narrow boards, and, if properly prepared in the first instance, it need not be polished. It is cleanly and labour-saving, for, of all the trappings with which we surround ourselves, the carpet will be found to be the most tyrannical, and, however we multiply door-mats and scrapers, muddy boots on a clean carpet will be a constant source of anxiety to a careful housewife.

CHAPTER THIRTY

CARPETS AND RUGS

IN the choice of carpets it would be well to avoid the dirty drab and biscuit-brown tones which make the average villa such a depressing place. Whatever else the carpet may be, it should at least be cleanly and pure in its colouring. It is well to secure, if possible, a colouring which will not show the dirt; but this principle may be carried too far, and while one may be content with dirty colours chosen on these grounds for railway carriages or steamboats, one can hardly be satisfied with them in the home, where the appearance of cleanness and freshness is invaluable. Better a floor of scrubbed deal than a frowsy carpet which, however clean or however unclean it may be, always looks dirty.

On the other hand, it would be well to avoid what is quaintly described as the "Art Square"; first, apparently because it is seldom square, and secondly, because there is little art about it. If we are to carpet at all, let the carpet extend right to the edges of the room. Round the margin of the art square custom has declared there must be a sort of Tom Tiddler's Ground of boards, stained a dark brown and varnished. This constitutes one border, and the art square provides a second inner border, which is one of those accommodating patterns which does not mind being cut to fit any size, and so the floor in a small room resolves itself into a series of borders. First there is the art square, which immediately breaks out into border, and then border again in the shape of varnished boards. All this frittering away of the

116

floor surface reduces the apparent size of the room, and the carpet is too large to be considered a rug and too small for the room as a carpet. It is usually adorned with flights of birds and trees laid out flat, and the pattern, instead of developing from centres, develops from the side. Surely, of all the furnishings labelled with that fatal prefix, the art square is the least to be desired.

Although, from a practical point of view, it is extremely desirable that rooms subjected to much wear should be uncarpeted, it must be confessed that nothing gives such a sensation of luxurious comfort to a room as a deep pile carpet, where footsteps are noiseless. Carpets like Brussels, which have no softness and depth, are unsatisfactory; and, if a carpet is decided on, it is best to get the full possibilities of this means of floor treatment. A plain green Axminster makes an excellent floor covering, and realises that meadow-life effect which has already been alluded to. Or a deep red carpet makes a fine basis for a warmer scheme of colour, while a good blue is almost equally desirable, though this colour is not quite so reliable. In all cases it is well to avoid borders and central ornaments, and to have an absolutely plain colouring, confining whatever pattern may be used to the rugs which may be placed at the fireside and at doorways.

The soft reds, blues and greens of the Turkey carpets are excellent for certain rooms, and the possession of an old Turkey carpet would indeed justify its possessor in taking it as the basis for a decorative scheme. Persian rugs and carpets are also of great beauty, and have been so long associated with Western furnishings, that they do not seem to demand an Oriental character in the treatment of the rooms they occupy.

This is not the case, however, with many other traditional types of carpet, which are only possible in rooms furnished in the traditional styles.

Cheap carpets may be obtained of jute, but when dyed these are rarely to be relied upon, and, if used, it is better that they should be undyed, and this natural "string colour" will form an excellent floor covering for a cottage-like room.

Some allusion has been made to that silent tyranny which inanimate things have the power of exercising over their possessors. This tyrannical attitude is chiefly noticeable in the carpet, and to reduce it to a proper subjection a yearly beating with rods is necessary. In the case of rugs, this annual drubbing is not demanded, and an occasional shaking is all that is required. In most cases it is therefore desirable that carpets should not be universally used in the house, and that they should be easily removable.

117

CHAPTER THIRTY ONE

THE HOUSE IN RELATION TO ITS SITE

If God has made the country, then may God
At least complete the country house;
So let the humble artist stand aside,
Prepare the canvas and the palette set
For those sure hands
Which touch by touch add purple to his roofs,
And clothe his walls with woodbine and with rose.

THE success of the artist in house-building will largely depend on his faculty for recognising the demands of the *genius loci*. Robert Louis Stevenson, in his "Gossip of Romance," has shown how the aim of the writer of fiction should be to fit to a particular place its appropriate story, to make the right thing happen in the right place, and so satisfy the imagination of the reader. And so the architect must try to express in his building the spirit of the country-side. So far from forming the blot on the scene which the modern country house or cottage so often is, it must be, if possible, an added beauty, appearing to interpret and explain the character of the surrounding country, and supplying that human note without which its appeal would be less intimate.

To explain this relation between the house and its surroundings, one must turn to the old buildings, and think first of some village in Kent or Surrcy, with its cluster of purple roofs and timber-framed walls. There is no inharmonious note here, unless it be the modern Board school, or a few smug modern villas or cottages. Or again, let us visit, in imagination, a Wiltshire village where the straggling cottages which line the wide High Street are all of pearly grey. And here perhaps the sole discordant note may be a modern arrangement of red bricks and tiles. Or, if we go further north, we shall find in a rugged mountainous district houses and cottages which express the same stern qualities as their neighbour hills. Again, in a chalk district, such as Norfolk for instance, we find that the presence of beds of flint in the chalk causes them to be used for building the walls. And so these old villages constitute a kind of geological map of the country. Much of the appropriateness of the old buildings to their positions was due no doubt to this use of the local materials. The stone house was thus of the very stone

118

of the hill out of which it grew, so that it became difficult to realise where man's work began and Nature's ended. Or the timbered structure was framed from the trees of the forest near which it stood, and in its curved braces and massive corner posts still there lingered some hints of the forms of the branches from which they were hewn. The step from Nature to building was a short one, and the materials were not subjected to the iron rule of the factory to lose their characteristic qualities under the steam saw and planing-machine. Not only were the conditions more favourable to the retention of local character, but the builders themselves were unconsciously closer to Nature and were almost as much a part of their natural surroundings as their buildings were. Their conceptions were the unconscious result of long hours spent in the open fields, and not the conscious and fantastic imaginings bred in offices and factories. And so it will generally be found that communities based on agriculture are usually characterised by buildings in harmony with Nature, while round the factory building becomes mean and sordid.

Modern facilities of transit, as well as the artificial conditions of modern life, the influence of machinery on the modern workman and his materials, as well as the growth of the commercial spirit are the main causes which have destroyed local character in modern building, and so on the bleak hillside we find the machine-made half-timbered picturesque villa showing in its rugged environment like a child's toy which has been left out in the rain. The town encroaches on the surrounding country like the spreading of some foul disease, and in the wildest and most picturesque scenery the traveller's enthusiasm is checked by the fatal glimpse of a desirable residence "pricking a cockney ear" over the tree-tops. Building, no longer an added beauty to the country, has become a nightmare of ugliness from which there is no escape, and soon the pictures in the railway carriages will be the last surviving record of the beauty of the past.

In modern building, while we may well learn a lesson from the old work, in using local materials, it would be unreasonable to forego the opportunity modern transit affords of importing materials which are more suitable for our requirements. Such importation, if judiciously effected, will not destroy the harmony between the house and its surroundings. It becomes dangerous when materials of an artificial character are imported to a district where the buildings are of natural materials. Stone, for instance, may not look out of place in a brick district, but it is not generally advisable to introduce a brick house into a stone locality.

It is desirable in country building to use materials which will colour naturally. Whatever artists we may employ to decorate the interior of the country house, it is well to invoke the aid of Nature in toning down its exterior till it harmonises with its surroundings and its walls are clothed with creepers. And so the materials for the exterior will be chosen with this end in view, and its tiles and bricks will not be selected for the smoothness of their surface.

In the town, on the contrary, this natural colouring cannot be included in the architect's scheme, and everything will tend to become black and dirty. Whatever beauty its buildings possess must be of an entirely artificial character, and the beauty of the whole must depend on some definite and conscious conception which should include a colour scheme. There is little to cheer the heart of man in the dingy buildings of stone or brick which comprise the modern town.

In the country or suburban house it may be noted that the more formal its surroundings the more artificial the house may be. Its terraces and lawns, like the frame of the picture, will help to isolate it from the surrounding country. In fact, instead of making the house harmonise with Nature in this case, we make Nature harmonise with the house. It will still be wise, however, to make concessions on both sides, so that house and Nature meet each other half way. But for the small houses, at any rate, it has been shown that the formal type of garden may not be altogether suitable, and the house which springs directly from its natural surroundings must be more natural and less artificial in its materials and their treatment. When, however, small houses occupy restricted roadside sites, a degree of artificiality is necessarily introduced which may suggest a more formal character for the house and its garden.

The choice between artificial and natural beauty will depend largely on the tastes of the individual. The first becomes reasonable wherever houses are grouped into communities, and the latter is desirable when they are built in the country, and the house will be judged not alone by its intrinsic qualities, but by the extent to which it adapts itself to its surroundings.

The position of the house on its site is a matter of primary importance, and too often the fatal mistake is made at the outset in this matter, in which, as in many others, the architect's advice may be duly considered, but is only acted on when it agrees with the preconceived ideas of his employer. Too much attention is usually given to the question of view, for houses nowadays are commonly so designed that it is only possible to endure to live in their apartments by resolutely and constantly looking out of the window. In most cases the best view is the outlook on to the garden, and the plans illustrated show how, in the placing of the garden in connection with the house, special vista effects should be arranged opposite the principal windows. But in some situations the question of a more extended prospect must be considered. Let us assume the case of a hillside sloping to the south. Here in the old days it is probable that the house would have been built in the valley at the bottom of the hill, because the builders valued shelter and cared little about outlook. But in modern times the tendency would be to place the house, if not on the hilltop, at least as near to it as possible, in order to get the most extensive outlook. In most cases it seems the wiser course to secure as far as possible both view and shelter by placing the house in such a case about half-way up the hill, so that the higher ground to the north shelters the house from cold winds and forms a fine background to the building, which rises above terraces formed in the hillside to the south. If the approach to the house is from a road which runs parallel to the hillside on the north side, the conditions will be favourable for the best possible arrangement of the grounds. It must not be supposed that the approach to a house from a higher level is necessarily undesirable. One catches then at first a glimpse of the building lying low amid its encircling gardens, giving an impression of sheltered homeliness which is perhaps preferable in some respects to the view from the valley, where the house is seen towering above its terraces. In discussing the question of steps and levels in the interior of the house itself this matter has already been mentioned, and here the same principles may be applied. It will be found that while the approach from a higher level suggests snugness and homely comfort in the house, in the approach from below these qualities are exchanged for dignity and impressiveness of effect. The distance of the house from the road is a question which demands careful consideration. In cases where the site is on the north side of the road, and the house must be approached from the south, the drive should be kept to either the east or western side of the site, and should be screened from the gardens opposite the south front. In such a case the conditions suggest that the house should be placed well back from the road, and the entrance to the house should be placed at the end rather than in the centre of the south front. But where the opposite conditions obtain, and the house is approached from a road on its north boundary, the house would then naturally be placed nearer the road to allow ample space for the garden opposite its south front. This arrangement is the best one for a country house, though the town-bred mind is apt to rejoice in making the approach to the house from the south, with the drawing-room bay window at the side of the front door. In cases where the road is to the east or west of the house the front entrance may well be placed facing the road, but the house should be kept to the north side of the site, so that the greatest possible space may be available to the south.

In thus fixing the position for the house on the site the question of aspect is here the main factor, but where the site is restricted it may be necessary to give up the idea of the south front overlooking the garden, and to be content instead with a garden outlook which faces west or east, but in such cases, wherever possible, windows to the south should be introduced to admit the sunlight. Special local conditions may often modify the principles advanced, but in most cases the question of aspect will be the dominant factor in determining the situation of the house.

CHAPTER THIRTY TWO

THE GARDEN

Awake O north wind; and come thou south; blow upon my garden that the spices thereof may flow out.

HAVING considered what changes are desirable in the conception of the modern house to meet the real needs of the average family, I next propose to deal with the garden in the same way, and to try and indicate a few general principles which should govern its design. The function of the garden is to grow fruit and vegetables for the household, and also to provide outdoor apartments for the use of the family in fine weather. This has led to a rough division of the garden into kitchen garden and pleasure garden, a distinction which implies there is no pleasure to be derived from the contemplation of plants or trees which are otherwise useful. We have already encountered this modern conception of beauty, allied solely to uselessness in the house and its furnishing, and need not therefore be surprised to find it arising again in the garden.

If rose leaves, like cabbage leaves, were found to have culinary uses, it is probable that the rose would soon be deposed from its position as queen of the flowers. In the kitchen garden one finds so many plants which have lost caste, as it were, by daring to be useful, and the scarlet runner would probably be as much admired as the scarlet geranium, were it not for the uses of its slender pods. The grey-green foliage and great thistle-like heads of the globe artichoke, the mimic forest of the asparagus bed, and the quaint inflorescence of the onion have each a distinctive beauty of their own which would be more widely recognised if these plants were not used for food.

But if for the sake of convenience we adopt this rough division of the garden into kitchen and pleasure garden, it may be concluded that for the cottager the kitchen garden alone is the most appropriate, including in its borders roses, lilies, and perennial flowers, with a background of cabbages, potatoes and other vegetables. Many old cottage gardens which are no more than this are to be seen in our villages, and show the possibilities of homely beauty which belong to such a union of use and beauty in the garden, and such a garden, worked in the spare time of its owner with a rough and ready lore which is his traditional inheritance, will be profitable as well as pleasant. But if we take a step from the cottage to the smaller type of suburban or country house, we shall often find its occupants have little knowledge of gardening. Under the specialising influence of modern civilisation they have lost the instinct for cultivating the soil, and they have neither the time, knowledge, nor inclination to grow their own vegetables and flowers.

"He who looks at my garden," says Emerson, "may see that I have another garden." The proper cultivation of the garden demands a considerable degree of leisure and thought, more than the man of affairs will usually be able to give it. And so the limited means of the dweller in the small house are often still further depleted by the hire of the professed gardener, whose ideas of gardening as an art are expressed in terms of bedding-out and general grooming, clipping and tidying. For such a household the best type of garden would be one which maintained its beauty with a minimum expenditure of labour. The growing of vegetables, in most cases where the labour is not supplied by the householder, will be found to be somewhat an expensive luxury. The lawn, too, will demand constant attention to keep it in order. Gravel paths will require weeding, and hardy annuals will require the preparation of the soil, the sowing of seed, and the removal of the plants after they have flowered. The whole situation seems to point to the natural or wild garden, with those departures that may justify themselves by their usefulness or beauty, secured without undue cost of maintenance. A visit paid to a copse in the spring, carpeted with primroses and anemones, followed by blue-bells, and later with groups of foxgloves, may, perhaps, suggest the thought that this kind of beauty can only be outdone by gardening of the more ambitious kind when it is at its very best. The woodland copse, moreover, demands absolutely no labour, and is a product of Nature unassisted by the art of man.

And so the small householder, in forming his garden, will do well to take Nature into his counsels and make a virtue of developing the local characteristics of his land.

On sunny hills, where purple heather grows, purple heather shall be the dominant note in his garden scheme; or by the sea, the thrift which blooms on the cliff shall be invited to lend its pink blossoms to edge his paths; and Nature, thus included in the garden, will be assisted and directed and raised to the nth power, so that it will seem but the apotheosis of the beauty of the country-side, and by the help of man in the battle for survival the coarser weeds will be severely handicapped. On these principles it will be possible to secure a garden which does not require constant grooming, and, once established, will take care of itself. Whatever labour may be given to it will be an investment repaid with compound interest, instead of that futile tidying and clipping which must be constantly repeated to keep Nature at bay.

But, apart from the wild garden, the orchard must find a place in the type of garden suggested for the smaller house. The trees, once planted in the grass, will require but little attention. Few things are more beautiful than the masses of blossom in the spring or the ripened fruit in the autumn. Under the trees the grass need not be constantly mown, and if the crop of hay is not profitable, it will at least repay for the labour of the scythe. In the spring the drifts of daffodils and crocuses will show to much greater advantage than if planted in flower-beds, where, on the bedding-out system, it will be necessary to remove them to make room for the next garden effect. It is in the orchard that use and beauty are most happily wedded, and the planting of fruit-trees should form an essential part of every garden scheme.

Having thus agreed to design the garden for the small house on natural lines, and to base it on the wild garden and the orchard, it will become a question as to how far mown grass, in the shape of lawns, should be included in the scheme. In many cases a lawn for tennis, bowls, or croquet is demanded, and, apart from these uses, I do not wish to undervalue the beauty of a well-kept lawn; but it will be well if the smaller householder, before including the lawn as a matter of course in his garden scheme, should realise that it implies a certain cost of maintenance, and that a garden can be formed, and not a bad garden either, without any mown grass at all.

Paths should be as few as possible, and should follow the lines of natural traffic. They should not wind, unless there is a reason for their winding, but should represent the easiest and shortest routes. If one imagines a garden without paths at all one would soon find certain beaten tracks appear, and these would represent the general lines for the fundamental paths. Wherever possible, paths should be paved instead of gravelled, and this is a luxury which may repay by saving the labour of weeding.

It is not, however, necessary to have a wild garden as the outcome of the conditions I have assumed. Plantations of flowering shrubs with the orchard and borders of perennial flowers will constitute also a type of garden which will require little cost for its maintenance.

A garden is expensive to maintain, chiefly in proportion to its artificiality and in the extent to which it includes mown lawns, bedded-out flowers, and clipped hedges. I do not wish to imply that these things are therefore inappropriate to the garden, but that they should be introduced in households of limited means at least with a full knowledge of the labour in maintenance they entail, and that it may be wiser in many cases to aim at that kind of beauty in a garden which can be achieved by assisting and directing Nature rather than by striving to mould her to an artificial ideal. The kind of garden I have tried to indicate is, in short, one for a man who, while fond of a garden, is unable, either through lack of time, means or ability to give it the attention it requires.

It has been my purpose throughout to show what is possible for the average householder, both in the planning of the house and its surrounding garden, and this has led me to dwell on the economic question in gardening designing which, as in the house, is often overlooked. But if these restrictions are removed, many possibilities appear in the development of a garden designed with artistic skill, and planted and maintained with expert knowledge.

The desirability of a natural or wild scheme for the basis of gardens will, of course, greatly depend on the nature of the site; and in the country it is often possible to obtain a site for the house which will require little modification in its essential features. Probably the best in this kind is an old orchard, but this is difficult to obtain. Of natural surroundings, however, there seems nothing quite so good as a setting for the house as a dark moorland covered with the purple of the heather, and that lesser kind of gorse which seems to have been clipped into neat round bushes by Nature's invisible shears. Add to this the background of a deep pine-wood and a few silver birches, and all the setting a house of grey stone will require will be a terrace enclosed with a rough wall of lichened stone. If a site of this ideal description is large enough, a portion of it may then be well enclosed as a garden of a formal kind; and if there is a stream, for no garden is quite complete without water, it may be carried in formal waterways and by fountains till, in the moorland, its course is marked by the emerald green of its grassy banks, and by the groups of iris, forget-me-nots, and other water plants.

But, in the suburban plots, there are few such possibilities, and a more formal kind of garden is suggested by the rectangular enclosure of the site and the somewhat artificial character of the surroundings.

In my previous indication of the lines in which a garden may be made which will need the minimum expense in maintenance, I have purposely assumed a somewhat extreme case. It will be mainly useful to the average man in showing what features of the garden are expensive to maintain.

In the production of a small suburban garden its practical application may lead to a reduction in the area of mown grass, and the avoidance of grass banks and edgings, which are difficult to keep in order. It may suggest the advisability of paved paths wherever possible, and when the site is large enough, the inclusion of an orchard and wild garden.

It will lead to the exclusion of bedding out geraniums, begonias, or pansies, and will take as a general principle of open-air flower culture that plants should be perennial, and not require removal in winter; and though dahlias, as well as some of the best annuals, may be included in the garden scheme, these will be recognised as worthy of a relaxation of the general rule. In preparing the flower-beds, the ground should be dug for at least a yard in depth, and where the soil is heavy, a drain formed with stones and filled up with good garden soil. The roots of the plants will then strike deep, and they will be little affected by drought. To protect the soil from drought, too, the garden beds should be well covered, and creeping plants may be introduced between the masses of perennials for this purpose. The borders should not be invariably planted with the smallest flowers nearest the edge, and the effect should be varied by bringing tall, bold clumps to the edge of the path, and this edge should not appear as a line, but should be formed by the plants in the border overhanging the path. When a change of level occurs in a garden, a grass bank should not be made, but a rough retaining-wall built of stone, and from the upper level roses and trailing plants should shower their blossoms. The joints should be planted with wall plants, and at its base flowers that will be grateful for the warmth and shelter it gives. The same rough and homely treatment should be used in steps, and these and the walls should be considered as not being mere masonry, but building which is to be clothed with plant life.

A garden of average size may include a lawn for tennis, croquet, or bowls, an orchard, a kitchen garden, and a flower garden in two main divisions – one a rose garden, which may be square or nearly square in form, and the other, which may be long and narrow, devoted to perennial flowers. All these outdoor apartments will be connected with straight paths, and one of these may form a pergola. In making the divisions of such a garden, it is important that sufficient space should be devoted to backgrounds for the flowers and garden ornaments. Of these background materials, the yew hedge is still the best, because of the depth and intensity of its tone. White lilies may look well against a brick wall or a shrubbery, but they will look their best against the sombre yew. And so will roses and other bright flowers. It is this use of the yew background which makes the old flower gardens so unequalled in their effect, and those who advocate its supersession by modern flowering shrubs, which may be more intrinsically charming, forget that the primary value of the permanent material in a garden is as a background to its passing show of blossoms – a stage on which the flowers present their yearly show. Having so arranged the plan that its transient brightness shall be seen in a proper setting, and not lost in the competing confusion of the shrubbery; the next important point to consider will be the connection of its apartments by paths where the vista effects are carefully studied. The beauty of the garden will depend to a great extent on its vista effects, and for this purpose its paths must be straight. The ends of these vistas require special attention, and may be treated in various ways – either by a semicircular recess, with a seat, or a summer-house.

The garden should not, moreover, be too open and exposed to the sun, but should be full of mystery, surprises, and light and shade. One of its most attractive features will thus be the pergola, with its paved walk checkered by the shadows of the climbing plants which form its walls and roof. It matters little what the structure of the pergola is. It may be rough poles with the bark on, roofed with branches, or it may be piers of stone or brick, with an open timber roofing. It should at any rate be rude and simple, and look as if it is meant for an outdoor life in rough weather. Other effects of shade may be gained by walks bordered with, perhaps, hazel or willow, and through these shadowed vistas we may look beyond to an open sunlit space bright with flowers. Actual size has little to do with the effect of such a garden, and a variety of effects may be achieved in a comparatively small area by careful planning.

The garden may include various features and centres of interest on the lines of the main vistas. The square rose garden may be focused in its central sun-dial, and round this wreathed climbing roses may form a circle supported by chains and arches. The angles of the square may be marked by single yews, and standard roses may be placed in regular symmetrical positions to realise a calculated effect, while the roses generally will be arranged in some definitely conceived colour scheme. Or in the perennial flower garden clumps of delphinium, phlox, hollyhocks, day lilies, &c., will be the subject of a similar scheme. The flowers, instead of being repeated at regular intervals, like the geranium and calceolaria formula of the villa garden, will be massed in single clumps, and the whole garden will be planted so that at each season of the year something is in bloom there, and in blooming forms a well-studied arrangement of colour. Here a central feature may perhaps be a dipping well for watering the garden. The garden seats, which should be of good design and solid structure, should be placed at those points in the garden which command the principal vistas to which they may form the terminal features, and in similar positions should be placed the arbours or summer-houses.

Amongst other features of the garden not to be overlooked are trellises to form screens or enclosures, and wreathed with rose or vine, tubs and pots for plants to be set at intervals on a terrace or stand, sentinel-like, to mark an entrance. Dovecots set on a pole will give a homely note to the garden, and fountains and statuary will be essential features in a stately scheme.

Terracing will form a necessary part of the garden on sloping ground, and where, as in the old Italian gardens, the slope is considerable, fine effects can be obtained with steps and terraces one above the other. They should be retained by walls rather than by banks, and these walls may be formed of rough stone and planted as previously described.

It would be impossible, with the space at my disposal, to deal adequately with all the features of the garden. I can do no more than indicate a few general principles. Neither have I any wish to pose as a partisan in the quarrel between the naturalists and formalists in its design. In the large garden each should have free scope, and natural garden and formal garden will enter into no rivalry there, but each will only enhance the peculiar charm of the other, and afford a solace for varying moods.

CHAPTER THIRTY THREE

WAYS AND MEANS

IT is a common belief that to build an artistic house a large sum of money is required. Art and ornament are often held to be synonymous terms, and the house which possesses the largest amount of ornament is often held to be the most artistic. It will be necessary, first of all, therefore, to state that the reverse of this is very often the case, and that a house is artistic in proportion to the amount and quality of the skill and thought displayed in its design, and not in proportion to the amount of decoration it possesses.

Again, the intrinsic value, or rather the market price of the materials of which a house is built, is often taken as the measure of its artistic merit, without regard to beauty of workmanship or design. Such a method of judging is almost as unreasonable as if one estimated the value of a picture by the price per pound of paint or per yard of canvas.

So far from being a luxury, the house which is rationally designed on economical lines is not only a source of pleasure and comfort to its possessor but also a wise investment.

In considering the cost of a house designed on the principles I have endeavoured to explain – principles which are claimed to be both rational and artistic – it is necessary to think of the house with its furniture and decoration ready for occupation, and to compare the total outlay required with the ordinary house, built, furnished and decorated in the usual way. And then, again, the cost of maintenance must be compared, the wear and tear of furnishings, and fabrics which perish in the using and which have to be replaced.

If one recalls to mind the ordinary house to let unfurnished, what a chilling and depressing vision is invoked! Think of its dreary wall surfaces, covered, perhaps, with three or four layers of dirty papers, its gas-fittings, its glaring windows with their broken venetian blinds, its mantelpieces and grates, and its floors with their borders of battered staining. To make all this endurable there must be curtains and carpets and drapings of all kinds; and in the furnishing it is often considered necessary to introduce a multitude of unnecessary things to distract and confuse the eye, and so to screen and palliate the original ugliness of the unfurnished room.

But in the house where the building itself has been the subject of careful study, beauty does not depend on furnishing or decoration. Unfurnished, it is still inviting and homely, and nothing but essential furniture is required for its habitation. The perishable fabrics, which form so large a part of the ordinary house, are here reduced to a minimum.

Its floors do not demand carpets nor its windows curtains, and the less furnishings and trappings put into it the better it will look. Where only a limited sum of money is available for the making of a home, it will be the best wisdom to spend as much as we can afford in securing a thoughtfully designed and well-built house, and as little as may be required for essential furnishings, and nothing at all in decoration.

If, later on, circumstances admit of further outlay, decoration can be added as a result of careful consideration, or cheap and temporary furnishings may be replaced by better, but the structure of the house cannot be so easily modified. Custom and habit are the tyrants who have settled for the non-reflecting majority the expenditure required for the furnishing of a house. It is usual to spend, say, £500 in furnishing a certain type of house, and the family is therefore invited to consider a scheme showing how to furnish for £500. The expense may be grudged, but it is paid because it is usual and customary so to do. And so the furniture arrives, and probably includes the very pictures for the walls. Given a certain station in life such surroundings are correct and usual. It is not merely that such furnishings are badly made and vulgar in design. They are for the most part quite unnecessary and merely a source of labour and an obstruction of floor spaces. The demand for such things is the creation of their manufacturers, for, it may be observed, that by continuously and patiently telling a man that he wants a thing, he will end by believing you, and whether it is an encyclopaedia or a drawing-room cabinet he offers himself a willing victim to the enterprising advertiser. And so the Englishman's house has become an indiscriminate collection of objects which he has been insistently told that he wants. It is a compound of the cabinet-maker's shop and the picture-dealer's gallery, and as such is surely the strangest medley which, since the world began, has ever been chosen as a setting for human life.

In this country it is not usual for the average man to contemplate the idea of building a house for himself. He is deterred by various considerations. He has been told that building is an expensive luxury, and that the cost of a house invariably exceeds initial estimates, while he fears that if it may become necessary for him to sell or let his house he may not realise his expenditure. His informants are generally those who have built houses, and whose experience in the matter he therefore values. Speaking from my own experience, I may say that I have designed houses which have been finished within the expenditure originally proposed, and others in which the initial estimates have been more than doubled; and I believe I am but stating the experience of architects in general when I say that the additional cost has always been incurred by the client's express demands. It has never occurred in houses designed for people whose means were limited, because they, knowing they could not afford to indulge in extras, were content to exercise a necessary restraint.

Generally speaking, the richer the client the more unchecked the tendency becomes to add to the original price, and this seems a very reasonable position of affairs for the man who in his daily life is accustomed to deny himself nothing; and, when the accounts have to be paid, it is perhaps merely human to cast the burden on builder or architect, and afterwards to nurse the conviction that this accumulative and unforeseen expenditure is an inherent part of the business of house-building.

To avoid such an experience it is necessary at the outset to determine once for all what is actually required and how much may be spent, and to allow a reasonable margin for unforeseen contingencies, and by keeping strictly to the original programme, or by departing from it only with the calculated knowledge of the cost involved in each case, there is no more reason why a man should spend more than he intends in building a house than in making a purchase in a shop.

If we assume the case of a man for whom it is necessary that economy should be studied, and who has no large sum to invest, and if we suppose that the rental he is prepared to pay allows of the expenditure of £1,000 on the house, it will be necessary for him to allow a certain sum for the formation of the garden and its enclosure, as well as for furniture and perhaps decoration, and in order to be quite on the safe side it will be well for him to think of the total sum as £900 instead of £1,000, so as to leave an ample margin for contingencies. The sketch-plans for the house having been prepared, unless the architect has had experience or special knowledge of the price of building in the particular district, it will be wise to get a preliminary estimate at this stage by submitting the sketch-plans, with a rough specification, to a local builder.

In the selection of a builder to carry out the work, the competitive system of tendering is not always the most satisfactory. It is better to make local inquiries and to try and find a man who has the reputation for being straightforward in his dealings, and give him the work on condition that his price is considered reasonable by the architect. The architect is thus spared the necessity of playing the distasteful part of the amateur detective, and the work is carried out with the minimum amount of friction. It seems, indeed, little short of disgraceful that in the ancient and honourable craft of building there are so many men who demand the services of a constant spy in the form of a clerk of the works to insure proper work being done. Apart from ethical considerations, this degrading and vulpine attitude is the worst sort of business policy, and the architect who has the misfortune to engage this type of builder does not continue to employ or recommend him. But the competitive system of tendering, assuming that all builders belong to the criminal class and need constant police supervision, gives the work to the lowest bidder without considering his reputation or inquiring as to his character. It is this competitive system which is to a great extent the cause of the degradation of the modern builder. Under the pressure of necessity he may be tempted to offer to do the work for a price which compels him to attempt to scamp it, and his dishonesty in this respect is a retaliatory measure. I do not say that competition between builders of reputation is necessarily bad, but in competitions between builders whose characters are not inquired into it will generally be the most unscrupulous – the one who counts on making up deficiencies by undetected scamping – who offers the lowest bid, and the whole process thus often results in the survival of the unfittest. To inquire into character after the competition has taken place is useless. The rules of the game demand that the work should be given to the lowest bidder, and the fact that a man has been invited to compete implies that he has been considered eligible.

Although an architect may be able to obtain from an unscrupulous builder a minimum standard of excellence in the work, not only is this achieved with much unnecessary friction, but in the absence of any pride in his work on the builder's part, it is impossible to obtain a really satisfactory result, for the best kind of work cannot be obtained under compulsion, and so the final result is never quite satisfactory.

Having succeeded in obtaining a reasonable price for the work from a reliable builder, it may next be considered how the man who has not a large sum to invest may set about the important matter of paying for the house. Assuming that the cost of the house is £1,000, it will not be a difficult matter to obtain a mortgage on the building as it approaches completion for three-quarters of its value, so that the actual sum of money required will be, say, £300. Assuming that the interest payable on such a mortgage is 4 per cent., the house may thus be equivalent to one for which a rental of £40 a year is paid. It might be considered necessary to allow a certain sum out of this for repairs, but in a house simply and solidly built this will be a much smaller sum than is usually allowed for old houses. The possibility of either selling or letting such a house eventually, should occasion demand, would depend very much upon its position and suitability to average requirements.

My own experience in this matter has shown that houses of average size, built in suitable localities, can be readily disposed of, for, while it is not the general public who at present demand rational houses, the minority who do are not catered for at all at present, and this minority, I feel assured, is increasing every year.

Those who have any faith in human nature at all must believe that the hideous outcrop of modern villadom is a merely temporary condition of affairs, and a veneer of so-called art will not for long be accepted as a substitute for comfort and convenience in planning.

The most economical house to build is one which is a simple rectangle in plan covered with an unbroken roof. In most cases, to aim at picturesque and elaborate roof-lines and plans full of nooks and corners, is to add to the cost and often merely to secure a restlessness and fussiness of effect. It is commonly supposed that the art of the house lies in complexity of roofing, in picturesque "skylines," and so on. In answer to an attempt to induce a client who held such views to accept a simple type of plan, I was told that a plain house could be obtained from any one, and that he had come to me because he wanted something unusual. To achieve the unusual in building nowadays, it is necessary merely to aim at being rational and simple, and to depend on proportion and the structural integrity for whatever beauty of an unobtrusive kind the house may possess. It does not by any means follow that a plain house is an ugly house, and conscious striving for picturesque effects often results in failure. The most telling and prominently satisfying buildings are generally those which are simple in outline and structure.

In estimating the cost of the various houses illustrated, it must be remembered that, as the price of building varies considerably in different localities, these can only be taken as approximately correct. In some cases I am able to give the cost for which the houses have been actually built. In London and its neighbourhood, within a certain radius which it is difficult accurately to define, as well as in certain popular or fashionable resorts in other parts of the country, the price of building is high. In country districts it is much lower, and is lowest in those where old traditions have been least influenced by modern ideas.

Large firms in most districts tend to maintain a uniform and somewhat high scale of prices, but in many country places the small local builder, who perhaps even works with his own hands, and who is not entirely consumed with the idea of making money, is perhaps the best type for building a small homely house. He does not possess elaborate machinery, and cannot produce that high mechanical finish in the work which represents the modern ideal of perfection, and which has made modern building so depressing. He may not be so intelligent or so expeditious in his work as the more up-to-date builder, but, on the other hand, he is often more conscientious and careful.

CHAPTER THIRTY FOUR

MAKING THE BEST OF IT

Ah Love! could you and I with Fate conspire,
To grasp this sorry scheme of things entire,
Would we not shatter it to bits – and then
Remould it nearer to the heart's Desire.

IN England, at any rate, the average man does not generally build a house for himself, and building is regarded as an expensive luxury to be indulged in only by the rich. My present purpose is not to inquire how far such a state of things is justified or what are its causes, but to accept the fact that many people who have their clothes, for instance, made to fit them, feel bound to accept the ready-made house. This might not be so serious a matter if the ready-made house were thoughtfully planned and adapted to the comfort of the occupant, but few, I think, who have experienced life in the average villa will claim so much for it as that! But assuming that such a house must perforce be ours, it may be useful to consider in what way its interior, at least, can be modified to make the best of it.

The task is not such a hopeless one as at first sight may appear, and for this reason: In the criticism of all art, an unconscious allowance is made by the intelligent observer for the limitations involved. We do not quarrel with the painter because, with his tube of flake white, he attempts to represent the brightness of sunshine. Unconsciously we make due allowance for the difficulties of his task. To make the best of the situation is all that any man can do, and the very difficulties of the task add to the interest of the final result, and make our triumph more readily applauded or our failure more easily condoned.

Those who have read of Japanese theatrical performances may remember that they include the presence on the stage of certain gentlemen in black who are not supposed to be seen by the spectator. In England, their duties would be performed out of sight; but the Japanese, while placing them in view of the audience inconspicuously attired, assume that the intelligent observer will consider it his duty not to see them. It is on some such principle as this that the undesirable features of the suburban house should be treated. One recognises at once, for instance, that its rooms are too high, and that an ugly plaster cornice divides wall from ceiling. In such a case, the decorator may finish his treatment of the walls, at the height of the doors perhaps, with a wooden rail. All the space above that line he practically ignores. It is not in the caste of his piece, and so it may be treated in the way which will best efface it from our impression of the room, and generally the best method is to whitewash all above the rail and then leave it contemptuously alone. There is nothing to be gained by picking out the cornice with colour, or by papering with elaborate friezes and ceiling-papers this upper portion of the room. All this will but help to draw attention to what we wish to ignore. Or again, the doors and woodwork generally will probably be enriched with all kinds of coarsely designed and mechanically executed mouldings. Here, again, the same principle will lead us to avoid any scheme of painting which emphasises these features by special colours for the mouldings, or different shades of colour for panels; and here again disapproval of features of this kind can best be shown by painting all the woodwork one uniform tint. Such a principle will, however, hardly serve us in dealing with such important features as fireplaces, for instance. The more important grates, which one may almost safely assume will be cast iron coarsely designed and finished in shiny black, with a few highly ornamental tiles let in the sides, and the overmantels, white enamelled probably, in the drawing-room with all sorts of niches and shelves, must, if possible, be removed to an attic, and a better and simpler fireside arranged, so that it can be easily removed if necessary, and the old one replaced when the house is given up. If, however, the house is an older one, even if it belongs to the much-abused Early Victorian period, the mantels may be of that simple type which was almost universal, and thus possess a sort of negative virtue in being at least not artistic! Here it will be necessary to remove the grate only and to fix above the shelf a small overmantel designed mainly as a background for ornaments.

In many cases a few slight structural alterations may be managed with an indulgent landlord. The house, if it is in a terrace, at any rate it may be assumed, will be of the plan shown in Fig. 1. It is the recognised formula. From the porch or vestibule, passing through the inner door with its leaded glass, of which the least said the better, one enters the narrow hall where the hat-stand is, and one looks beyond to the long flight of stairs, with possibly a varnished pitch-pine newel-post, which is as much too large as the balusters above it are much too small, and which seems to have absorbed the whole art of the stairs. Here, the first step in improving the plan will be to remove the partition between the narrow hall and the front sitting-room – the opening being spanned with a beam behind which a curtain is fixed. The hall now becomes a recess in the front room which may be screened with the curtain when required. The dismal passage has disappeared.

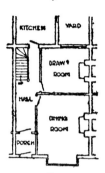

FIG. 1
The inevitable
terrace plan.

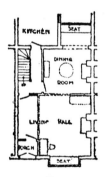

FIG. 2
The above plan
modified as
suggested.

A further improvement may be made by forming a ceiling of wood panels perhaps on fibrous plaster and wood at a low level to this recess, for its ugliness as a passage even is much increased by the excessive ceiling height, for in the suburban villa the height of its largest room is the height of its narrowest passage.

The staircase will also be shut off by another low opening with its beam and curtain or even by a door.

On entering from the porch of such a house, we are at once in a recessed portion of the hall or house place, with its liberal suggestion of space and freedom, instead of that chilling passage which no art of man can make homely and inviting.

Let us now consider the back room, which in a house of this kind will be the dining-room. It is generally small and cramped, and in spite of its sheet of glass, which makes it impossible to escape from the insistent presence of narrow back premises, it is also dark. It is assumed that the kitchen premises form an annexe in the rear, and are not in the basement; and their

136

position will make it difficult to light this room properly, while the prospect from its window can hardly be anything but cheerless. But the window of the front room will give a large amount of light, and more in fact than is needed there.

A further modification of the structure would therefore take the form of making an opening in the partition which divides the two rooms, which may be either fitted with glazed doors or with the beam and curtain as before. A small conservatory might then form the end of the vista outside the dining-room window, or if the window itself is merely modified it might take the form of making it solely a means of letting light into the room without disclosing the barrenness of the outlook. This may be done by fitting shutters glazed with leaded glass on the inside face of the wall. These could be easily removed, and besides forming a screen, they would have all the advantages of double windows and counteract those disadvantages of the large window which have already been referred to.

In making such a modification of the stereotyped villa plan, I fully recognise that it will only appeal to the more intelligent inhabitants of villadom. The conception of the house, which includes the sacrifice of the front room to the visitor, and the furnishing of it with superfine and highly polished cabinets and occasional chairs and tables, will not gladly accept for mere family uses the most important room in the house easily and comfortably furnished, with materials which will stand, and not be the worse for, constant service. In considering how such a modification of the plan will meet the conditions of family life, the question may first of all be considered from the fundamental standpoint of heating. In such a villa, the family will often be normally a "two-fire" family, and will only keep in constant use the kitchen fire and that in the back sitting-room. The inevitable result of this will be that the back sitting-room in the winter months will be the general and only sitting-room and feeding-room for the family group, or if the front sitting-room fire is kept in use the family must necessarily have their meals in the cold. When, however, the whole area of the two rooms is treated as one apartment with a good fire in the front room, the dining-room becomes a sort of recess in the hall, and shares in its heat as well as light, and the whole interior forms a roomy and comfortable setting for the family life. On occasions when it is necessary to receive visitors without infringing on the family life, this may be done either in the back or front portion of the plan, according to the convenience of the occasion. The separate uses of the back room would depend on the possibility of including another fire in the minimum heating arrangements, or a heating apparatus might be used to warm the greenhouse and dining-room, and the possibility of other retreats for members of the family would depend on the number and disposition of the bedrooms, and the possibility of heating them either by artificial means or by additional fires, while in some cases a reception-room may be placed on the upper floor, which could be reached without disturbing the privacy of the lower rooms. In cases where additional frontage allows of a garden of reasonable width at the back, the space outside the dining-room window may be used as a garden-room, and if the wide doorway to the front room is still retained this will not make the dining-room itself too dark.

Figure 4 shows another modification of the normal plan which is

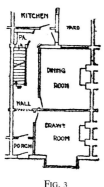

FIG. 3

particularly adapted to houses where there is an outlook at the back on to the garden, and especially when this is to the south, the partition between the back room and the staircase hall being removed and a beam and curtain introduced. The whole of the back portion of the house now becomes the hall, and the front room communicating with it by double doors becomes the part of the plan set apart for the reception of visitors. As the staircase now becomes an important feature a slight modification in its form is often desirable, and this can be effected by forming a square landing as shown. This arrangement is specially adapted for houses where the back room is fairly large, and in its altered form it will become the dining-hall. Here, as in small dining-rooms generally, a folding table will be desirable which can be removed when not in use, and in its reduced size used as a side-table.

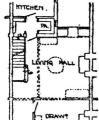

FIG. 4

In the decoration and furnishing of the villa thus modified in its structure the general principles advanced elsewhere will equally apply, and it only remains to note a few of the special conditions which it presents. In the new house it is advised that the structure should in itself be complete and satisfying and not depend on superficial decoration, which when applied takes the form of clothes designed to display bodily beauties of proportion rather than to conceal defects. In the villa, however, decoration must be palliative. It is not so much a case of a house to be decorated as a disease to be alleviated, and the decorator thus becomes a physician who advises the proper treatment for each case.

It has already been shown how features which cannot be removed may be made at least inconspicuous, and how others too important for such a system may be removed and replaced by something better. A few notes may be added as to the treatment of the floor, which, in a house built as one would wish, should, as far as possible, be structural. In the villa the best treatment of the ordinary floor is to cover it with a veneer of parquet prepared with a dull glossy surface which does not require polishing. This treatment should at any rate be adopted, if possible, in the principal sitting-rooms, and considering the saving in the cost and wear of carpets its cost will be justified.

In other rooms, linoleum or plain colour or cork carpets will form a satisfactory basis for rugs. These materials will form useful palliative remedies for bad floors, and they are considered in this connection merely because, in the house as it should be, the real floor should not require covering except to gain that sense of luxury which the deep pile of a good carpet conveys. Certain labour-saving appliances may be easily added to the house. A lift from the kitchen when it is in the basement, and a speaking-tube, and a few washstands, fitted with taps, in the bedrooms, and the use of tiles for wall-covering as far as possible in bathrooms and kitchen premises – all these will help to reduce the labour of the house.

To make the best of some old country farmhouse will constitute a more congenial task. Old houses in the country are full of inspiration and suggestion. But how seldom is the *genius loci* regarded, and how often one sees the serene dignity of an old house marred by all kinds of up-to-date artistic furnishings and decorations.

Whatever is done to an old building should be so conceived in harmony with the house that one should not be able to detect where the new work begins and the old ends. All should show alike an old-world beauty, comfortable, serviceable and homely. The ancient glories of the house, many of which may have been since obscured, may be replaced with only such slight modifications as may be required to meet modern demands.

In suggesting these schemes for the modifications of the average house, I am fully conscious that each case will have special conditions demanding special treatment, but in the average house this will largely consist in the judicious removal of partitions, so securing a sense of spaciousness instead of the cramped confinement of the house, which consists of a series of small compartments.

CHAPTER THIRTY FIVE

THE TERRACE HOUSE

MUCH has recently been written on the improvement which it is assumed has taken place in recent years in the design and adornment of the home. If the prevalent use of "art" wall-papers and "art" furniture, and the continuous construction of "art" villas may be taken as an evidence of progress, there may indeed be some reason for congratulation on a national advance in this important matter. But to the better informed this artistic progress is a mere chimera and only evidences the ignorance of the general public as to what constitutes beauty and fitness in domestic surroundings, and the commercial acumen of the various tradesmen who pander to the popular taste. It is true that here and there, in isolated instances, houses are built and furnished with modest comeliness, but in the rank and file of building, in the average home of the average family, modern progress has chiefly consisted in the substitution of spurious art for confessed ugliness.

A great part of this rank and file of modern houses is made up of row upon row of terraces – houses built on plots of standard width and designed on a standard plan, so that an absent-minded occupant of one of them might be excused for entering his neighbour's house in mistake for his own, and would find little in its interior arrangements to undeceive him. All this regularity and similarity might find some excuse for itself if it represented the final outcome of a logical scheme. It has again and again been urged that the standard plan represents the best solution of the terrace problem, and that attempts to modify it have not been successful. If it were conceded that in the planning of the terrace house it is first of all essential that there should be a seldom occupied sitting-room with a bay-window commanding a view of another similar bay-window on the opposite side of the street – that kitchens and other compartments of the house connected with domestic service are shameful things, and should be hidden at the back, regardless of aspect – that the interior of the house should be subdivided as far as possible into as many little apartments as possible, which, though they must needs be small, may at least be lofty – that the comfort of the family is really quite a secondary matter in comparison to the proper respect due to furniture, for the proper display of which the house is built, &c. &c. one might, perhaps, then admit that the stereotyped plan is the best that can be arrived at, and it is in accepting these unwritten canons without question that attempted modifications have failed. One of the primary factors which induces variety of plan is the aspect of the houses; but this question is not considered at all in the plan of the terrace house. In view of the importance of sunlight in the principal rooms, it seems unreasonable that the houses on the north side of a road should be of the same plan as those on the south. In the case of a terrace with a north aspect towards the road, is it really the best arrangement to make the principal sitting-room sunless, and in this case, at any rate, is it desirable to place there the usual bay-window with its plate-glass, lace curtains, venetian blinds, and other upholsteries? Were it not better done to place the kitchen premises here, and thus gain the full breadth of the garden at the back, and make there the principal room, with its bay-window overlooking a sunny garden, thus reducing to a minimum the line of communication between the kitchen and the road, and obviating at once all that traffic across the house which the position of the kitchen premises at the back usually entails?

The conception of the house, which primarily consists, as I have endeavoured to show it should consist, of one good-sized living-room or hall, makes the position and outlook of this room a fundamental question. There the family live, and there, at any rate, they must have sunlight, a pleasant outlook, and cheerful surroundings.

In the ordinary terrace house there is no such dominating room for the family use. The principal apartment overlooking the road is usually preserved for visitors, and a little dining-room at the back is badly lighted by a window blocked by kitchen premises which leave only a narrow strip of ground available for a garden.

If you ask me where the family live I cannot tell you, but, judging from the unlighted rows of front bay-windows, one may at least conclude that they support existence somewhere in the back, and reserve their front apartment to display all those evidences of advance in modern domestic furnishings on which we congratulate ourselves nowadays.

If, however, the family life is centralised in one large apartment, the position of this apartment, in its relation to the road, would vary according to aspect, while the general tendency of the occupants of houses in terraces to live at the back, where freedom from dust and noise and an outlook on to a private garden may be enjoyed, suggests the advisability of a complete reversal, wherever possible, of the present scheme for the terrace house described in the phrase "Queen Anne in front and Mary Ann at the back," a reversal which would place the kitchen premises adjacent to the road and the sitting-rooms overlooking a garden at the back.

In such cases the house with its back to the road may be placed as close to it as possible without the usual disadvantages of such a position. In other cases, where considerations of aspect suggest that the principal sitting-room should be placed towards the road, it would be better for the houses to be set well back.

In the case of roads which run east and west, it would be best if these divided each single set of plots, so that in all the house would face south. In roads which run north and south, the question of aspect will have less influence on the plan. Thus one is brought to consider the question of laying out an estate, not entirely with a view of convenience for traffic, but to allow the best conditions for the individual house, and where terraces are introduced it is desirable that these should run east and west, and, instead of being planned with houses facing the street on both sides, should have houses close up to the road on the north side and gardens on the south.

Special local conditions must necessarily modify such arrangements in special cases, but the estate plan should be evolved in this way from the individual house, which should be again evolved from real requirements, and not based on fantastic chimeras and conventions.

As to the amount of frontage given to the houses, some variety may also be introduced, and a terrace with a liberal frontage allowance is better than detached houses set close together, because in the latter cases the spaces between the houses are practically useless for light or outlook.

It is, moreover, unreasonable in building a terrace that all the houses should have exactly the same accommodation.

The tailor who sells ready-made clothes recognises certain variations from the normal in the human frame which it is impossible to ignore, and the same variations occur in families. So that while the majority of the houses may contain normal accommodation there should also be a certain number adapted for abnormal cases. It will thus be seen how many factors there are which tend to suggest variety in the plan of the terrace house, and when to these are added the peculiar local conditions which it is impossible to deal with here, it may well be urged that there is no rational excuse for the standard terrace plan, and, so long as the large majority of the population are doomed to live in such dwellings, it is doubtful whether there is much cause for congratulating ourselves on the improvement of the British homes of today.

In the two plans for terrace houses shown, the first would be appropriate for a terrace where the road is on the sunny side, and where it is therefore

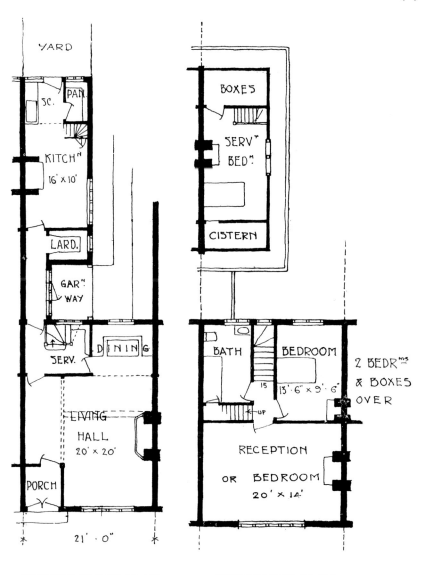

YARD

SC. PAN.

KITCH^N
16' x 10'

LARD.

GAR^{GE}
WAY

SERV. DINING

LIVING
HALL
20' x 20'

PORCH

21' · 0"

BOXES

SERV^T
BED^M.

CISTERN

BATH BEDROOM

15 13' 6" x 9' 6"

UP

RECEPTION

OR BEDROOM
20' x 14'

2 BEDR^{MS}
& BOXES
OVER

GROUND FLOOR PLAN   FIRST FLOOR PLAN

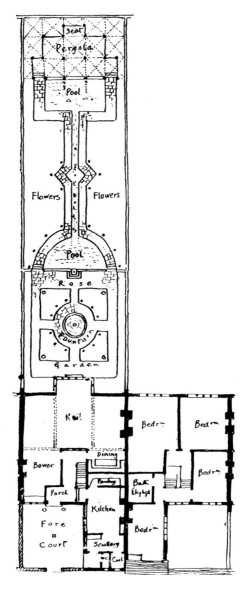

GROUND FLOOR PLAN   FIRST FLOOR PLAN

PLANS

desirable that the principal windows should look towards the road. In such a case it would be desirable that the houses should be set well back, so that the garden space should be in front, and the house should be to some extent free from the dust and the noise of the road.

The straight walk leading to the front entrance might be flanked on the one side with a range of posts and roofed with branches so as to form a pergola, of which one side is formed by the division-wall between the houses, and the other afford glimpses of a long flower border. This path would then appear as a simple kind of cloister. The whole of the ground plan of the main block of the house would then consist of one large room, with its dining recess, serving-room and staircase. In this room the usual passage at the side is incorporated, and is merely divided by a curtain, for it seems unreasonable that so much space as is usually occupied by this passage should be entirely cut off from the house for only occasional use. This large room is heated by a fireplace of ample proportions, and the whole effect on entering from the porch is one of homely comfort and breadth (see colour illustration p.15).

In order to get the maximum amount of light at the back, the kitchens are treated as a separate block, and represent a little additional house for the servants, with its separate stair and bedroom accommodation over the kitchen. In the main block the family bedrooms are provided on two floors, of which the upper is in the roof.

In the second plan for a terrace house it is assumed that the road is on the north side, and so the kitchens are placed on the road side and the whole of the south front then remains to be treated as a private garden. The frontage is here about twenty-eight feet, and here, as before, the essential feature of the ground plan is the large hall. Instead of the usual three small sitting-rooms there is this roomy hall, with the other two sitting-rooms represented by the relatively small bower or reception-room and the dining-recess, both of which appear as mere appendages to the principal room. There is no attempt to secure the usual apology for a garden towards the road, but a certain character is given to the approach by introducing a little square paved court which is approached from the road by an archway in the wall. Under the kitchen wing would be a basement which would afford space for a larder, washhouse and cellar.

On the upper floor the bedroom accommodation consists of two rooms facing the south, and two smaller ones overlooking the entrance court. The position of the bathroom admits of a domed ceiling carried into the roof-space, and lighted from above with a central circular skylight. The main

A TERRACE HOUSE (B)

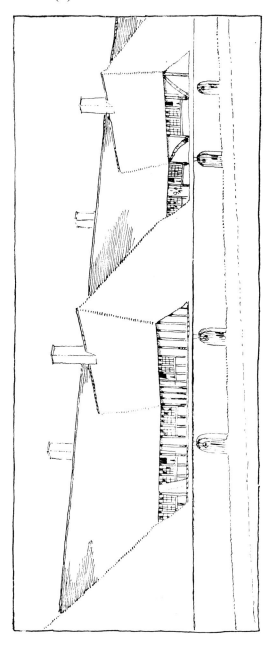

VIEW FROM NORTH

146

VIEW FROM SOUTH

roof-space would contain, besides the servants' bedroom, two additional attics which might be used either as additional bedrooms, children's playroom or study. It is doubtful whether such a plan as this would appeal to the speculative builder who is at present the sole arbiter of the fate of those who dwell in terraces. Not because of its cost, because it could be built as cheaply as the ordinary type of house, but merely because it is unusual and runs counter to those cherished accepted traditions which have made the terrace house so irrational and inartistic.

The miniature gardens to these houses would admit of a variety of treatment, and it is not suggested that they should all be similar in plan and arrangement. In the garden, of which a plan (p.144) and views (p.147 and colour illustration p.17) are given, a more liberal use of water has been made than is usual. The little square rose garden, with its central fountain, overlooks a semicircular pool in which is reflected the terrace wall and sundial, and beyond this a narrow stream conducts the water to the lower pool, beyond which is the pergola forming the termination to the garden. The posts of the pergola would be made of pine-trunks with the bark on. In their natural state these are a little dark in tone, so they could be whitewashed and would thus eventually show that pearly grey tone which may be noticed in the tree trunks of old fruit-trees which have been treated in this way. The importance of the proper study of reflections in the use of water in a garden has suggested that the pergola should begin at the edge of the water so that its columns and the lantern which marks the line of the central vista are reflected there.

CHAPTER THIRTY SIX

COTTAGES

IN the planning of modern cottages under the guidance of the general principles which have already been advanced in the consideration of the plans of houses, it will be observed that the problem is here much simplified by the absence of the servants, while the increased rigour of economical restrictions eliminates all but the absolutely essential. In seeking for a basis for the plan, the essential fact to be borne in mind is that the cottage household in most cases maintains but one fire and that fire fulfils the twofold function of warming the kitchen and cooking the food. It may be at once deduced from this that the cottage family lives in its kitchen, and such will be found to be the case. In many modern cottage plans this essential fact is hardly realised, and one finds a large living-room, perhaps with a small kitchen attached, while others are sub-divided into equally minute parlour and kitchen. In all these plans it is the kitchen which will be lived in, and the parlour or living-room will be filled with pretentious furniture and kept for show. And so as the villa apes the mansion we shall find again the cottage struggling to attain the coveted elegance of the villa. The possession of a parlour with its recognised appointments is in this case not an expression of the requirements, tastes, or habits of the family, but rather the symbol of one of the degrees in that spurious scale of excellence on which the modern social system is based. Just as to the vulgar the term "carriage people" is used as a caste distinction, and the possession of a carriage is held to be a sign of merit, so on a lower plane the owner of a parlour acquires precedence over the family not ashamed to admit frankly its custom of living in its kitchen. The central feature of the cottage plan should thus be a roomy kitchen. If a parlour is added it should be relatively small, and the kitchen should dominate the plan, while an intermediate type of plan might, by including the parlour as a recess in the kitchen, obviate the necessity of the second fire.

In addition to the kitchen living-room it is desirable that a scullery or back-kitchen should be added, where the washing of dishes and other work may be done, and here, unless a separate washhouse is provided, there should be a boiler. In addition to this accommodation, a coal-store and water-closet are required, and these may often be placed in a detached position, while the pantry is generally more conveniently placed in the main building. The typical cottage should have at least three bedrooms, of which one should be larger than the other two.

The question of the bathroom as a feature in the modern cottage plan is a somewhat difficult one. It must be frankly admitted that the average cottager would have little use for it, and in such families it is often only the children who enjoy a weekly "tub." A recent inspection of some model cottages in which the greater part of the scullery floor-space was taken up by a full-sized bath, left one wondering as to the probable uses to which it would be put – whether the cottager would find it a handy place for storing potatoes, for instance, or whether, as in an actual instance, the visitor would find its dusty interior embellished by a slipper and an orange. If a bathroom is introduced it should not be on the upper floor, unless connected with a hot-water system arranged in connection with the kitchen fire. It is better on the ground-floor, because, while it is easy to come downstairs it is difficult and laborious to carry water upstairs to the bath.

The best arrangement for the bath is, then, adjoining the scullery, so arranged as to levels that the water heated in the boiler can be drawn off by a tap placed directly over the bath. Both on account of the limited supply of hot water as well as to economise space, the bath should not be five or six feet long, but modelled on the sensible American bath-tub, which allows of complete immersion with a limited water-supply.

Where there is no hot-water system it is doubtful whether there is anything to be gained by making the bath a fixture. It is much better to give the cottager the option of where ablutions shall be performed, and in cold weather in the case of the children, at any rate, the tub in front of the kitchen fire can hardly be improved on. A few cottage plans are illustrated. In those in which the cottages are shown as terraces, separate washhouses, earth-closets and coal-sheds would be provided besides the accommodation shown in the plan – the washhouses being common to two or more of the cottages.

The more advanced type of cottage plan – the parlour cottage, as it may be called is represented by the plan of the lodge at Falkewood, and the pair of cottages illustrated under the title of Elmwood Cottages.*

In these the small parlour is so arranged that, divided from the living-room by a wide doorway, it represents a recess in the house place.

Here, as in Boffin's Bower, the cottage housewife, who, like Mrs. Boffin, wished to indulge in a higher flight, might define the elegances of the household by a chalk-line on the floor as Mrs. Boffin did.

Crossing that frontier the more material male would tread with mincing footsteps – speak with bated breath; and there on a Sunday the family would assemble, and find perhaps a welcome relief from the workaday associations of the kitchen. The district visitor and all those charitable and well-meaning persons who have so little respect for the privacy of the cottager would here be entertained in a portion of the house place, which, while not so entirely isolated and self-contained as the usual musty and ill-ventilated cottage parlour is, would yet be sufficiently screened from the kitchen itself.

In the kitchen the treatment of the range gives it something of the broad

---

* Since writing the above these cottages have been realised at the Letchworth Garden City, where they were entered as No. 65 in the exhibition of cheap cottages.

They were designed as a protest against the merely utilitarian ideals of modern building generally, and the cottage exhibition in particular, and attempted to show how the beauty of the old cottage is not incompatible with modern requirements.

EXTERIOR

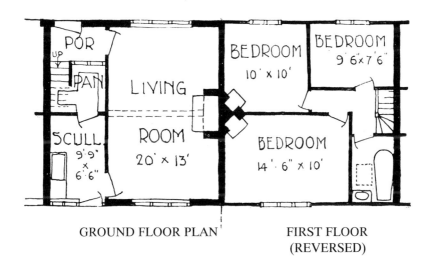

GROUND FLOOR PLAN   FIRST FLOOR
(REVERSED)

ROW OF COTTAGES (B)

EXTERIOR

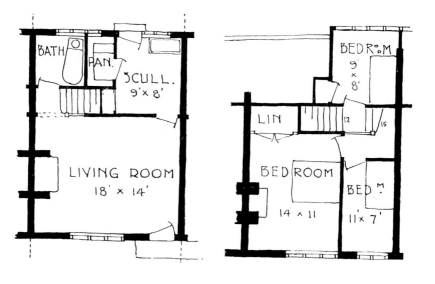

GROUND FLOOR PLAN   FIRST FLOOR PLAN

FALKEWOOD LODGE

EXTERIOR

GROUND FLOOR PLAN

FIRST FLOOR PLAN

and inviting character of the ingle and less of the repellent and unhomely appearance of the modern utilitarian cooking-machine. As of old pots hang suspended over the open fire, while broad hobs on each side give ample space for cooking-utensils. In the centre of the brick floor stands the table of scrubbed deal, while the settle, the dresser with its array of homely china, and the sturdy Windsor chairs complete the furnishing of a room, which, instead of the heartless and brutal utilities of the model dwelling, would seem to minister to something more than mere material needs.

In the scullery, besides the boiler, there is a small fireplace, which is always a welcome adjunct to the cottage household. It is here that in sultry summer weather the simple cooking, which in such a season is all that is required, is effected without lighting the kitchen range.

The little square court set in patterns of cobble-stones crossed by paved ways is common to both cottages, and this merging of garden paths and garden gates simplifies the approach and obviates the competing duplication of these features.

On the south side, however, the gardens are completely separated by a dividing hedge. The actual extent of the garden should be such as to amply provide the family at least with all the vegetables it requires, if not fruit, while its borders would also be set with all the old-fashioned cottage flowers. Such accommodation as is provided here should not be too much for the average cottager to expect. It is difficult accurately to estimate the cost, but in most districts this pair of cottages should be built for from £400 to £500.

It is impossible entirely to sympathise with the earnest desire of the modern philanthropist for the cheapest possible kind of country cottage, or to object entirely to restrictive by-laws in so far at least as they prevent the wholesale use of galvanised iron in country dwellings.

It is true that cottages constructed of wood might reasonably be erected in many cases with roofs of pantile, but it should not be forgotten that while the temporary building is cheaper in its cost, its shorter life and need for constant repairs makes its eventually more costly than the permanent building. Temporary building may possibly enrich the fathers, it will surely impoverish the sons, and the only possible excuse for temporary structures is that they are only built for temporary purposes. One cannot but deplore modern commercial conditions, which seem to make mean dwellings inevitable, and the work expended in building the cottage, so grudgingly bestowed by a contractor and workmen, who will do no more than is in the bond, and not so much in many cases. Under the more human conditions of rural England in the past, cottage building was done in a different spirit. One

EXTERIOR

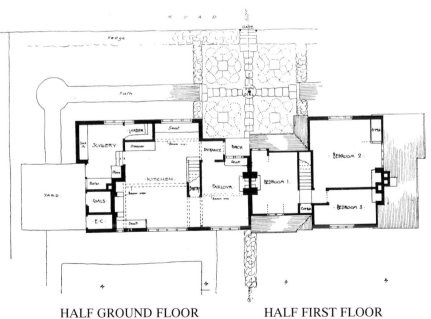

HALF GROUND FLOOR   HALF FIRST FLOOR

may suppose that a man then, who needed a dwelling for his family, would call together his neighbours and friends, each of whom would contribute their share of labour. All would be imbued with the primary idea of making a comely little dwelling. This would be the first consideration, and however important the financial side of the question, it would still be secondary. And this is the rule in all good work – a rule which cannot be too often insisted on. A man working in such a spirit would be ashamed to stint his work, when, by perhaps a few hours more labour he could do it well. It has been truly said that a thing of beauty is a joy for ever, but it is a saying which implies its converse – that an ugly thing is a disgrace for ever – and it may be noted how the composition of the word disgrace implies the shame one ought to feel in the creation of an object devoid of grace. It is well that cottages should be as cheap as careful and ingenious planning can make them. The time is passed for those great unbroken roof-spaces or these massive chimneys like castle towers which make so much for beauty in old cottages, but while in totally ignoring the claims of beauty, it is an easy matter for any one to design a cheap country cottage, the difficulty of the problem lies in achieving a building reasonable in cost, and not without that kind of beauty which will make it seem at home in rural surroundings.

It seems to be generally supposed by landowners who build cottages that to be practically satisfactory they must needs be ugly, and that sanitary cottages cannot possess any of those beauties which belong to old cottages and farm-houses, or, if such beauties are possible, that they can only be added by excessive cost. So widespread is this conviction that ugliness in building is generally accepted as evidence of practical qualities, of which it is held to be the natural and inevitable outcome. And so the modern cottages which are gradually destroying the beauty of English country, and which appear as hideous ulcers on the fair face of many an ancient village, are supposed to represent the inevitable result of modern progress instead of the ignorance and callousness of their builders. And so the beautiful village streets, where each cottage contributes its share to the whole effect, are gradually being transformed into sordid slums.

The only alternative to such ugliness of cottage building at present seems to be the artistic community of model dwellings, where the earnestness and reality of the ancient village is replaced by complacently picturesque semi-detached cottages, which seem to constitute a sort of high-class suburbia, and where all the superficial artistic features cannot compensate for the omission of that real beauty which seems to be rather the unconscious outcome of sound building than a quality which depends on the designing

THE KITCHEN

of front elevations, picturesque half-timber work, and the like.

Such buildings rarely appear as confessed cottages, but all seem to strive to pose rather as little villas, and, on the whole, one seems to prefer the unashamed ugliness of the average modern cottage to their shallow artistry. It is, perhaps, needless to add that by the general public the modern artistic community is taken at its own valuation, and its owner is content with the minimum percentage on his outlay in the fond delusion that he has been instrumental in producing an object-lesson in the art of cottage building. It is only here and there, in isolated exceptional cases, that cottages are built which are really cottages; modest and unassuming, and without any taint of the suburban villa or that underlined art which is everywhere accepted as an evidence of the advance of modern architecture.

The question of the cheap cottage has assumed such importance in recent years that it seems desirable to include plans for a pair of cottages which could be built in most country districts for not more than £175 each, and which would, even for this price, be something more than mere wooden shanties.

The irreducible minimum of accommodation for such cottages consists of a good-sized kitchen and scullery, three bedrooms, pantry, coal-shed, and earth-closet. In some cases the scullery may be included as a mere recess in the kitchen, but this is not desirable where the scullery is also the washhouse and bathroom.

Although in the normal cottage household three bedrooms are required, there are many families in which two will be sufficient, and thus it seems desirable that one of the three bedrooms should be placed on the ground floor, where it can be used as a parlour or bedroom as required. In this way the planning of the cottage is simplified, for in the main block two rooms are placed over two rooms, and the scullery is added as a lean-to at the back.

This pair of cottages is designed for a site in which the approach is from the south. They should, therefore, be set well back from the road, so that the outlook from the windows overlooks the garden.

The common entrance, which in the pair of cottages illustrated on p.155 was justified by conditions which led to the placing of the cottages near the road, with the gardens at the back, is here not so admissible, and the whole scheme serves to show how the position of cottages, in relation to a road, should vary with varying aspects, and how such conditions as these lead naturally to variety in position and plan, which adds to the interest and beauty of any group of detached buildings, and which, though appearing accidental, is actually the logical outcome of a proper study of the problem.

VIEW FROM ROAD

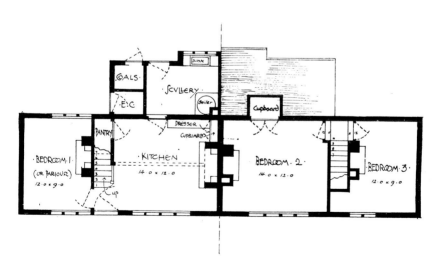

GROUND FLOOR PLAN   FIRST FLOOR PLAN

CHAPTER THIRTY SEVEN
SEMI-DETACHED HOUSES

THE semi-detached house might, perhaps, be better described as semi-attached, for it is its attachment which forces itself upon its tenant as its salient characteristic. It generally represents a hesitating compromise which is fatal to success, and secures for itself neither the advantages of the terrace nor the detached house, while it seems to combine the drawbacks of each. It represents a builder's expedient for making the most of his frontage, and inasmuch as it ranks higher in the conventional scale of excellence than the terrace house and commands a higher rent, it is often to be seen on the outskirts of the modern town, where it has been built for those who cherish the illusion that a semi-detached house is necessarily superior to one in a terrace.

This type of house generally consists of the ordinary terrace plan with the addition of a narrow passage at the side by which the butcher's boy is enabled to reach the back premises. The rational planning of a house on such a frontage would not sacrifice three feet of it for the use of the butcher's boy, but would rather, in building a continuous terrace, give this space to the principal rooms, and would then rather consider the possibility

VIEW FROM NORTH-WEST

of bringing the back premises to the butcher's boy instead of sacrificing space and spoiling the garden by placing the kitchens at the back of the house regardless of aspect, and thus involving difficulties in their approach from the front. Here one is met by the same traditional follies which have been alluded to in the case of the terrace house, and comfort and convenience are alike cheerfully sacrificed to a convention which decrees that the kitchens must be placed at the back.

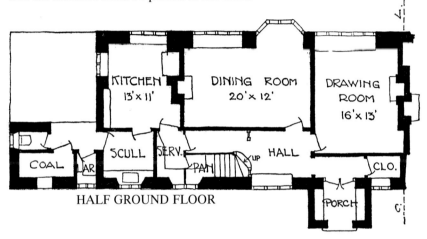

HALF GROUND FLOOR

If there is any rational excuse for the semi-detached house it is that the unattached side should be utilised for light, but in the class of houses which gain their title with the least expenditure of frontage this excuse cannot be urged. But there is a secondary class of semi-detached houses with more ample frontages, which seem to have all but realised the dream of complete detachment, and it is this type which has some degree of reason for its existence. In such houses light can be obtained from three sides, although this is not in all plans essential or desirable. On the other hand, the lack of privacy which is inevitable in the open parts of the garden of the terrace house is equally felt in the semi-detached one, while for those who appreciate the isolation of the detached house the enforced attachment to one other establishment is more felt than if they were merely one in a row. The houses represent a series of families arranged *tête-à-tête*, and neighbours can hardly be ignored as in the terrace. Under these circumstances it is doubtful whether the slight reduction in the cost of the houses caused by the common wall between them is sufficient compensation for these disadvantages.

161

From the artistic point of view the semi-detached house presents the advantage of an extended frontage which enables the designer to gain that long, low proportion which is specially desirable in country buildings, and this may be noted in the examples of semi-detached houses illustrated. But while special conditions of site and demands of occupants may make the semi-detached house suitable in exceptional cases, as a rule it is better to avoid the compromise it affords and to build either terraces or detached houses.

CHAPTER THIRTY EIGHT

HOLIDAY HOUSES

THE term holiday house is here used to include all those dwellings which are adapted to life in the country or at the seaside during a holiday, when the formal routine and conventionalities which have to some extent dictated the plan of the permanent home are set aside for a freer and less restricted existence. The possession of a little holiday house in some favourite summer resort has many advantages, especially for those who do not wish to occupy it during the popular period, when it may be let. A house for this purpose should be as compact and simple as possible. Its windows should all be provided with solid shutters, so that it cannot be easily damaged when unoccupied. Its furniture should also be of the simplest kind, without carpets, curtains, and other unnecessary fabrics, so that even the most ruthless tenant of the furnished house will be unable to injure it.

Such a house should contain one large sitting-room, as well as four or five bedrooms, bathroom, and the usual kitchen premises, reduced to their simplest form, while a verandah or garden-room is an important feature in the holiday house.

In the general scheme of the house and its decoration, a wider scope for fancy is admissible in a dwelling only occasionally occupied, which should be adorned in a holiday mood. The general characteristics of the exterior should be governed by locality, and here the seaside house demands a special treatment, widely differing from that of the country cottage set among trees, and local traditions of building should in all cases be carefully considered, so that it does not appear as an importation of the town into the country. There is something essentially illogical in following the common practice of choosing some country site for its beauty, and then deliberately defacing that beauty by the erection of a cockney villa, which calls itself a cottage; or perhaps constructing there one of those galvanised iron "artistic bungalows," lined with match-boarding, as per catalogue. One finds these charming structures gravely discussed in magazine articles. For a few pounds extra a barge-board or a finial are added as an artistic finish, or aesthetic quality is imparted by "breaking the line of the ridge." Or, again, one is shown how a dwelling may be made out of three railway carriages, and various schemes are illustrated for enlarging and disfiguring old country cottages. Mr. So-and-So has constructed a tin bungalow of horrible aspect in the sacred solitudes of the New Forest, for £230 7s. 6d., and when he can afford another pound or two, he will probably make the recognised concessions to the claims of art involved in the addition of finials perhaps to the roof. And yet it is so easy to construct the simplest kind of dwelling without offence to the artistic sense, and the best course is to follow the local customs of the district, to employ local labour and local materials. In many parts of the country tarred weather-boarding, with roofs of pantile or thatch, are used for farm buildings, and suggest a basis for a scheme which would be quite satisfactory, both artistically and practically, for the holiday house, and in all the details of the house safety from ugliness may be found in eschewing as far as possible the products of the town factory.

The simplest type of holiday dwelling is the tent, which, although only suited for use by hardy people, in favourable weather at least, brings one closer to Nature than any more permanent habitation. And what possibilities of beauty are to be found in the artistic treatment of the tent. One may imagine it striped in shades of green, showing as some strange tropical growth in a meadow, or in some dainty little encampment one may catch a glimpse of gay banners. But, beautiful as the tent may become, it is essentially a fair-weather dwelling. For permanent dwellings of the simplest kind, one may try to realise some of the primitive types of human habitations. The huts of savage races may be studied as examples of how it is possible to achieve a romantic beauty in the simplest kind of structure.

And for those, in these material and commercial days, who still dare to "think nobly" of the home – as Malvolio of the soul – it may be possible to realise in the dim recesses of some woodland such a dainty dwelling as to some chance wanderer from the town might seem to sum up and express the very spirit of the forest.

At the seaside, it must be remembered, you cannot count on that natural weathering and vegetation of the exterior which helps to harmonise the house and its surroundings in country districts inland, and so, instead of

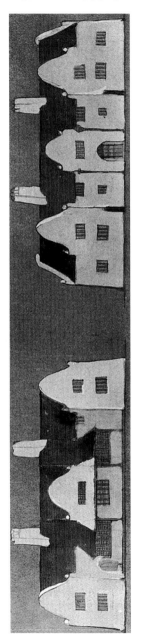

ELEVATIONS

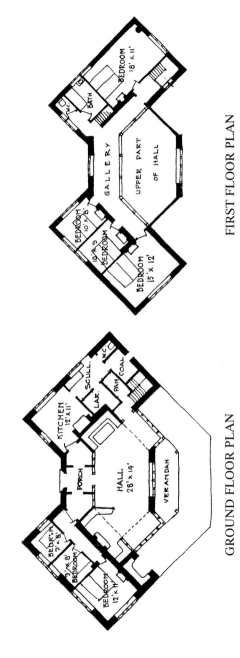

FIRST FLOOR PLAN

GROUND FLOOR PLAN

164

painting the coast red with bricks and tiles, it will generally be better to adopt the formula of white walls and green slate roof. In chalk districts, the local use of flints may be noted and adopted, or walling may be constructed of beach-stones.

In the smaller kinds of holiday houses, however, a wooden structure, which is so designed that it can be readily moved, may meet the demands of those who are content to dispense with material comforts in a temporary shelter from the elements. Here the roof may be formed of prepared canvas, and the dwelling represent but a slight improvement on the tent or the gipsy's caravan. The whole of the appointments of such a little dwelling, modelled on those of the yacht, should be compact and serviceable, and it might well be fantastically adorned with brightly painted chamferings.

Of the four designs for holiday houses illustrated, the first has been described in the *Studio* for July 1904.

One of the disadvantages, from an economical point of view, of the house which consists of one storey only, is that much space is often wasted in the roof, especially in cases where the use of tiles makes it desirable that this should be high-pitched. In the plans for the country cottage "Springcot," it has been arranged that the roof-space should be fully occupied by making the bedrooms partly on the ground floor and partly as attics in the roof, while in the hall the inclusion of the roofing in the room gives a constructive character which it is difficult to obtain in a room with a flat ceiling. The hall thus appears to be, indeed, the house itself, and not a mere compartment. The broad and low passage which crosses the building from front door to garden-room serves the artistic purpose of providing at the threshold a fine vista effect as the first impression on entering the house, and the grey-brown of its homely timbers, the creamy white of its plastered surfaces, and the subtly varied shades of grey in its stone-flagged floor form a frame to the brightness of the court beyond and the sun-flecked pavements and posts of the pergola, while a hint of the hall is conveyed through the panes of dim greenish glass in the screen.

Practically this passage serves to disconnect the kitchen premises from the rest of the house and to provide a ready means of access to the garden. A small staircase, which does not attempt to assert itself as an artistic feature in the plan, and which is concealed by the panelling on the passage wall, gives access to the gallery which overlooks the hall and the servants' bedroom over the kitchen. At the opposite end of the house, on the ground floor, is the principal bedroom, with bathroom adjoining, and a second little stair gives access to two attic bedrooms over these. An enlargement of the

SPRINGCOT. VIEW FROM ROAD

SPRINGCOT. VIEW FROM KITCHEN GARDEN

SPRINGCOT.
THE CORRIDOR

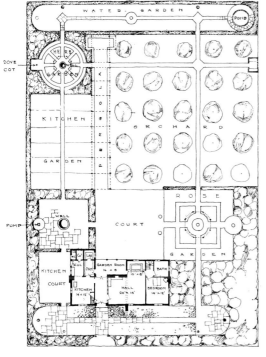

GROUND PLAN

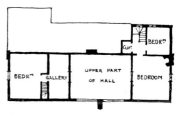

FIRST FLOOR
PLAN

plan, where more bedrooms were required, might consist of an extension of this wing, and this might suggest the use of the principal bedroom as an additional sitting-room, opening with a wide doorway into the hall, and thus adding to the general floor-space of the house.

In this little house it will be noted how structure everywhere replaces superficial decoration. The modern tradition of house-building, which strives to make of each room a rectangular box, lined with smooth plastered surfaces, and which then proceeds to decorate these surfaces with superficial materials covered with patterns, is here set aside in favour of the decorative claims of mere building. Such decoration as is included in the scheme is introduced mainly for some definite purpose, and thus the ornament on the walls of the dining-recess gains in richness of effect in contrast to the relative plainness of the hall itself, and helps to deepen the shadow under the beam over this little alcove.

The plan for the garden shown in connection with this country cottage is submitted mainly as an illustration of certain principles of design in garden-making. It is not suggested as a suitable scheme for any site, for each will demand a special treatment. And in such treatment much will depend on the due recognition of the possibilities of local features. In a cottage which is only occupied for certain portions of the year, it is important at least for those for whom the economical aspect of the matter cannot be ignored, that both the building and the garden should be able to take care of themselves, and the house and garden, as usually designed and furnished, may often prove in this respect a costly incubus, demanding for its maintenance considerable labour in repairs of the structure as well as much clipping and grooming and weeding in the garden.

As far as the house is concerned, it is not a difficult matter to make it self-sustaining. It is only necessary to apply those principles which have already been dwelt on, and to omit all those cumbrous and useless fabrics and furnishings which demand so much attention in the average house.

And in the garden it might be suggested, in view of the labour required in weeding, to decide to give up that unequal conflict and to have a garden composed entirely of triumphant weeds. But in order to do this it will be necessary to choose a site where the right kind of weeds grow. There are many such country places where the flowers which grow naturally and quite untended might well form the basis for a wild garden in which the skill of the gardener would be shown mainly in recognising and accentuating the natural characteristics of the place, for it is easy to spoil natural beauty by the introduction of sophisticated plants and shrubs. But

SPRINGCOT. THE HALL

where it is not possible to obtain a site which possesses natural advantages, there are still many types of garden suitable for the occasionally occupied house, and labour in maintenance may be reduced to a minimum by the substitution of an orchard for the lawn, and by the use of paved paths instead of gravel walks.

In referring to the garden illustrated by the plan (p.167), one may note first of all the importance attached to vistas – vistas arranged with definite terminal effects. One may also observe the usefulness of shade in the garden as well as light, and how embowered paths may be contrasted with the brightness of open spaces.

The most important of these vistas is the one which, beginning at the garden gate, extends through the passage which crosses the house and beyond across the open courtyard to the pergola, where it is terminated in a garden seat, and a glance at the plan will show how much it depends for its effect on such vistas, and how widely it differs in this respect from those gardens full of winding paths which never fulfil the promise they seem to convey of some vision of the beyond. On the other hand, the defect of the formal treatment often lies in a certain barrenness, a lack of mystery, and those surprises and dramatic effects of light and shade which are such essential attributes of the garden. Open flower gardens are best approached through dim and shady alleys, and everywhere broad and open sunlit spaces should be contrasted with the shade of pergolas and embowered paths. In passing through these enclosed ways one loses all conception of the garden scheme till, at the intersection of a path, one suddenly perceives through vistas of roses and orchard trees some distant garden ornament, or perhaps a seat or summer-house; and so one becomes conscious of a scheme arranged to secure definite and well-considered effects. As in a dramatic entertainment, apartments of the garden full of tragic shade are followed by open spaces where flowers laugh in the sun; and by such devices the art of man arranges natural forms to appeal in the strongest way to the human consciousness.

In the treatment of the exterior of this country cottage, a simplicity of form has been adopted which conveys something of that air of repose which belongs, as a matter of course, to old farm-houses and cottages, but which may be sought in vain in the average modern country dwelling.

The second design for a holiday house (the House with the Purple Shutters) is especially adapted for a seaside site, where its simple roof-plan and long low eaves-line would seem to harmonise with somewhat bleak and wind-swept surroundings. Here the use of slates for the roof permits a

THE HOUSE WITH THE PURPLE SHUTTERS

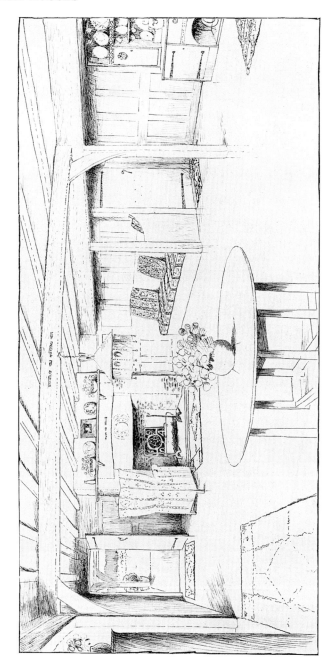

THE HOUSE WITH THE PURPLE SHUTTERS. INTERIOR OF LIVING ROOM

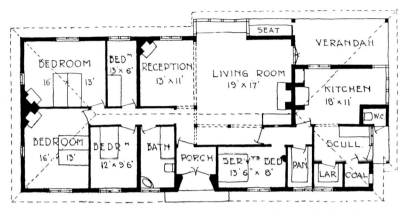

THE HOUSE WITH THE PURPLE SHUTTERS. PLAN

low pitch, so that, although the whole accommodation is provided on the ground floor, there is little space wasted in the roof.

The central feature of the plan consists of the large hall, or living-room, a portion of which can be screened off if required. Access to the front door and the bedrooms can be obtained from the kitchen premises without passing through the hall itself. Under a slight extension of the roof is also included a verandah or garden-room.

The treatment of the garden in such a seaside house might well include all those flowers and shrubs which flourish by the sea. The feathery foliage of the tamarisk, the blue-greens and purples of the sea-holly, the puce-pink flowers of the sea-thrift, the sea-lavender, the sea-poppy, and many other seaside flowers, would combine to make an interesting and unique garden. Here, too, might be grown that group of plants which, originally dwellers by the sea, have been trained to live in inland gardens, and all these plants would not present that air of protest which one often seems to discern in flowers removed from their proper home, but would seem to rejoice in the salt air and sea-breezes.

The third plan for a holiday house was originally designed to meet the demand in a special case for rather more than the usual number of bedrooms, some of which are placed on the ground floor.

The form of the plan, while giving a wide outlook from the hall by placing the little terrace to the south between the protecting wings on each side, shelters it from cold winds and makes it a trap for the sunlight.

173

CHAPTER THIRTY NINE

FLATS

THE ordinary town house, in distinction from the country house, may be considered as a dwelling which, owing to its restricted size enforced by the costliness of land, cannot expand laterally. As the land is sold in pieces like cloth of a constant width it is capable of easier extension to the back, and the form of house which results from these arbitrary conditions is long and narrow, and as the plan is unable to expand laterally it develops vertically, and its rooms, instead of being placed side by side, are placed on top of each other.

But in the flat, the houses instead of being packed laterally are packed vertically, and so a block of flats is really a series of one-storey country houses placed on top of each other. But the conditions which have led to the development of flats in modern towns have not been favourable ones. Built as commercial speculations on restricted sites to meet a demand which is generally in excess of the supply, the object of their existence has been to secure the highest rent for the minimum of space and convenience. But as the flat is more economical to work than the town house, and as it possesses several other advantages over it which will be alluded to later on, its tenant is prepared to put up with certain restrictions which do not essentially belong to the flat at all but only to the flat as it is now built. Tradition has fixed the lowest standard of comfort demanded in the house, but no tradition applies to the modern flat, and the fact that in its present state it still competes successfully with the more commodious house of equal rent seems to show that it is more adapted for town life.

In the flat one might suppose the utilitarian spirit which prides itself on its practical qualities and sound common sense would at least find expression. Here it might be assumed there is no margin for the art of the house, and the lift, the electric light and the other modern conveniences seem to bear witness to the prevalence of conditions with which it is popularly supposed that art has little to do.

And yet a visit to the average flat will impress the intelligent observer chiefly with the extraordinary ignorance of planning which it displays, the reckless squandering of space, and the want of any sort of arrangement in the rooms.

He may be duly impressed with the imposing façade, but on opening the

174

front door of the flat he is visiting he will be confronted with an apparently interminable passage, narrow and lofty. On each side of this dismal thoroughfare are rows of shut doors, each opening into minute compartments having no definite arrangement or sequence, so that the unattended visitor on opening one at a venture may find himself confronted by the elegance of the miniature drawing-room, or precipitated into the more homely if less pretentious appointments of the kitchen. And such a dwelling is cheerfully regarded by its occupants as a "cosy flat," and its inconveniences and restrictions are considered as essential parts of the scheme, the defects of the qualities for which they pay so dear.

The popular view as to dwellings seems to be that they grow like trees in certain shapes, and with certain internal defects beyond the control of mere human agencies, and so the flat, like the villa, is accepted without criticism.

The plans for flats which I illustrate may be found to be somewhat more liberal in their accommodation than those to be obtained at a moderate rental, in London at any rate; but the present high rent of flats seems to be due to temporary artificial conditions, and there is no valid reason why a flat should not provide the same accommodation as a terrace house for approximately the same rental. Moreover, the plans submitted are mainly to illustrate certain principles of planning which would apply to small flats as well as large ones.

The first essential is to secure a roomy and spacious ensemble in the sitting-rooms by such modifications as we have already considered in the ordinary house plan, and this is a more pressing requirement in the flat because its rooms are generally small, and there is no garden to afford relief to those prisoned within its cells (see colour illustration p.18). The apartments for the servants should not be jumbled up with the family rooms, but should be definitely planned and isolated, and while the sitting-rooms can be connected to give an ample floor-area, there should be rooms also which may be entirely quiet and private. A balcony is also a desirable feature in a gardenless dwelling.

On referring to the larger plan illustrated, it may be noted that the servant can reach the front door and the bedrooms without passing through the sitting-rooms. On entering from the porch the visitor, instead of finding himself in a narrow passage, is at once welcomed in a roomy hall, beyond which a glimpse may be caught of the drawing-room. In both hall and dining-room the planning has led naturally to recessed fireplaces, and in spite of the ingle-nookeries of the modern villa it is maintained that such a type is unequalled for comfort. The bedrooms are five in number, including

175

the servant's bedroom, and thus afford the full complement of rooms which the average family demands, while the furnishing of some of these as bed-sitting-rooms would afford private retreats for the individual members of the family.

The whole scheme is practically a house built round a court which affords light to the servants' premises and to the passages from which the bedrooms open. This passage, with its side lighting and ceiling at a low level, will be entirely different to the narrow and lofty one which has already been mentioned. Its windows will not afford an outlook into the court, but with their leaded glazing will merely let a toned light into the passage.

There is a lack of storage-space for boxes, but it has been considered that space in the flat itself is too valuable to be used in this way, and the basement or roof space of the building would afford the necessary accommodation of this kind required by the tenants. In the treatment of the exterior of such a building simplicity and economy should be the ruling ideas, and the use of cleanly whitewash is recommended, which with some bright window boxes and a roof of green slates will make an ensemble which would possess the qualities of freshness and gaiety which are the essence of beauty in building, and worth miles of grimy pedantic façades.

Let the money which would otherwise be spent in trying to impress the indifferent passer-by by all sorts of architectural features be spent instead on the interior, or in adding a few more square feet in area to the rooms.

Such a building, placed in a town where the inhabitants are not forced by the unchecked greed of the speculator to huddle their houses together in restricted sites, would naturally be surrounded by foliage, and its white walls with their gay window adornments would rise out of green leaves. Within easy reach, if not actually surrounding the building itself, would be the public garden, which would replace that private garden which its occupants are unable to obtain. I am aware that the term public gardens conjures up a sorry vision of winding walks, carpet bedding, and notices to keep off the grass. Very different is the public garden I should ask for as a satisfactory substitute for a private domain. It would be selected first of all for its natural beauties, including, if possible, a piece of woodland, and a stream perhaps, and these would be developed on natural lines, while within its bounds would also be included enclosed apartments for the culture and display of flowers and fruit.

The inclusion of natural features in such a garden would of course only be possible in certain cases, but if the garden is entirely artificial and formal it should be designed with thought and feeling, and with plenty of light and

176

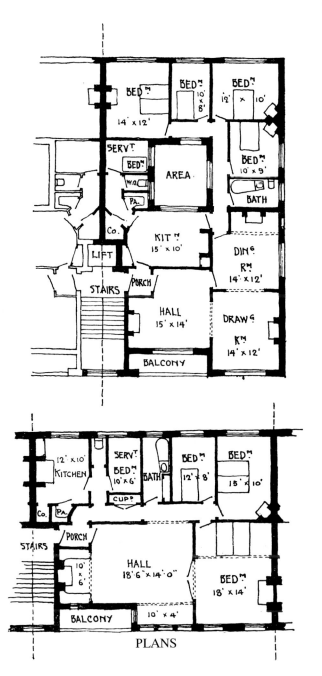

PLANS

VIEW OF ENTRANCE

shade, and some good vista effects.

The smaller plan for a flat shows the application of the same principles in a flat which, lighted only from the front and back, might be built as a continuous terrace. Here there is one good-sized sitting-room, with ingle fireplace and balcony, adjoining which is a bed-sitting-room, in which the beds can be entirely screened by curtains. The bedroom furniture would be designed in the form of little cabinets, which when closed would help to convey the character of a sitting-room. Besides this bed-sitting-room are two other bedrooms at the back, and a servant's bedroom isolated from the family rooms, a bathroom and kitchen premises. If the bedroom accommodation thus provided is not all required, the bed-sitting-room adjoining the hall could be furnished as a drawing-room, and if necessary it could be cut off from the hall by closing the sliding doors and entering it from the small door at the back, to which access from the front door is afforded by means of the passage adjoining the kitchen.

CHAPTER FORTY

CO-OPERATIVE HOUSES

ANY one who has penetrated to the less fashionable outskirts of a modern town must have observed those long rows of mean dwellings which encroach on the surrounding country, and must have felt what a melancholy thing it must be to live there. One cannot but think that there should be some better way of living than that which finds expression in these sordid streets. The house of a civilised people should convey something more than the callous commercialism of the speculative builder, and should be arranged on some better principle than that which merely aims at crowding as many as possible into a given space. In this matter the savage who decks his primitive dwelling with brightly painted carving is more advanced than we, and of all the habitations of man, surely none have quite reached such an expression of sordid meanness as the modern street of modern villa residences.

Let us a consider for a moment one of these rows of little houses, all exactly alike, and each with its gas-meter under the stairs, its scraper on the front doorstep, its linoleum in the narrow hall, the patent cooking-range and its incapable cook in the kitchen.

Here it would seem that a great saving of labour and expense might be effected by centralising the functions of cooking and heating in these houses, and by providing one large fire and one capable cook to take the place of a dozen incapable cooks and a dozen miniature cooking-ranges.

The difficulty of such a reform would appear to be that in the combination of the family units, which it would involve, what is gained in convenience and economy may be lost in privacy and comfort; for while, as the copybook maxim says, "union is strength," the strength of the community is generally obtainable only at some sacrifice of its individuals, and while the bundle of arrows is not so readily broken as the single shaft, their feathers may be sorely ruffled by their close contact with each other.

And so the centripetal force, which urges the desirability of combination, is opposed by a centrifugal one which, in the interests of individual developments tends to keep our houses isolated and self-contained. And thus the problem seems to resolve itself into a compromise between these opposing tendencies to secure the benefits of union and co-operation, and yet not to lose the advantages of privacy.

It is proposed, in the scheme for an arrangement of small houses here illustrated, to replace the servants of the individual house by a central staff of trained domestics under skilled supervision, and to provide the necessary accommodation for their work and habitation in the shape of one well-appointed kitchen, with the necessary offices, sitting-room and bedrooms, thus removing from the house all that portion of the premises devoted to the servants.

Again, the small dining-rooms of the houses are replaced by one large central apartment, where the occupants of a group of houses could enjoy well-cooked food in spacious surroundings, while still, where required, food could be conveyed to the separate houses where special conditions made it desirable.

Having thus centralised the functions of feeding and service, the next consideration would be the centralisation of heating, which would be effected by hot air or hot water supplemented in the separate houses by the open fire.

In seeking for the type of plan which would be most suitable for such a group of houses, the college court with its central hall and cloisters at once suggests itself. A covered approach to the central hall from the various houses is thus provided, and the whole arrangement is one which is admirably adapted to artistic treatment.

In the plan illustrated, such an arrangement on a small scale is shown,

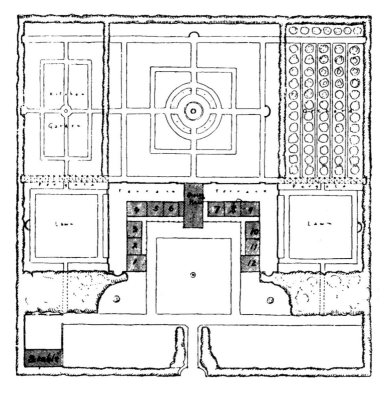

GARDEN PLAN

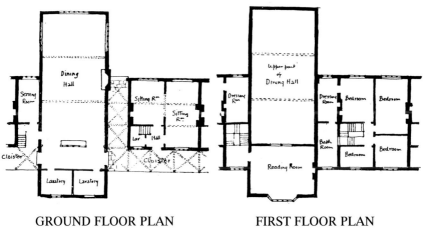

GROUND FLOOR PLAN   FIRST FLOOR PLAN

comprising twelve separate houses, which vary slightly in their accommodation, but contain on an average two sitting-rooms on the ground floor, with four bedrooms and bathroom, &c., above, and in the roof one or two attics.

These houses are placed round three sides of the square, which a further addition to their number would enclose, leaving merely a covered carriage entrance. In the centre of the south side is the central hall, beneath which is the kitchen and offices, and over which are the bedrooms for the servants and accommodation for the mistress. Adjoining the hall are lavatories and cloak-rooms, and over this lower portion, in a mezzanine floor, is a reading-room.

The building is surrounded by ample garden-space, where, instead of curly paths and shapeless shrubberies of the villa, there are square lawns enclosed by yew hedges, an orchard with brick paths set in the grass, pergolas and arbours, and all the other features of the old English gardens. It may be questioned whether such a setting is altogether admissible in a scheme which professes an economical basis, but it is not suggested that this group of houses should be tied to a railway station, where land is dear and space limited. One of the promised results of modern advance in locomotion has been the practical possibility of living in the country, and one of the features of the scheme proposed is a motor 'bus, which would convey the occupants at stated times to their business or pleasure.

It is a question as to what degree the features of the individual house should be retained or merged into the general use, and it might possibly be advisable to set apart a portion of the garden to be divided up into small private gardens for the individual houses; or again, in the central dining-hall, on a larger scale a series of recesses might be arranged, allotted to individual families. For the benefit of those who wish to retain the possibility of the simpler forms of cooking in their own house, such as the preparation of a simple breakfast or tea, at least one of the fireplaces in the sitting-rooms would be of a type suitable for such purposes, and the presence in the room of necessary appliances for such operations would help to give it that quality of homeliness which is so difficult to obtain in a room where the china is merely for show. Many minor improvements would probably suggest themselves in a more complete and exhaustive study of the scheme, which is here advanced in a tentative way, but the central and inevitable fact is the economy of labour which must result from the co-operative system of dwelling.

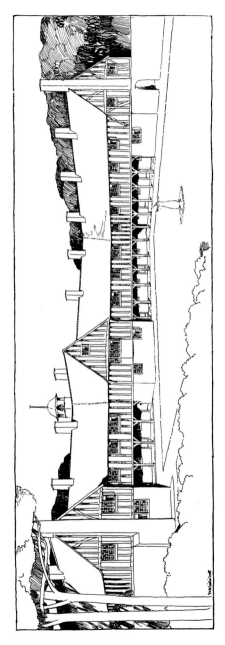

ENTRANCE FRONT

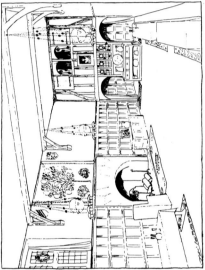

THE DINING HALL

A HOUSE AND GARDEN IN SWITZERLAND

THE house and garden which forms the subject of the following illustrations was designed for a hillside site in Switzerland. The site is a somewhat small one, only slightly more than one-third of an acre in extent, and is bounded on its upper and lower sides by roads which do not run parallel to each other. The house is placed parallel to the upper road, and gains a certain air of snugness by being placed somewhat below its level, so that from the entrance gate one descends eight steps into the little square entrance court. From this court vistas to right and left end in garden ornaments backed by clipped hedges. The house is symmetrically disposed, with its central arched doorway with black door relieved by metal, and on each side this recessed central portion is flanked by the projecting gables with their chimneys.

Turning to the right from the entrance court and passing the angle of the house is a small part of the garden specially arranged for children, with its swing, giant's stride, and flower beds, while in one angle, the masses of dark shrubs which surround it are cut out into a circular recessed retreat, one of those enclosed nooks which especially recommend themselves to children. The woodwork of the swing and giant's stride is painted in gay colours, and in the centre of the four flower beds is a circular tank, lined with turquoise-blue tiles, in which gold-fish and other aquatic pets are kept. The furnishing of this part of the garden would also include a low garden seat and table.

Descending some nine steps which pass the bay window to the children's room one reaches another terrace, at a lower level, from which access may be gained, through a verandah or porch, to a billiard-room on the lower floor. From this terrace also opens a small garden pavilion from which one reaches the flower garden and lawn below by means of a sloping path on the bank of shrubs above which the house and its terrace rise. On turning the corner of the house by the drawing-room bay-window one passes along the terrace which runs parallel to the garden front of the house. At the opposite end of this terrace one turns to the right down a wide flight of steps leading to the rose garden. Half-way down these steps is a landing from which to the right one looks through a shady archway of clipped shrubs into the bright flower garden with its central dipping well and terminal pavilion. To the left from the same landing one looks into the pergola. The rose garden is laid out in square form with a circle of climbing rose on arches round another dipping well. Here also is a semicircular recess for a seat, and passing down another flight of steps one reaches, through an iron gate under an arch, the lower road. Divided from this rose garden by a hedge is the lawn with a semicircular recess at the end for another seat, and adjoining the rose garden to the north is the shady pergola with its roof of leafage on the level of the court which adjoins it to the north. In this pergola one passes through a door, not without a suggestion of mystery, up a flight of steps into a square court. To the north of this are the kitchen premises with a drying-yard for linen which is placed half outside and half under the arched wall of the house, so that the clothes can be dried under cover in wet weather. This drying-yard immediately adjoins the washhouse and laundry. Above this one passes the back entrance, and turning the corner of the house reaches the entrance court again.

It is a garden of many vistas, a garden of mysteries and dramatic effects of light and shade, and within its narrow confines are included apartments for all weathers and all moods. From the rose garden, as shown in the sketch, the house soars above its terraces and steps, and so this aspect of the building is in marked contrast to the view from the upper road from which it appears so low and so snugly ensconced in its surroundings.

On entering the house one finds oneself in a roomy square low porch from which an inner door opens into the central hall, which one sees beyond the low-ceiled gallery which forms a picturesque approach to the dining-room from the drawing-room. The drawing-room is divided from the hall by folding doors, and these two rooms together afford an ample floor-space. In each the open fireplaces are important features. In the hall the fire is placed under a wide arch of masonry, and in the drawing-room a corner fireplace is arranged with copper hood open hearth, and tiled wall-spaces. The dining-room has a recess which would be used for the less formal meals, and adjoining this and conveniently placed for service are the kitchen premises. The hall is two storeys in height with a gallery and lofty bay-window overlooking the terrace and garden.

From the deeply recessed doorway adjoining the fireplace of the hall one reaches a garden-room and little upper terrace, from which the lower terraces and garden are reached by a flight of steps. The children's room and study occupy the opposite wing of the house to the kitchen, and both open out to another square verandah.

Below this main floor-level is another floor which from the garden side becomes on a level with the main terraces. Here, besides the necessary washhouse, laundry, heating-chamber, servants' hall, bathroom and w.c., and the cellars, there is also a billiard room with large ingle fireplace and verandah opening on to the terrace.

On the bedroom floor are four bedrooms, three dressing-rooms, two bathrooms, and a linen-room over the porch. Two of the bedrooms have wide balconies with flat roofs.

On the attic floor are four attics and a large studio.

The walls of the exterior are finished in creamy white with red tiled roof.

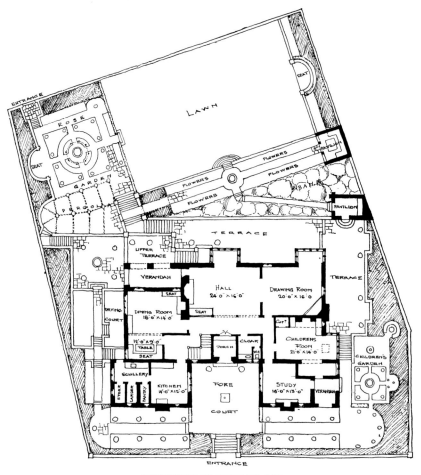

GROUND FLOOR PLAN

186

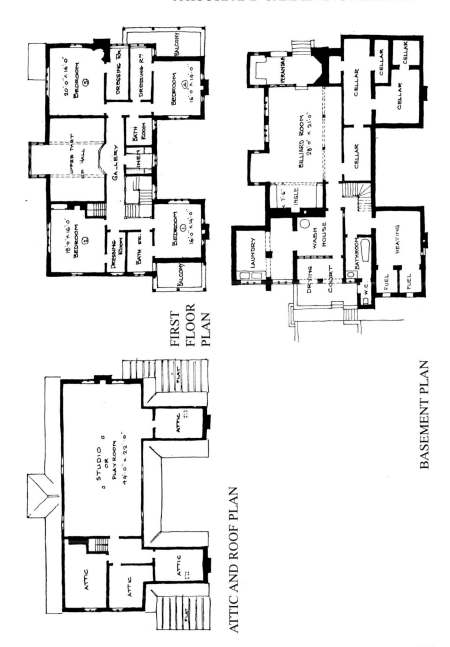

FIRST FLOOR PLAN

BASEMENT PLAN

ATTIC AND ROOF PLAN

GARDEN FRONT

A HOUSE AND GARDEN IN SWITZERLAND

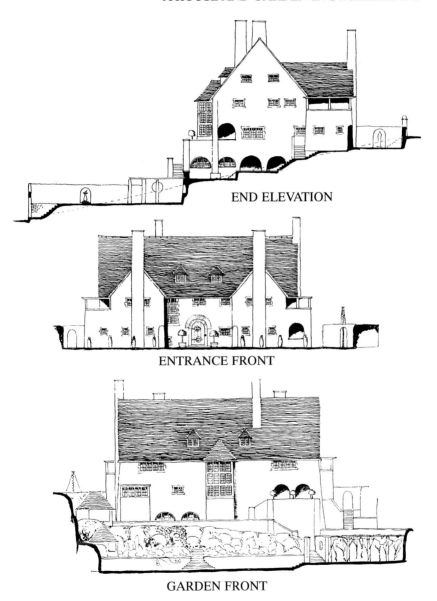

END ELEVATION

ENTRANCE FRONT

GARDEN FRONT

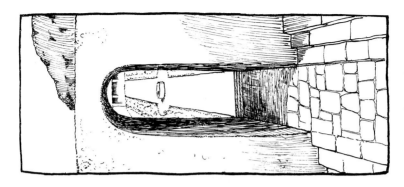

VIEW OF FLOWER
GARDEN FROM STEPS

ENTRANCE COURT AND VISTA

A HOUSE IN AMERICA

THE house which is illustrated here was designed for a site in America, under somewhat severe restrictions as to cost – restrictions which suggested the simplicity of its form and roof plan. In these respects it resembles "Findon."

The low square porch is designed on somewhat the same lines. This opens into a small hall-space, from which the staircase ascends. The drawing-room and dining-room form together the main living-rooms of the house, and each have ample fireplaces. The study is smaller and more isolated, while the kitchen premises are simplified by the absence of the separate scullery and by the partial use of the basement for storage. Five good-sized bedrooms occupy the first floor, with bathroom and linen-closet, and above these are five attics with servants' bathroom. The basement contains heating-chamber, laundry and cellars. American characteristics will be recognised in the ample cupboard-space provided in the bedrooms, and the servants' bathroom.

In the arrangement of the ground plan the hall forms a recess in the drawing-room, from which it can be cut off when required by sliding doors. When these doors are open, the drawing-room and hall together form a spacious reception-hall, and when the doors to the recess are closed it obtains the privacy which may be required for its uses as a drawing-room. The hall recess does not attempt here to pose as a room. There is, therefore, no fireplace, and its whole treatment suggests it is but a recessed portion of the larger room.

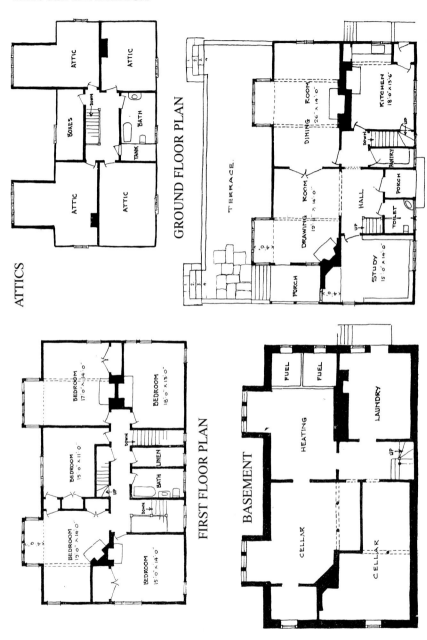

ATTICS

GROUND FLOOR PLAN

FIRST FLOOR PLAN

BASEMENT

A HOUSE AND GARDEN IN POLAND

THE house now to be considered is one designed for a site in Poland, where the rigour of the winter climate demands some modifications of the normal English plan. The chief of these modifications consists in the reduction of the windows as far as possible, and the construction of these with double thickness of glass with an air-space between, and also in the thickening of the walls, and by these means reducing to a minimum the influences of outside conditions on the internal temperature. It further became desirable to create an interior world which in its warmth and brightness would, to some extent, compensate for an enforced seclusion within its walls for half the year. A large floor-space and a somewhat irregular disposition of the apartments was specially desired so that the interior would be rich in pleasant vistas, and the occupants feel something of that sense of unconfined freedom which the rectangular plastered box cannot give. The plan which is illustrated shows but a modification of a scheme which was originally designed by my client with a view to realise such a spacious and unconfined interior effect.

In the scheme for the roof it became necessary to consider the question of snow and to avoid all internal gutters. The heating question is also an important one, and involves, besides the ample open fires, a complete system of hot-water heating.

The conditions under which this house is to be built are peculiarly favourable to that human expression in workmanship which, under modern conditions, it is so difficult to obtain. The brick for the walls are all made on the spot, and the timber for the trees felled in the neighbourhood. In the working of this timber it does not pass under the fatal rule of the steam saw and plane, and so the beams of the house seem still to retain some of their original characteristics, and are eloquent in signs of human handicraft. It is all the difference between the orange picked from its native tree and the orange bought from the greengrocer's shop, and the associations of Nature still cling around the beams and posts in the house. In the effect of the interior it is the art of mere building which is principally relied upon, and posts, beams, braces and arches all contribute their aid to the whole constructural scheme.

The final notes of the general effect of the interior, which consists for the main part of broad spaces of creamy plaster with the grey-brown of timber, are supplied by brilliant concentrated notes of colour in heraldic decoration.

A HOUSE AND GARDEN IN POLAND

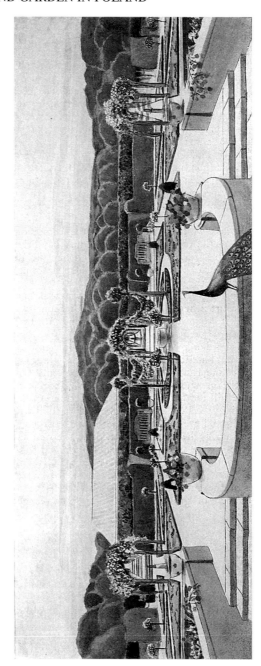

PART OF GARDEN SHOWING THREE RADIATING VISTAS

In some of the rooms a more extensive use of superficial decoration is arranged for, and the bedrooms are each adorned with a special flower motif (see colour illustration p.19).

The scheme for the garden shown in connection with this house is based on existing features in the grounds surrounding a previous house, and also the natural levels, so that lawns and terraces can be formed without excessive cutting and filling. In thus modifying and developing an existing garden, impediments which one is apt to regard a little impatiently at first seem gradually, when the matter has been exhaustively considered, to become the means of realising unexpected effects, and like the grain of sand in the oyster, form the nucleus for what may at last become a pearl. As an example of this may be instanced the hothouse shown on the garden plan illustrated, a building of solid structure which could not be easily removed. Other and more vital considerations led to the placing of the new house at an angle which bears no definite relation to this building, and as the lines of the new garden plan necessarily followed those of the house, the hothouse seemed to become a discordant element in the scheme. A reference to the plan will show how, by the introduction of diagonal paths which follow the lines of the hothouse, this building is brought into harmony with the scheme, and the sketch of this portion of the garden shows that thus, from a given point of view, one may look along the lines of three radiating vistas – a special garden effect which resulted from the necessity for incorporating the hothouse in the garden scheme.

An important feature in this garden is the circular drive to the north of the house where the horses may be exercised, and viewed from the house or from the seats in the recess which forms the terminal feature to the main drive vista.

One of the principal factors which have governed the choice of the position for the house as well as the main lines of the garden has been the relation of both to existing old trees, so that they should so group themselves round the building and form points of interest in the garden so as to make it appear that the trees were a part of the general scheme.

So too the existing tea-house, by the extension of its verandah and the introduction of a paved court in front of this, becomes a terminal feature to one of the main vistas, and is brought into relation with the rose garden.

It will be noticed that this garden plan chiefly extends to the east of the house. This is owing to the fact that it is in this direction that the slope of the ground, which falls towards the lake to the south, is less steep. On the south and west of the house the ground falls rapidly, and here the principal feature is a pergola cut in the hillside and open on one side to the lake, the

195

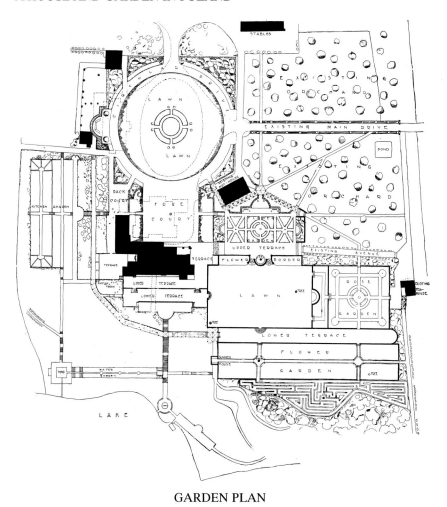

GARDEN PLAN

196

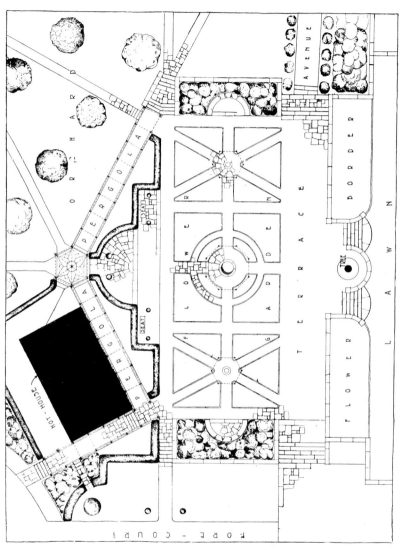

PART OF GARDEN

197

A HOUSE AND GARDEN IN POLAND

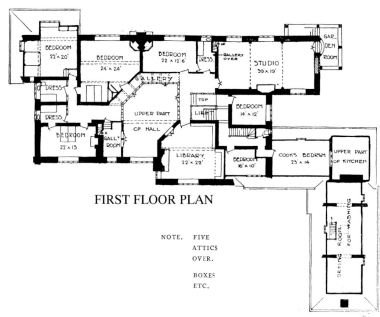

FIRST FLOOR PLAN

NOTE. FIVE
ATTICS
OVER.

BOXES
ETC.

GROUND FLOOR PLAN

THE STUDIO

other being formed by a retaining-wall. This follows the natural lines of the hillside round the south and west sides of the house, and connects the terrace below the lawn with a kitchen garden formed on the west side of the house. In this part of the garden plan is also included a broad flight of steps which forms a descent from the centre of the lower terrace of the house to the lake and boathouse.

Amongst other features of the garden scheme may be noted the maze, which occupies an irregular piece of ground, and the long flower garden adjoining this to the north.

THE HALL

LE NID

I N modern times the house of the average citizen is necessarily a somewhat prosaic affair. It has been my endeavour to show how far some quality of romance may be introduced into its scheme, so that the man who is justly not content with bread alone may find in his home some solace for the imagination – some stuff of which dreams may be made.

In the dwelling, which it is now my purpose to describe, less rigorous restrictions have made possible a fuller expression of decorative ideals. To describe it I must transport the reader to a dim pine-wood in Roumania, a wood such as that of which Swinburne sings:

> Far Eastward and Westward the sun-coloured lands,
> Shine bright as the light on them smiles,
> While fairer than temple uplifted by hands,
> Tall column by column the Sanctuary stands,
> Of the pine-forest's infinite aisles.

There is surely nothing in Nature quite so architectural in character as a pine-wood. Under foot is the brown carpet of the pine-needles, and around in endless perspective the tall columns of the trees, while above one catches glimpses of dusky orange branches set in sombre green. The air is heavy with the incense of the trees, and no tangled undergrowth obstructs the floor save where the pale green of bracken shimmers in a misty light amidst the purple trunks.

If in such a wood one were to seek a dwelling, surely one would expect to find, as Psyche did, the hostelry of a god, or at least the woodland retreat of some goddess of the groves.

It would not seem unfitting that these columns should support such a structure perched like a nest under the vaulting of the spreading branches.

It is in such a wood that "Le Nid" is built. The floors of its chambers are formed by horizontal pine-trunks secured to the trees enclosing a somewhat irregular space. Its walls are of a like rustic character, and its roof of dark-toned thatch, so that the whole structure seems in harmony with the trees which support and surround it.

But while this general roughness and rustic character seems essentially appropriate in such a situation, it will be necessary to explain that it differs materially from those arrangements of squirming and tortured branches

201

which have so corrupted modern rustic work with evil associations. The columns which support the roof and the balcony, which partly surrounds "Le Nid," present the subtle vital curves of healthy unobstructed growth, and not the contorted and bizarre convulsions of trees stunted and highlighted by unfavourable surroundings.

On reaching this balcony, poised so high above the earth, it seems inevitable that the mystic influences of the dim incense-breathing wood should suggest Rossetti's lines :

> The blessed damosel leaned out
> From the gold bar of Heaven.

Under the deep shade of the roof one perceives the entrance door to "Le Nid" bowered in an interlacing framework of carved branches and leafage, in the midst of which birds flutter and cling, and over which gleams a gilded nest.

On entering, one perceives that the brown and rough outer husk of this aerial dwelling is richly lined with jewelled and brilliant colour.

Some indication of the effect from the entrance may be gained from the illustration which forms the frontispiece to this book. The apartment represents the room of the sun and sunflower, and in all its various decorations the same symbol is presented. The tiles, the seats and the windows all represent different treatments of this sunflower motif, while the ceiling represents an attempt to convey in conventional terms something of the effect of glimpses of sky and sun seen through the upper branches of trees. In contrast to this golden room is the cool recessed *ercker,* of which the lily is the symbol flower. Its floor is set with a mosaic of water lilies disposed in lines which converge to the shrine on which a dim light burns. Towards this shrine, too, the lilies of the frieze bend their heads, and the pictured Madonna is framed by branches intricately interwoven. On the opposite side of this little oratory is the organ enclosed by doors, the inner sides of which are bright with flights of angels painted on a gilded ground.

The lines from Rossetti –

> We two will stand before that shrine,
> Occult, withheld, untrod,

lines which seem to have been struck out with masterly precision as by a sculptor's chisel – seem especially appropriate for inscription over this shrine so remotely enskied.

Adjoining this principal apartment – the salon of the sun and the sunflower – is a bedroom where the drowsy poppy prevails. Over the door the inscription is from the Ancient Mariner:

> To Mary, Queen, the praise be given,
> She sent the gentle sleep from Heav'n
> Which slid into my soul.

Here the hangings of the bed are embroidered with poppies. Poppies are painted on the walls, and are inlaid in the panels of the furniture. Beyond the bedroom is the kitchen, daintily appointed, and completing the whole plan of a dwelling probably unique in its situation, structure and adornments.

LE NID (detail)

FINDON

T HIS house was designed for a client who had no delusions about picturesque roof-lines and quaint arrangements of gables, but who recognised the merits of simplicity both from an artistic as well as an economic point of view. The house is a simple rectangle, roofed in one span with a plain hipped roof, thus avoiding the expense of lead gutters, and the unbroken eaves-line runs round the whole building.

Half-timber work was adopted for the wall framing because it seemed peculiarly adapted to the district where its cost was no greater than a nine-inch brick wall. It is framed of solid timbers which in some cases show inside the house, and the same framing is carried out in internal partitions.

The site, which is practically level, is laid out as shown in the garden plan illustrated. The house is placed in the centre of the ground, and the space is divided into definite compartments of lawn, forecourt, rose garden, orchard, &c. as shown, which are connected with straight paths giving some good vista effects.

From the inner door at the side of the wide and low porch one enters a recessed portion of the dining-hall under the overhanging gallery above. This recess may be divided by a curtain from the dining-hall itself, and thus the drawing-room, study and kitchen premises can be reached without passing through the dining-hall itself – the whole of the traffic of the house being confined to this recess. The principal room of the house, which constitutes the focus of the plan, is the dining-hall, which is about fourteen feet high, and is boarded round with wide planks to the height of its doors, above which are broad spaces of whitewashed plaster, and a ceiling of rough woodwork also whitewashed. As the house was designed for a lady, the drawing-room is rather large in proportion to the other rooms. It is low and homely, and from it to the south are casement doors which open on to the terrace.

On the south-west corner is a small study, in which the walls are chiefly lined with bookcases. A fixed seat is placed near the fireplace, with a little window above it. The writing-desk is placed in a corner of the room where it enjoys a left light. This disposition of the furniture shows how a small room may be arranged to make the most of a limited floor space. In the other sitting-rooms the principal pieces of furniture are shown on the plan – the grand piano in the drawing-room, with its special window, and the couch at the side of the fireplace. In the dining-hall the central circular gate-table, which can easily be moved to one side when required, stands in the centre of the room. The sideboard is placed under the overhanging gallery, and a long and wide seat occupies the bay-window, from which one looks on to the terrace and the central vista of the rose garden beyond.

A feature in connection with the dining-hall which must be noted is the serving-cupboard which has already been described. The fire is placed on a wide hearth of stone under a brick arch. The kitchen premises are completely isolated, but conveniently placed for service, and are all floored with red tiles. In the kitchen itself the window to the east, which overlooks the rose garden, is glazed with obscured glass, and the outlook for the servants is into the orchard on the north.

On the upper floor are four bedrooms, bathroom, w.c., and linen-cupboard. The positions for the beds are shown on the plan.

On the attic floor is a large central attic bedroom – the servants' bedrooms, and boxroom and cistern-room.

It will thus be seen that though in some ways a specialised house, it yet provides ample accommodation for the average family requirements. It requires but little furniture, and that of the simplest kind. Whitewash is its principal decoration. It demands little outlay to furnish, less to decorate, and can be maintained with the minimum of labour.

On the whole it may be taken as a fairly typical example of the average house built as a practical realisation of the principles which I have advocated.

ENTRANCE FRONT

FINDON

GARDEN FRONT

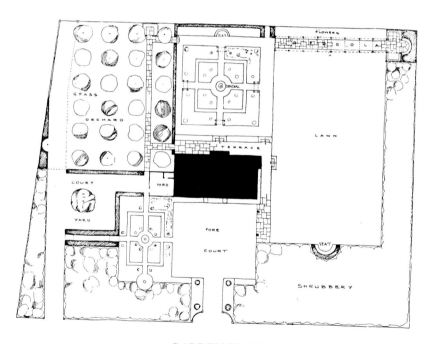

GARDEN PLAN

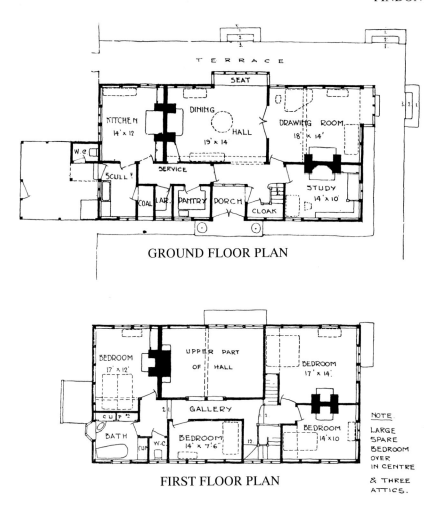

T E R R A C E

SEAT

KITCHEN
14' x 12

DINING

HALL
19' x 14

DRAWING ROOM
18' x 14'

W.C

SCULL?

SERVICE

COAL LAR. PANTRY PORCH

CLOAK

STUDY
14' x 10'

GROUND FLOOR PLAN

BEDROOM
17' x 12'

UPPER PART
OF HALL

BEDROOM
17' x 14'

GALLERY

BATH

W.C

BEDROOM
14' x 7'6"

BEDROOM
14'x10

CUP

FIRST FLOOR PLAN

NOTE.
LARGE
SPARE
BEDROOM
OVER
IN CENTRE
& THREE
ATTICS.

THE DINING HALL

THE DRAWING-
ROOM FIREPLACE

THE STAIRCASE

TRECOURT

THE title of this house was suggested by the fact that the grouping of its structure involves the formation of three courts. Of these the central or fountain court is completely enclosed by the house, and, so far, the traditional model of an ancient type of plan is followed. There seems little doubt that this formation was originally adopted mainly for purposes of defence, and some excuse may be required to justify the perpetuation of such a plan in these days when conditions demanding the fortification of dwellings no longer obtain. It may be urged then that there are many other advantages, practical and æsthetic, which make the plan of building round enclosed courts advisable in modern times. The form of plan which resulted from the necessity for defence inevitably secured the quality of seclusion, and led to the creation of a little inner world, an enchanted territory of courts and enclosed gardens which owed the greater part of their charm to such enclosure. And this idea of the house and its garden as a little fairy-land, sheltered and defended from the bleak influences of the common every-day world without, can only be adequately conveyed by the same expedients which would be adopted by those who were obliged to fortify it against the attacks of enemies.

The court system of house planning has, moreover, other advantages, leading as it does to compactness of plan in a large house, and to an increased facility for lighting the various rooms and passages. Another ancient device for the defence of the house may here be noted in passing as an example of that process of rational adoption and reluctant rejection of the features of old houses which results in a building which fulfils modern conditions. The enclosure of a house by a moat has much to recommend it from an æsthetic point of view. The reflection of its walls in the still water from which they seem to spring, conveys the idea of a little island home set like a jewel in a zone of silver. But the obvious inconsistency of creating an obstruction to the approaches of the house with no practical object, and then making bridges for transit over it, makes the enclosing moat to a modern house appear an archaic affectation, and the most one can learn from it is the beauty of the conjunction of architecture and still water, and the value of reflections in design.

Referring to the illustrations, it may be noted that the use of colour in architectural sketches, especially when it is of that accidental character which the weather gives, has often been somewhat unfairly reprobated. As, however, in the choice of materials for country building, it has been urged that they should be adapted for Nature's painting, some suggestion of this process must necessarily be conveyed in illustrations of exteriors. Some indication might also have justly been added of the growth of creepers on the walls, and these have only been omitted in order not to confuse the forms of the structure. The relative plainness of the building is an indication that its grey stone walls will be partially adorned with climbing plants, and its red roof stained by the weather with tints which can only be dimly suggested by the sketches illustrated (see pp 212 and 213 and colour illustration p.20).

Referring to the plans of the house, it will be noted that the arrangement is entirely symmetrical; but it is a symmetry which is not incompatible with practical considerations, and does not involve those anomalies of plan which the rigours of the Palladian style enforced on the designers of English country houses in this respect. From the central entrance in the long north front one enters a porch which opens on to an arcade revealing the central paved court, with its fountain and bright tubs of flowers. Immediately adjoining the porch on the right is the business-room communicating with the private study beyond, and in the wing which forms the extension of the north front to the west is the billiard-room with its open timber roof and gallery. Passing along the wide low corridor on the west side of the fountain court, it will be noted that this forms the direct approach from the entrance to the drawing-room; and adjoining it, and forming the connecting-link between drawing-room and study, is the long and low library; its unbroken wall-surfaces lined with books, and its central bay-window commanding the garden court, and beyond it one of the chief garden vistas.

The corridor, which bounds the fountain court on the south, extends east and west, and its lines are extended in the form of pergolas emphasising the unity of design in house and garden. At its centre a bay-window overlooks the fountain court with its arcade to the north, and to right and left, in summer weather, one may catch glimpses of garden vistas checkered with light and shade, and bright with flowers.

From this corridor the great hall, fifty feet in length, is entered, and here broad white wall-spaces contrast with the darker tones of panelling, and the principal features are the great open fireplace and the bay-window overlooking the terraces and gardens to the south. From this hall, drawing-room and dining-room open with wide doorways, and so the route from the former to the latter is another vista of which the terminal features are the alcoves in both rooms, more richly decorated than the rest of the walls, and with little windows where stained glass show like gems in the shade.

In the drawing-room the realities of the structure, the display of which gives a certain earnest character to the whole interior, will be modified by a more elegant treatment, and in the boudoir adjoining it the same feeling suggests the octagonal form developed from the square, and the introduction of slender white columns, above which a domed ceiling represents a miniature firmament adorned with flights of birds.

At the eastern end of the hall is the panelled dining-room, adjoining which the breakfast-room has an eastern aspect. The remaining portion of the ground plan is occupied by the kitchen premises, which provide the usual accommodation required for a house of this size. Of these the kitchen itself has an open timber roof, and the lower part of the walls lined with Dutch tiles.

The first floor provides eleven bedrooms and four bathrooms, as well as two of the servants' bedrooms, the remainder of which would be in the floor above, the further development of which would provide a number of additional attic bedrooms. The bedrooms generally have been arranged to form suites, each including a bathroom and dressing-room.

VIEW FROM SOUTH-EAST (detail)

ENTRANCE FRONT

TRECOURT

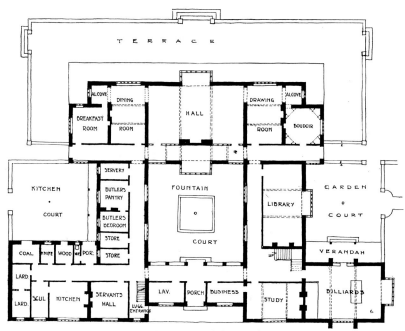

GROUND FLOOR PLAN

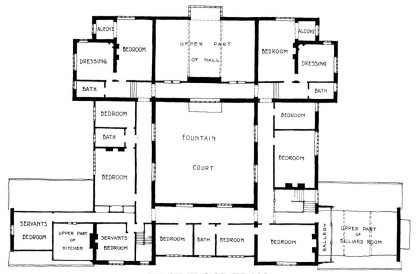

FIRST FLOOR PLAN

214

TREVISTA

THE house now to be considered is one specially designed to suit one of those rectangular plots of ground so commonly to be found in suburban and even country districts, where estates are laid out with little regard for anything but commercial and utilitarian ends. In such districts it is not permitted to advance the house beyond what is called the building-line. Such beauty as might be gained by a certain irregularity as one may find in old villages, where here a cottage abuts on the road itself, and there one stands back from the highway, is here impossible, and the houses appear as if drawn up on parade, toeing the line with dreary and inevitable regularity. The land so divided is generally sold by the foot of frontage to the road, and the plots are generally of considerable length, as it is assumed that the back land is of no great value. A house is considered, apparently, as primarily a place where one sits in a bay-window which commands a view of other bay-windows and an outlook on the road. Whether the sun looks in at your window is apparently a minor consideration as long as an expanse of plate-glass reveals to the passer-by the elegance of your furnishings. The house illustrated here follows no such canons, but deliberately turns its back on the road because the road is to the north, and its occupants prefer the sun and the beauties of a secluded garden to the traffic and dust of the street.

Although thus cut off from the drawbacks to a roadside situation, it yet keeps as close to the road as the building-line permits, in order to gain the more land for the garden on the sunny side.

In its frontage of a hundred feet three gates form the starting-point of three main vistas, which extend to the back boundary of the site. On entering the centre gate in the paling of cleft oak one finds oneself in no miserable apology for a front garden set with rows of bedded flowers or choked with amorphous shrubberies; but, instead, in a cleanly open court from which one catches glimpses right and left of pleasant vistas appropriately terminated. On opening the front door, one enters a wide and low passage, and beyond its cool shade one sees the garden-room, and, beyond that, one catches a glimpse of a garden vista which, beginning with the rose garden, ends in the semicircular recess at the end of the lawn. This definite connection of the garden paths with the passages of the house helps to make house and garden parts in a comprehensive studied effect.

215

It is impossible to consider them entirely apart from each other, for taken together they form a single conception. It is not a case of first designing a house and then laying out its immediate surroundings as a garden bearing a certain relation to it, for house and garden are here the product of a single initial idea which comprehends the whole.

In the consideration of the ground plan it will be observed that the central passage serves to separate the main living-rooms of the family from the kitchen premises and the children's room. The central feature is the large hall, house place or living-room, of which a sketch is given, in which some indication is conveyed of its great hospitable open fireplace, and its broad spaces of wall, where homely whitewash forms an economical and satisfactory substitute for superficial and mechanical artistry. Adjoining this hall is the dining-recess, a feature which has already been described. The drawing-room is also so arranged in connection with the hall as to give, when required, a combined room over forty feet in length, while the position of the fireplace in the drawing-room not only gives a certain seclusion, but allows of a window there to the south.

The functions of the garden-room have already been dwelt on, and it is here placed to command the main garden vista.

Turning to the consideration of the rooms on the left of the central axis of the plan, it will be noted that the staircase is so situated that a separate staircase for the servants will not be required. The children's room is long and low, with a sunny outlook to the garden, and a wide ingle fireplace. Here, as elsewhere, the structure is all, or nearly all, the decoration, and so the interior acquires a certain dignity and reality which cannot be realised by the cunningest schemes of paper and paint. To the north of this the kitchen premises are well isolated, and in occupying the position of honour overlooking the road represent a radical departure from the average scheme for a house. A covered way or entry here isolates, but gives dry access, to the coal-cellar and w. c., and forms a part incidentally of one of the three vistas which are the basis of the whole scheme.

On the upper floor there are four bedrooms and bathroom, while above in the roof the space admits of further development; and besides the servants' bedroom, cistern-room, and boxroom, a study or studio might be formed there, or additional bedrooms if required.

In considering the garden scheme, it may first be noted that in addition to the three main vistas there are two subsidiary ones, one of which is opposite the bay-window to the hall, and the other opposite the window to the children's room, and these help to confirm the unity of plan in house and

VIEW FROM ROAD

BIRD'S EYE VIEW OF GARDEN

THE HALL

218

FIRST FLOOR PLAN

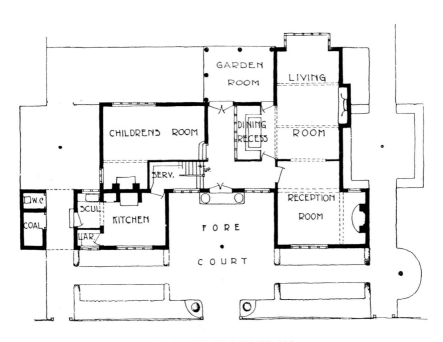

GROUND FLOOR PLAN

219

garden, which has already been alluded to. The regularity of the outline of the site and the assumed absence of natural features on an approximately level site are all attributes which suggest, and indeed demand, formality of design. There are occasions and places where it would be equally reasonable and inevitable to admit natural features as the basis of the scheme, and to depart from the rectangular in the formation of paths. But here to do so would be to indulge in unreasonable affectations of design, and so the rose garden opposite the south front of the house is symmetrically disposed, culminating in the central dipping-well, a feature so practically useful for watering flowers with water which has been exposed all day to the sun, surrounding which roses wreathed on arches, and festooned on chains seem to join hands as in some ancient country dance round the maypole.

This rose garden is flanked on each side by semicircular recesses for seats, and from the lawn it is divided by an open screen of climbing roses. The lawn itself presents an open space of shaven turf, flanked on each side by pergolas, which seem to be the side aisles of a floral church, while at the end of the lawn another semicircular recess forms the terminal feature to the central axis of the plan. Between the pergolas and the boundary hedge is a long narrow flower bed where lilies and other flowers show their beauty to the best advantage against a dark background, and gleam at intervals between the pergola posts. Beyond this pergola, where the paving is dappled with shadow, a little garden of perennial flowers completes the vista, which is terminated by an arbour. The possessor of such a little garden will find scope enough within its boundaries to create a little paradise of flowers. But it should always be borne in mind that the flowers are for the garden, not the garden for the flowers. As in the house, the collector of furniture and *bric-à-brac* comes to regard his home as a mere shelter for art treasures, so the gardener is apt to consider the merits of the individual bloom before the general effect of that little outdoor world in which it is but a unit. It is not enough to grow the right sort of flowers, but it is necessary that they should be arranged in right relation to each other, and considered in this way, the materials of which the garden is composed are as the colours which a painter uses to make a picture, and he who chooses a small canvas may rival the efforts of a whole staff of gardeners employed without the controlling influence of artistic skill in the grounds of the millionaire's mansion.

ROSE COURT

THE little house and garden now to be considered is adapted for the ordinary type of building plot, and requires a frontage of about sixty-five feet. Its equivalent in the house agent's lists would be represented by the villa with three or more reception-rooms, each reduced to dimensions which would make them cramped and uncomfortable – each demanding, too, its separate fire. The best room would be one facing the road to the north, and this would probably be to some extent preserved from vulgar daily use, and the family would probably be crowded into a little back room where a cumbrous dining table would occupy most of the floor-space. The garden would be 'tastefully laid out' with winding walks and shapeless shrubberies. In fact the whole scheme would represent the usual congestion of absurdities for which the dweller in villadom is content to pay a high rent. In the plan here submitted the central feature is necessarily the hall or living-room, and adjoining this the dining-room and drawing-room have dwindled to mere recesses sharing in the warmth of the great central fireplace, and adding to the spaciousness of the hall, of which they are a part. The small study occupies a more isolated position, and the kitchen premises towards the road are conveniently placed for service while they are completely isolated from the family rooms. On the upper floor are four good-sized bedrooms and bathroom, and over these the full development of the attic space would admit of additional bedroom accommodation, or perhaps a children's playroom, in addition to the servants' bedroom, boxroom, and cistern-room. The general character of this interior is structural and homely, and would present that earnest reality of effect which belongs to the confessed elements of its structure. It is the quality which is to be found in old farmhouses and cottages, but may be sought for in vain amongst the uncharted wildernesses of modern villadom. The plan of the garden is somewhat similar to that previously described, especially in that it presents three main vista-lines, each bearing a definite relation to the house. It presents a somewhat similar artistic scheme to a church, and if one considers its central rose garden as a square nave flanked by the aisles which the pergolas suggest, it will be at once apparent that the central flower garden beyond, with its screen of roses, must be the chancel where at matins and vespers pale lilies are the choristers. The orchards are thus side chapels, and between nave and chancel will be seen a miniature transept completing the vista to right and left. The reader will be able to complete still further this picture of a church of flowers which was designed merely to meet the condition of the site, and with no conscious ecclesiastical idea. The small sketches indicate the general character of the house, and the view from the garden-room looking down one of the pergolas is also shown in colour (p.21).

It will be noted, in this and other of the roadside houses illustrated, a site is indicated with a frontage to the north. This is generally not difficult to obtain on most building estates, because the average builder, obsessed with the fixed idea of the bay-window overlooking the road, and who prefers to display all the glories of the house and garden to the man in the street, naturally selects a road frontage facing south. In adopting the opposite arrangement not only is privacy obtained and that air of seclusion which is essential to the ideal garden, but the house itself constitutes a substantial screen to northern winds as well as to the dust and noise of the street. In placing the kitchen premises towards the road, the route to the back door is reduced to a minimum, and the whole of the kitchen premises are isolated from the garden. In the case of a house facing a frontage to the south, it would be desirable to place it well back from the road so as to allow of a garden in front of it. The front door should then be placed at one end so that the approach to it can be formed at one side of the plot, and may be screened with a hedge from the garden. In the case of a house having a frontage to the east, it will often be desirable to adopt the same scheme as I have suggested for a northern frontage, making in this case a western garden frontage, and by the use of bays securing still a share of southern aspect. Each site will demand its own special treatment, and in those with an eastern or western frontage, where the frontage admits, it will often be desirable to place the house with its end towards the road, an arrangement which may often be met with in old villages.

That the majority of people really demand as a *sine qua non* that they shall have a bay-window facing the road it is difficult to believe, and its continual recurrence, I feel assured, is owing merely to a fixed idea on the part of the builder whose commercial training leads him to forget the essential difference between the house and the shop.

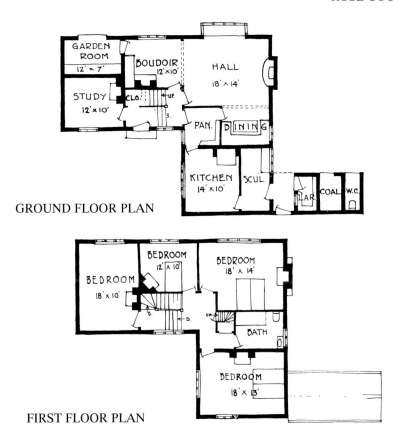

GROUND FLOOR PLAN

FIRST FLOOR PLAN

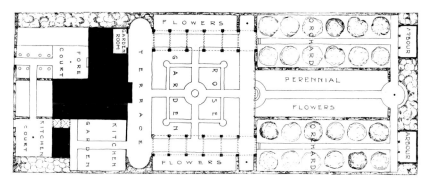

GARDEN PLAN

THE HALL

VIEW FROM NORTH

VIEW FROM SOUTH-WEST

WHITE NIGHTS

I N this plan a small house is shown which in many respects resembles the last. It is adapted for a fifty-foot frontage to the north. Here, however, the building-line has been ignored, and the house brought right up to the road. This allows of a little high-walled square court, with the front entrance through an arched gateway, and with the back entrance through an entry, as in the previous plans.

As one approaches the front entrance of this little dwelling, and, looking through the bars of the entrance gate, as one begins to realise the character which the house obtains from this treatment, the Dutch primness and cleanliness of the paving and cobblestones, with a few tubs of flowers and some central ornament – a little lead figure, perhaps, on a well-designed pedestal – one may, perhaps, be excused for preferring it to the inevitable 'drive' and shrubs of suburbia. Such a little grey court, with its indefinable hint of romance, is worth a dozen front gardens and sweeping drives, which are the pretentious preludes to such mean habitations. In the plan of the house it will be noticed that the hall, with its appendages of bower and dining-recess, occupy the whole of the garden frontage to the south, while the kitchen premises, as in the previous example, are placed towards the road. On the upper floor the plan shows the arrangements of the bedrooms, while the attic accommodation is a variable quantity, and may include additional rooms for the family as well as the usual servants' bedroom, boxroom and cistern-room. The plan of the garden is not shown in this example, but the central position of the bay-window, as well as the position of the window in the boudoir, will be sufficient to indicate that its main lines have already been determined.

The coloured sketch (p.22) gives a suggestion of the general character of the interior. In the dining-recess here it is proposed to stencil the walls with a pattern of trailing vine, with grey-green leaves and purple grapes; and this vine motif will perhaps suggest an appropriate selection from the 'Rubaiyat' on the beam above.

> Ah fill the cup: what boots it to repeat
> How time is slipping underneath our feet;
> Unborn tomorrow and dead yesterday,
> Why fret about them if today be sweet.

226

Such a sentiment may not commend itself to all, but except in its opening phrase it seems but another way of repeating the canonical command to take no thought for the morrow.

It will be noticed that this little space of vine adornment is the only superficial decoration made in this apartment, which almost constitutes the house. All the rest is grey-brown timber, red bricks, and whitewash. It may also be noted that there is only one picture in the room and but few ornaments; and if one examines the materials which go to make up this interior, it will be found that there is little but has its definite structural function. It is no histrionic reproduction of a farm-house kitchen, such as the modern furnishing firm will construct for you, where beams and joists are arranged for effect, and where the whole is as much like real building as a piece of street scenery on the stage.

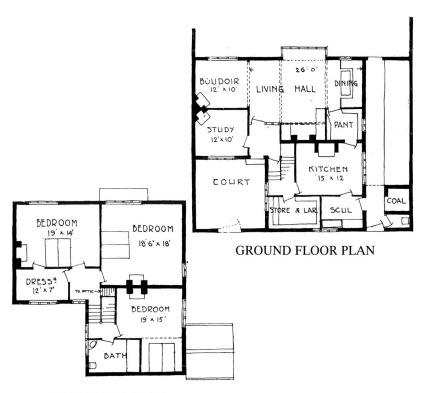

GROUND FLOOR PLAN

FIRST FLOOR PLAN

VIEW FROM ROAD

THE CLOISTERS

THIS house was designed for a site divided from the road on the north by a high wall, the line of which was not parallel with the main axis of the site. The ground plan shows how this difficulty has been met by the formation of a forecourt of irregular pentagonal shape. Paths paved with old flagstones radiate from the centre of the court, and the triangular spaces between them are set with cobble stones in patterns of grey and white. The little grey court, enclosed with its high wall, is brightened by its marginal areas of mown grass, and in its centre a little lead figure completes the focus of the scheme.

The house is grey, too, like the court, relieved by the varied tints of purple and gold in its roof of old tiles, by the toned whiteness of the panels in the half-timber work, and by the twinkling lights of its windows of crown glass.

The plan of the house itself is based on the traditional model of many an old manor-house. One enters from the porch a paved passage, which crosses the house and forms the starting-point for the main garden vista. To the right of this are the three principal sitting-rooms the hall, two storeys high, in this case used as a dining-hall; the drawing-room and study – each with its comfortable fireside and separate approach.

To the left of the central passage are staircase and lavatory, and beyond these a children's room, which opens on to a cloister walk open to the south, a place for meals in summer weather and for the children's play.

The remainder of the ground plan is occupied by the kitchen premises.

On the upper floor the hall, with its galleries, divides the bedrooms into two groups. That at the west end comprises two bedrooms and dressing-room as spare rooms, and that at the east the family rooms – the principal bedroom having a dressing-room, with bath adjoining the principal bathroom. The roof-space contains the servants' bedrooms and boxroom, and the development of the space over the hall would admit of a possible billiard-room there. The position of the children's room on the ground floor, in relation to the kitchen premises, suggests that a modification of the plan might consist in making this room the dining-room, the children's playroom being placed in the attics.

A portion of the garden scheme is shown on the ground plan. The path which forms its central vista-line divides the lawn from the rose garden, and, the latter being sunk, this path becomes a terrace. A few old trees seem to adapt themselves naturally to their positions on the edge of the lawn, and the rose garden is focused in the central dipping-well. Beyond, to the south, are kitchen garden and orchard; and the house is so placed that the bay-window of the hall looks down the centre of an existing avenue of old fruit-trees beyond the lawn.

Another feature of the garden scheme which may be noted is the little square court to the west of the house, from which an arcade opens communicating with the study.

The cost of this house would be about £2200.

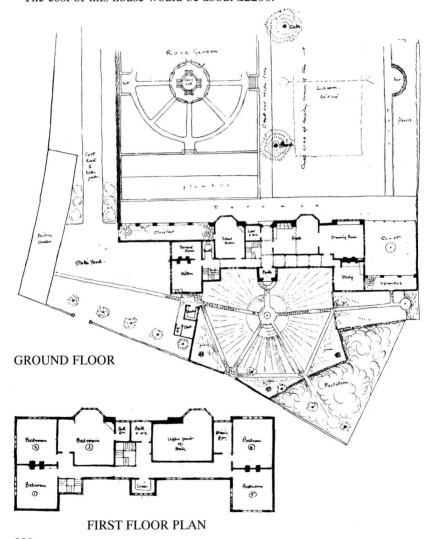

GROUND FLOOR

FIRST FLOOR PLAN

GARDEN FRONT

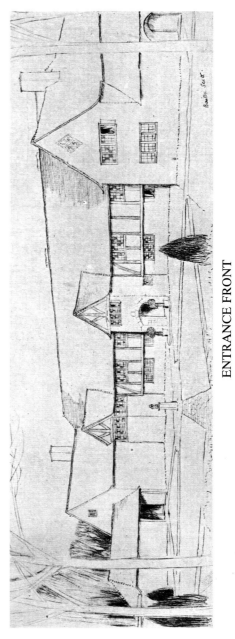

ENTRANCE FRONT

BLACKWELL

THIS house in the Lake District is chiefly noticeable for its large central hall, in a recessed portion of which a billiard table is placed. The principal feature in this hall is the great ingle fireplace with its open hearth and seats, and over this a little stair, with stone-vaulted roof leads to a small chamber overlooking the hall. From the front entrance a broad and low corridor gives access to drawing-room, dining-room, and kitchen premises, without infringing on the hall itself, so that it never becomes a passage-room. The first floor and attic floor give ample bedroom accommodation. In the adornment of this house it was specially desired that the mountain ash should form the subject for decoration, and this appears in the form of carving, leaded glass, plaster-work, and stencilling in the various rooms.

Two of the most important features in the metal-work are the drawing-room grate and hall electric light pendant. In each of these the ironwork is brightened by white enamelled flowers and scarlet berries.

In the carved trees, which appear in the staircase screen and on the hall ingle, birds' nests are interwoven in the branches and birds flutter amongst the leaves and fruit. In the brackets to the lower beams and in the bosses to the ceiling various local plants are represented. One is entwined with bryony, another shows the blooms of the wild guelder-rose, while the bloom and berries of the hawthorn and the wild rose are amongst the features of the carving. The same variety of carving occurs in the white drawing-room, where, in the capitals to slender columns, the foliage and branches of various trees are represented.

THE ENTRANCE HALL

VIEW FROM SOUTH-WEST

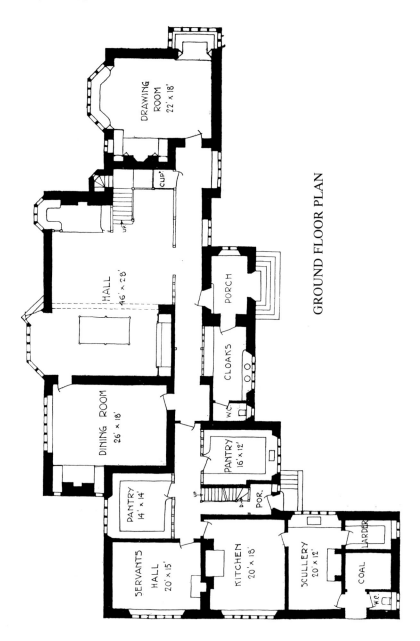

GROUND FLOOR PLAN

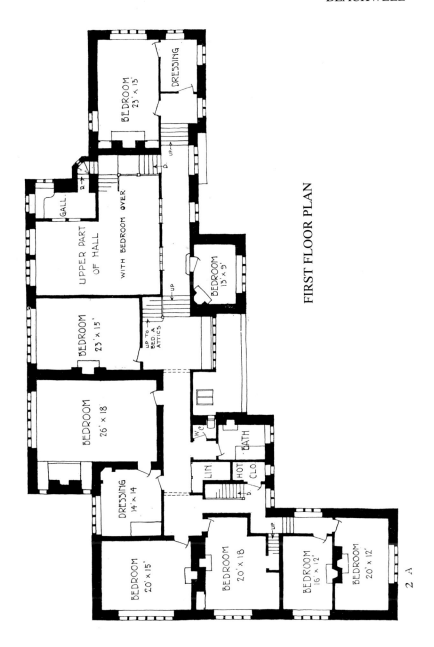

FIRST FLOOR PLAN

2 A

THE HALL

THE DRAWING-ROOM

THE DRAWING-ROOM INGLE

THE DINING-ROOM

THE UPPER CORRIDOR

A HOUSE FOR AN ART LOVER

THIS 'Haus eines Kunst-freundes' was awarded the first prize by a jury of German architects in a competition organised in Germany. The accommodation shown in the plan was specified in the conditions of the competition, and the complete set of drawings in colour have been published as a portfolio by Herr Alex. Koch, of Darmstadt, who has kindly allowed me to reproduce here, on a small scale, a selection of the illustrations. The form of the plan was suggested by the fact that both on ground floor and first floor the required rooms seemed to divide themselves naturally into a group of four, connected by the central hall. This hall was therefore made six-sided, with the projecting wings attached to four of the six sides. On the ground floor these consist of kitchen premises and dining- and breakfast-rooms on the one side, ladies' and reception room, with study and business-room on the other, while on the upper floor the four departments or suites consist of guests' rooms, parents' rooms, children's rooms, and rooms for daughters and governess.

The advantage of the projecting wings, as enclosing and sheltering the terrace to the south, follows naturally from this arrangement as well as the variety and interest given to the vista effects of the interior, which, like those arranged on the stage, vanish at an angle from the picture plane.

Some suggestion of the character of the interior may be gained from the illustrations. Here, as in other schemes, unity of effect is aimed at by making the principal apartments combine into one coherent whole.

The whole of the route plan of the house is carefully studied, so that the occupants of the various suites have their special private approaches to the rooms. The principal bathroom is a special feature, octagonal in form, and lined with marble and mosaic. The children's breakfast-room may also be noted as an octagonal room with a domed ceiling. The lines of the house on the exterior suggest the scheme for the garden.

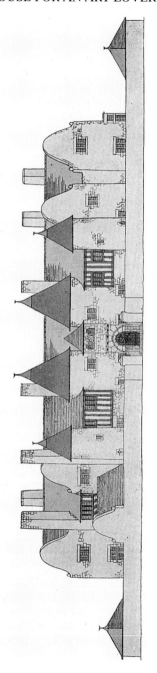

NORTH ELEVATION

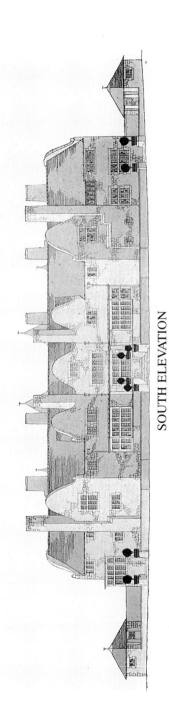

SOUTH ELEVATION

A HOUSE FOR AN ART LOVER

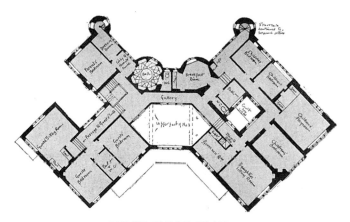

FIRST FLOOR PLAN

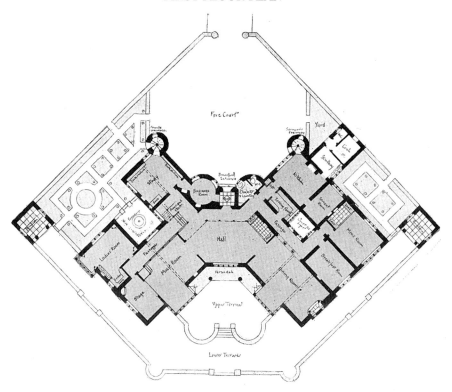

GROUND FLOOR PLAN

THE HALL

THE DINING-ROOM

THE MUSIC-ROOM

LADIES' ROOM

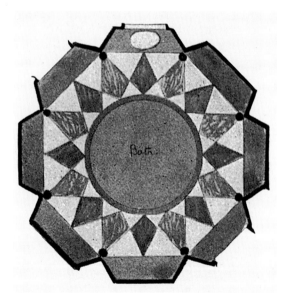

PLAN OF BATHROOM

PARENTS' BEDROOM

SECTION OF BATHROOM

THE PLAY-ROOM

THE STUDY

THE HAVEN

THIS is a house, designed for a site in Surrey, having a hundred feet frontage to a road on its north boundary. The type of building is ground floor and attics, low enough to give breadth of effect, but not so low as to look like a bungalow instead of a country house.

The plan encloses a central court, from which covered entries lead to kitchen and stable-yards. From the main entrance one looks into the central court. The shade of the entry frames the picture, as it were, and in this arrangement of light beyond the shadow, there is the symbol of Hope and the suggestion of a little inland haven enclosed and sheltered. Crossing this main court and entering the front door one approaches the hall by a wide and low corridor. Part of this corridor is included as a recess in the hall, which may be curtained off, if required, when the hall becomes the dining-room. The drawing-room opens into the hall with a wide doorway, and over it a little special stair leads to the billiard-room, which has an open gallery overlooking the hall.

The south-eastern end of the house contains six bedrooms and two bath-rooms, with a studio, while there are also two servants' bedrooms in the western wing. At each end of the south front are open verandahs or garden-rooms.

Under the bathrooms is a heating chamber, which is utilised for heating the house generally and also the hot water for the baths.

The contract price for this house, with the stable and other outbuildings, in a somewhat expensive district in Surrey, including all the structural wood-work in English oak, and the floors in oak and maple throughout, was £2300.

THE HAVEN

GARDEN FRONT

ENTRANCE FRONT

THE HAVEN

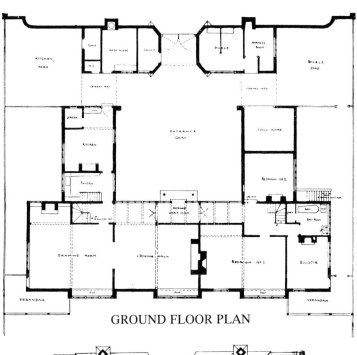

GROUND FLOOR PLAN

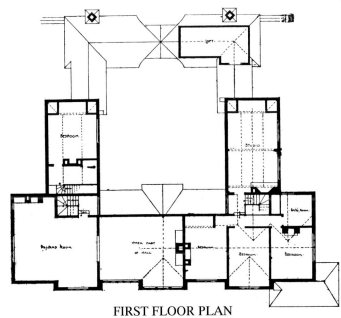

FIRST FLOOR PLAN

THE HAVEN

BILLIARD ROOM

THE INNER COURT

250

THE DINING HALL

BEXTON CROFT

THE plans and photographs of "Bexton Croft" represent the realisation of a scheme for a house described in the *Studio* for January 1895, and somewhat rashly entitled there an ideal suburban house. A study of the ground plan shows that it consists mainly of three sitting-rooms, of which the centre one, the hall, is two storeys in height. These three rooms may be combined by sliding back the wide doors which divide them, forming a spacious interior effect focused in the central hall. The passage on the north side of these three rooms allows of access to all of them and to the front door without infringing on the privacy of the house. The kitchen premises are isolated but conveniently placed for service. Under them is a larder and cellar.

On the upper floor there are five good bedrooms, with bath and w.c., and over them again a central attic, which is used as a study or 'den', as well as a boxroom and servants' room.

A special feature of the plan is the little secret staircase which opens in the panelling at the side of the drawing-room bay and gives access to the south gallery in the hall and beyond this to the principal bedroom.

The photographs give some idea of the homely character of the wood-work in this house, though they do not show the brilliant colouring of the heraldic decoration which, in the hall ceiling and elsewhere, relieves the dark oak. In the fittings of this house considerable use was made of old panelling and balusters.

252

VIEW FROM DRIVE

THE DINING-ROOM

BEXTON CROFT

THE PORCH AND CORRIDOR

THE HALL

254

THE SOUTH GALLERY

BEXTON CROFT

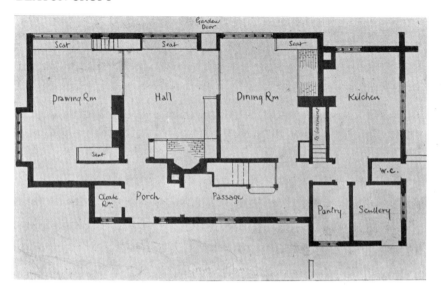

GROUND FLOOR PLAN

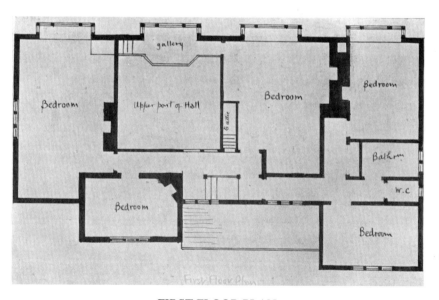

FIRST FLOOR PLAN

THE FIVE GABLES

THE house now to be described represents a realisation of a plan illustrated in the *Studio* for December 1897. In this realisation some slight modifications were introduced which may be noted in comparing the *Studio* plan with those now illustrated.

Unlike other plans which have been illustrated in the *Studio* this one was originally designed to meet the special requirements of clients and site. It will be noted that the wide doorways between the rooms on the ground floor are used as an expedient to make these appear to combine to form one large apartment, and to avoid that impression of confinement in separate and isolated boxes which constitutes one of the essential defects in the plan of the modern small villa. Further study of the problem of the small house suggests a more complete combination of dining-room and hall, with a possible separate route to the front door from the kitchen through the space occupied by the bicycle-room on the plan; but the plan, as it stands, represents a fairly effectual compromise between the ordinary plan arranged on the separate box system and the logical conclusion arrived at by the study of the actual uses to which the rooms would be put, which might condemn the hall, in so far as it is not used as an extension of the dining-room floor-space, as an inadmissible luxury in a small house. Another feature which might also be considered a luxury is the separate staircase for the servants, and this is mainly justified by special conditions of plan, which make it possible to introduce it with the minimum sacrifice of space.

One of the greatest difficulties in the planning of the small house is the proper isolation of the kitchen premises from the family apartments. A reference to the plan will show how this difficulty has been met, partly by the interposition of a brick wall, and partly by the use of the serving-room or pantry as a disconnecting space between the rectangular block containing the kitchen premises and the rest of the house, while the odours of cooking are disposed of by a ventilating shaft carried up at the side of the kitchen flue.

THE FIVE GABLES

VIEW FROM SOUTH

THE HALL

THE DRAWING ROOM

THE DINING ROOM

THE FIVE GABLES

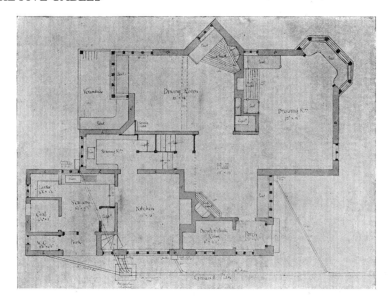

GROUND FLOOR PLAN

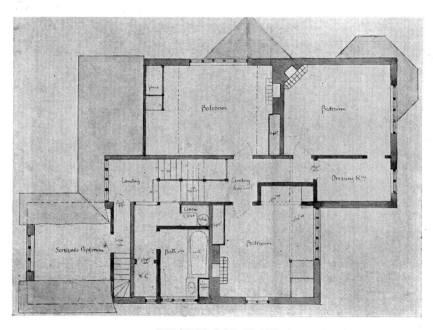

FIRST FLOOR PLAN

HEATHER COTTAGE

IN the plan of this little house and garden on a hillside, the levels of the ground formed the most important factor. It is long and low, but while at one end it consists of merely a ground-floor room with attic over, at the other the sloping ground has changed it into a house of practically two storeys. To the north the hill rises considerably and helps to shelter the house. It serves, indeed, as a practical illustration of the principle of placing a house, not on the highest point in the site, which is so often done, but at an intermediate level, which gives both shelter and view. In the garden the pergola is a notable feature, serving to screen the drive from the lawn, of which it forms the northern boundary. One of the objections sometimes raised to the pergola is that the flowers of the creepers which clothe it are all outside, and not seen from the inside, where the effect, save for such flowers as may bloom in the borders, is mainly one of light and shade. This suggests the placing of the pergola so that its exterior may also form a garden feature, and in this case its sunny side comes into view both from the drawing-room window and the lawn.

In the house, the dining-hall, with its open timber roof and wide ingle, is the central and dominant apartment. The dining-table is placed at one end across the room. The drawing-room is small and low, and over it the study forms a little attic-room with its private stair and gallery overlooking the hall. The arrangement of the bedrooms allows of the treatment of the dressing-room as a second bathroom, with comparatively little extra cost in plumbing, while a third little staircase gives access to servants' room over the kitchen. At the time of writing this house is in process of construction, and coloured drawings must replace photographs in its illustration (pp. 23, 24 and 25). These at least admit of some suggestion of the colour, in which the heather, from which the house takes its name, is a notable feature.

HEATHER COTTAGE

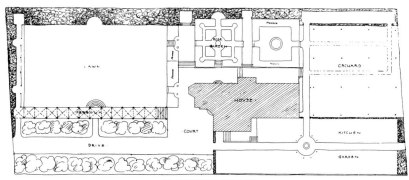

GARDEN PLAN

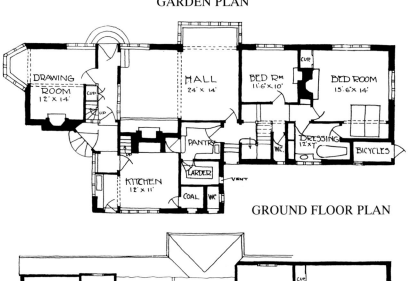

GROUND FLOOR PLAN

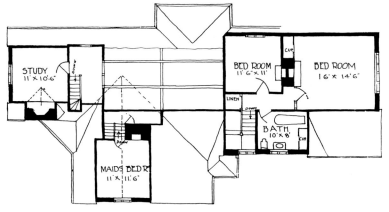

FIRST FLOOR PLAN

EVERDENE

IN many of the country houses illustrated it will be noted that the favourite formula is that in which the garden front faces the south and the entrance front the north. One enters at the back. And this arrangement is usually most to be desired. In the present case, however, the road being on the south side of the plot, it is desirable that the entrance should be either on the west or east front, while the accommodation required seems to suggest the possibility of a house built round and enclosing an inner court (see colour illustration p.26). The house is low – one storey with attics – an arrangement which admits of a hall with an open timber roof, and which, in bringing the attics down to the first floor level, makes them more valuable than when they can only be reached by a long climb. In country districts, where land is not too expensive, this broad and low manner of building has much to recommend it, for not only does it make use of all the roof-space, and that in ways which add greatly to the picturesque character of the interior, but by bringing the rooms so formed within easy reach it makes them of greater value.

In the disposition of the ground floor, the important feature is the three rooms to the south, culminating in the central hall, while the bedrooms and kitchen premises enclose the court on the remaining three sides. The bathroom on the ground floor, with a bath, perhaps, of circular form sunk in its floor, is capable of special treatment, which would make it somewhat more interesting than the bathroom of the usual utilitarian type. The study, with its little special private stair, forms an attic-room, with shuttered openings overlooking the hall.

In this type of plan, indeed, the claims of romance seem to meet most happily economical limitations. Its cost, at the average country price of eightpence per cubic foot, amounts to about £2000. In some districts it would be less than this, and in others, near London, it would amount to perhaps £2500, at tenpence per cubic foot. But the use of the roof-space gives for this sum a considerable accommodation.

The treatment of the garden illustrates the application of the principle of carefully studied vista effects applied to an actual site of somewhat irregular form on a practically level piece of ground (see colour illustrations pp. 27 and 28).

THE HALL

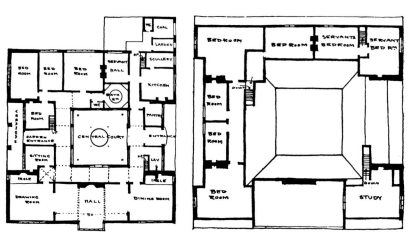

GROUND FLOOR PLAN   FIRST FLOOR PLAN

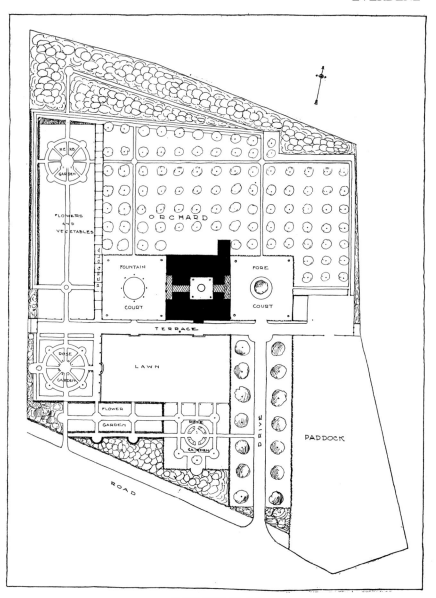

GARDEN PLAN

LINGFIELD

THE plan of this house somewhat resembles "Falkewood", its central feature being the dining-hall, with which drawing-room and study combine to make a spacious interior, which thus has a certain unity of effect.

The remainder of the ground floor is taken up by kitchen premises of the usual type.

On the first floor are three bedrooms and dressing-room, as well as bathroom and w.c., while the roof-space contains, besides the servants' rooms and boxroom, another large bedroom.

The inclusive cost of this house was £1500.

The garden scheme, of which a plan is given, represents a carefully studied arrangement of vista effects, and includes a considerable area of natural heather garden, with silver birches and pines. From the front gate there are two main vista lines, one looking down the pergola, and the other along the grass path which leads to the sunk rose garden, and ends in the drawing- room bay, while, in proceeding up the drive, several other cross vistas occur. The circular carriage court is set with formal yews.

From the point of view of the house itself, the two principal bay-windows form the outlook of studied effects From the seat of the bay-window in the dining-hall three vistas spread fan-like through the heather – three narrow brick paths go to meet the curved path which forms the edge of the fan.

From the drawing-room the outlook is immediately on to the little square sunk rose garden, and beyond this along a grass path through a plantation of silver birches and pines carpeted with woodland flowers.

LINGFIELD

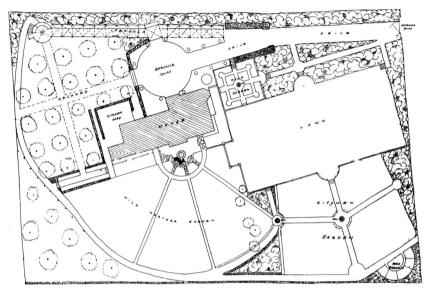

GARDEN PLAN

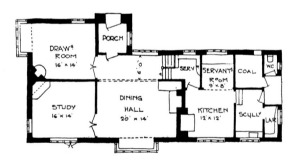

**GROUND FLOOR
PLAN**

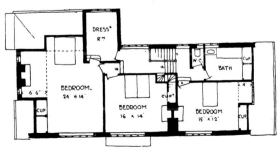

FIRST FLOOR PLAN

267

THE WHITE HOUSE

THE White House, in the general arrangement of its plan, may be compared with "Bexton Croft." It presents the same arrangement of the three sitting-rooms connected with a passage at the back, and combining to form a spacious interior effect.

The importance of the outlook towards the south-west, however, led to the corner bay-window there, and the placing of the kitchens in a return wing instead of as an extension of the south front.

The general character of the house also became changed in response to local influences. Occupying an exposed position on the Clyde, not far from the birthplace of that modern revival known as the Glasgow School, and designed for a client who already possessed some of Mr. E. A. Walton's beautiful furniture, without any conscious effort the conception of the house seemed to be modelled by these factors to a greater severity in its external lines and to a general character throughout which suggests little of the old-world houses.

THE NORTH FRONT

THE SOUTH FRONT

THE ENTRANCE GATE

THE HALL

270

THE DRAWING-ROOM

THE DINING-ROOM

THE WHITE HOUSE

GROUND FLOOR PLAN

FIRST FLOOR PLAN

THE CROSSWAYS

THIS house is somewhat inadequately represented by the plans and the sketch of the hall. Some idea of the effect of its exterior can be gained by referring to the house described as "Findon." It has the same simplicity of roof plan and outline, and is thus essentially economical.

The hall or house place, with its large ingle fireplace, occupies the greater part of the ground floor, the dining-room and drawing-room having dwindled to recesses. The garden-room or verandah occupies a corner of the south front, and the study is an isolated compartment of the plan. The design, as it stands, was made to meet the demands of a special client. It would be improved by omitting the partition between scullery and kitchen and the lavatory by the front door. The back stair is hardly necessary, and a door might be added giving access to the garden-room from the bower. The upper floor contains five bedrooms and bathroom, and the roof would give space for two more bedrooms as well as the servants' room and boxroom. The cost would be about £900.

THE CROSSWAYS

THE HALL

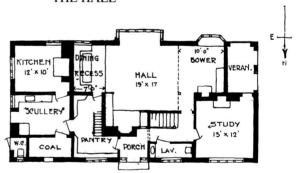

GROUND FLOOR PLAN

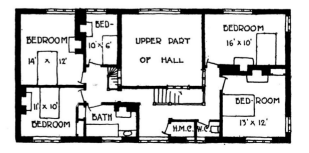

FIRST FLOOR PLAN

HALCYON COTTAGE

THIS little house has recently been built in a site within sixteen miles of London. The central feature of the plan is the roomy living-room or house place, which, as in various other plans illustrated, appears as the hall, and, indeed, almost the house itself. The whole of the traffic of the house is confined to the little recess in this room opposite the front door, which can be screened by a curtain from the room itself. The remaining accommodation of the ground floor consists of a small study and the usual kitchen premises, while on the upper floor there are four bedrooms, bathroom and linen-closet in which the hot-water cylinder is placed In the attic there are servant's bedroom and boxroom. The plan shows the proposed treatment of the garden, and the sketch of the living-room the general homely treatment of the interior.

The inclusive cost of this house was £525.

HALCYON COTTAGE

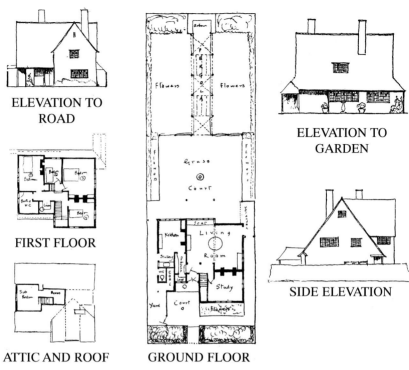

ELEVATION TO
ROAD

FIRST FLOOR

ATTIC AND ROOF

GROUND FLOOR

ELEVATION TO
GARDEN

SIDE ELEVATION

THE LIVING-ROOM

FALKEWOOD

THIS house was designed as a summer dwelling, and by special request the principal rooms were placed to face north. The basis of the plan is the 'dining-hall' scheme, in which the dining-room when not in use appears as the hall. The remaining sitting-rooms are the drawing-room and children's room, and both these can be reached without passing through the dining hall. Both of these rooms open on to a square garden-room. The kitchen premises are unusually large for the size of the house, and include servants' hall and butler's pantry, with back staircase.

On the first floor there are four good-sized bedrooms and sewing-room, bathroom, &c., and in the attics are two servants' bedrooms and a boxroom. The two colour illustrations (pp. 29 and 30) show the proposed treatment of the interior of dining-hall and drawing-room, and plans are also shown of the stable and garden, while the lodge is illustrated in the chapter on cottages (p.153).

FALKEWOOD

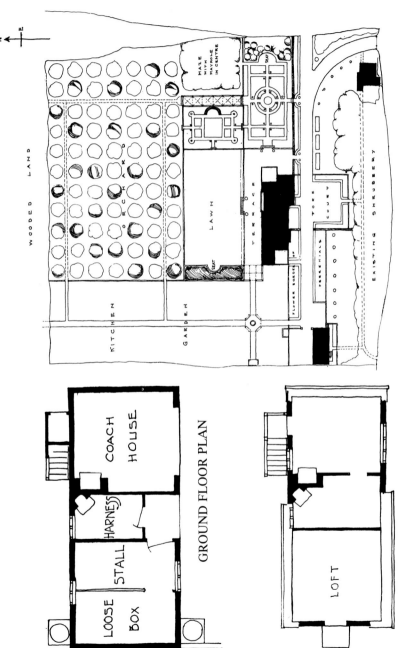

GARDEN PLAN

GROUND FLOOR PLAN

FIRST FLOOR PLAN

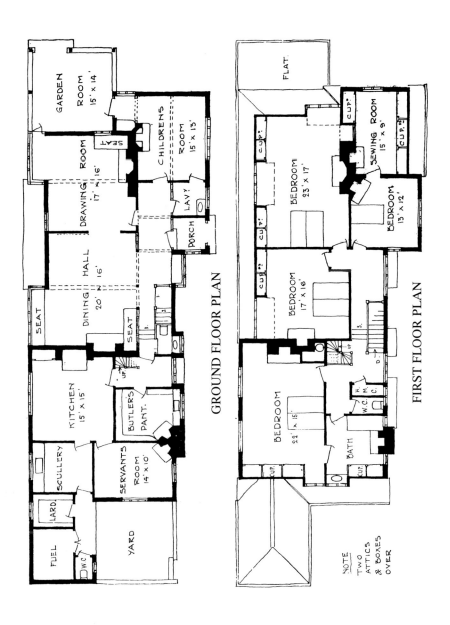

GROUND FLOOR PLAN

FIRST FLOOR PLAN

GARDEN ROOM 15' x 14'

DRAWING ROOM 17' x 16'

SEAT

CHILDREN'S ROOM 15' x 13'

LAV!

PORCH

DINING HALL 20' x 16'

SEAT

SEAT

KITCHEN 15' x 15'

BUTLER'S PANT.

SCULLERY

SERVANTS ROOM 14' x 10'

LARD.

FUEL

W.C.

YARD

UP.

FLAT

CUP.

CUP.

SEWING ROOM 15' x 9'

CUP.

BEDROOM 23' x 17'

CUP.

BEDROOM 13' x 12'

CUP.

BEDROOM 17' x 16'

UP.

D.

H.M. W.C. C.

BEDROOM 22' x 15'

BATH

CUP.

CUP.

NOTE TWO ATTICS & BOXES OVER

AN OLD HOUSE REMODELLED

THIS little house, now occupied by the present writer, is illustrated chiefly as an example of simple types of cottage furniture.

It is essentially a house of small rooms, and the principal structural modifications consisted in forming a hall by the removal of a partition. The fireplace in the room so formed was then removed and the brick arch which formed its structural basis left exposed. A coarse sacking was then fixed on the walls as a background for the old furniture.

In the small dining-room the upper part of the walls and the ceiling were whitewashed, with a dark blue dado beneath.

The exterior, thanks to its long low roof of weathered tiles and its setting of trees, required nothing but a little white paint on the woodwork.

THE HALL

THE DINING-ROOM

AN OLD HOUSE REMODELLED

VIEW FROM GATE

VIEW FROM LAWN

DANESTREAM

THIS house was designed for a site which slopes towards the north, and the floors of the rooms follow the natural slope of the ground. At the front door one enters a wide low passage which runs across the house to the garden-room, and beyond this is extended in the line of one of the garden vistas. On the south side of this passage are the two principal sitting rooms – the drawing-room and study; while, on its north side and at a lower level following the slope of the ground are dining-room and kitchen premises. On the first floor are four bedrooms and bathroom, and in the attics, servants' bedroom and boxroom. The cost of this house was £1250. The plan of the garden includes an old gravel-pit developed as a rock garden.

DANESTREAM

VIEW FROM NORTH-EAST

VIEW FROM SOUTH-WEST

THE DRAWING-ROOM

THE
CORRIDOR

DANESTREAM

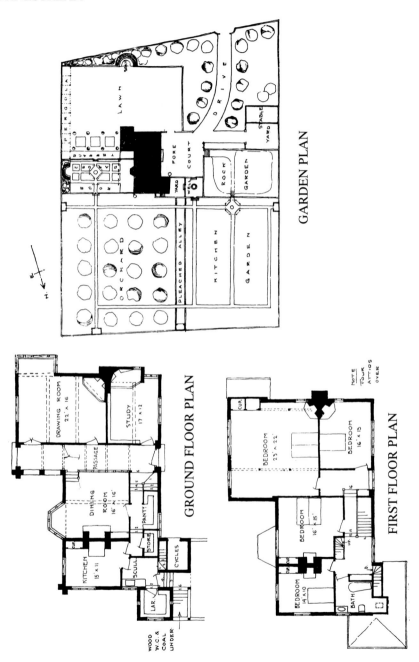

GARDEN PLAN

GROUND FLOOR PLAN

FIRST FLOOR PLAN

A STONE HOUSE

THIS house was designed for a somewhat exposed position in a stone district.

Three sitting-rooms occupy the greater part of the south front, culminating in the central hall, which extends through two storeys with a gallery.

The morning-room, or study, occupies one of the wings, and the remainder of the plan is taken up with kitchen premises.

On the upper floor are five bedrooms and bathroom, with servants' rooms and boxroom, &c., in the attics. The general character of the exterior, with its central porches on both fronts flanked by gables, represents the traditional model of many small manor-houses.

A STONE HOUSE

THE GARDEN FRONT

THE ENTRANCE FRONT

SANDFORD COTTAGE

THIS little house was built in Scotland in a district where thatching with reeds was still understood, and so this method of roofing was adopted. The plan consists of dining-hall and parlour, the traffic being concentrated in a recess in the former and the rooms made capable of combination by a wide doorway. The rest of the ground plan is occupied by the kitchen premises, which include a separate washhouse.

On the upper floor are three bedrooms and dressing-room, with bathroom and w.c., and servant's room with boxroom in the attics. The inclusive cost was £850.

SANDFORD COTTAGE

VIEW FROM NORTH

THE HALL FIRESIDE

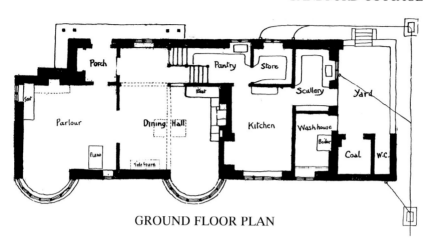

GROUND FLOOR PLAN

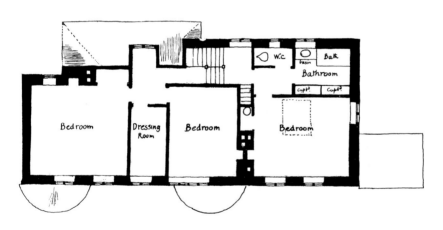

FIRST FLOOR PLAN

A ROADSIDE HOUSE

THE plans of this house represent a fairly simple and economical arrangement. The central feature, as in other cases, is the dining-hall, which here extends through two storeys (see colour illustration p.11), and from this room the drawing-room opens with a wide doorway. In the two wings are study and children's room, besides which, on the ground floor, there are the usual kitchen premises. On the upper floor are four bedrooms, bathroom and linen-closet, and in the roof over these are two good attic bedrooms, besides the servants' rooms and boxroom. The cost of this house would be about £1300.

VIEW FROM ROAD

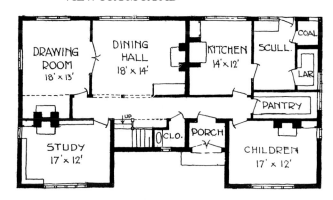

GROUND
FLOOR PLAN

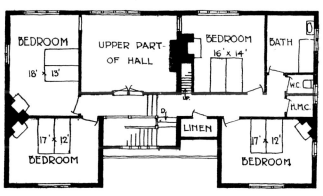

FIRST FLOOR
PLAN

ST. MARY'S

THIS is a somewhat special type of plan in which there are less than the normal number of bedrooms and a drawing-room on the upper floor. The staircase, as the approach to the drawing-room, is therefore somewhat wider than usual and is supplemented by a back stair for the servants. The hall and dining-room are divided by a partition with a wide doorway, and in the study a little Eastern oratory is a special feature.

THE ENTRANCE FRONT

GROUND FLOOR PLAN

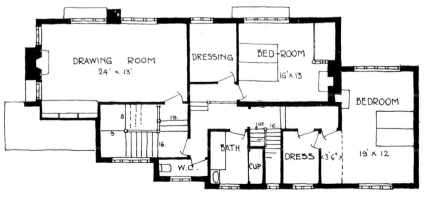

FIRST FLOOR PLAN

THE GARTH

IN this house the main block of the ground plan consists of four good-sized rooms which, by the use of double doors, combine to form a spacious interior effect, while the kitchen premises, which include a somewhat large pantry and small servants' sitting-room, occupy a projecting wing.

On the upper floor are five bedrooms, two dressing-rooms and bathroom; the attic space contains the servants' bedrooms and boxroom.

The photographs give a fair idea of the interior and exterior of this house.

THE GARTH

VIEW FROM ENTRANCE COURT

297

THE GARTH

THE GARDEN FRONT

THE HALL

THE DINING-ROOM

THE LIBRARY

THE GARTH

GROUND FLOOR PLAN

FIRST FLOOR PLAN

FURNISHED ROOMS AT DARMSTADT
AND MANNHEIM

IN looking back on the record of past work, and in recalling the flavour, not always entirely delicious, of ten or fifteen years ago, one is chiefly struck by the strange irony of fate which has made one's employment consist of building houses for other people to furnish, or furnishing houses which other people have built. In no single case in the houses illustrated by photographs am I responsible for the furniture, and the sympathetic reader will perhaps realise this in glancing at some of these illustrations.

In the two examples now given of Continental work, it has been my task to decorate and furnish only.

In work of this kind, which depends so essentially for its effect on colour schemes, photographs are somewhat inadequate.

In the sitting-room at Darmstadt the panelling is ivory-white, and above this the wall is orange. The central electric-light fittings, designed by Mr. Ashbee, are grey pewter, and the furniture is chiefly in tones of green and blue. And this arrangement of white, orange, grey, green and blue is supplemented by touches of brilliant pink in the flowers.

In the dining-room a more sober scheme prevails, the wall above the panelling being covered with embossed leather.

In the music-room at Mannheim the panelling is again white, and on the white ground of frieze and ceiling are set trees and wreaths of mountain ash and rose modelled in plaster, and painted their proper colours with flights of silver birds.

The fireplace presents a space of white marble with a central rosette of pink-toned 'midnight sun' marble surrounded by rays of black. The grate is *repoussée* brass, and the slender shafts of the columns are crowned by capitals, where white lilies bloom between pale green leaves. The electric-light fittings are of armour-bright iron, with touches of green enamel.

The principal piece of furniture is the large music cabinet, specially designed for the use of a composer. It is of oak, inlaid with ebony, pewter and pearl.

The special piano for this room has not yet been executed. The little inlaid semicircular chairs which appear in this room have recently been much exploited by furnishing firms.

The double windows used in German houses gave an opportunity for the use of stained glass, designed to not unduly obstruct the light. The flowers are in shades of pink with grey-green leaves. The boudoir, which opens into this music room, follows much the same scheme of colour.

The corner fireplace is lined with turquoise-blue tiles, and the furniture of oak is inlaid with ebony, ivory and pearl.

Other rooms in Germany, not illustrated here, which have been decorated and furnished, consist of exhibition rooms, designed for firms in Berlin and Dresden. It appears to be a growing custom with the principal furniture firms in Germany to invite representative architects to contribute to such periodical exhibitions, and in these it has been Mr. Mackintosh and myself who have represented the British section. In thus recognising the claims of the individual artist in this field of design these German firms seem to set an example which might well be followed in this country, where, so far, furniture is still considered a commercial product merely, and its design as hardly worthy of serious study as an art.

The examples of furniture illustrated are selected from designs made for Mr. J. P. White of Bedford, and published in a book of furniture which may be obtained from him. The rose bedstead and dressing-table are part of a suite designed for a bedroom in which the rose prevails. The walls and ceiling are decorated with a trellis of roses. Gleams of pale blue sky show between the flowers, birds cling and flutter amidst the branches.

The daffodil dresser is part of a room where cool fresh spaces of green and grey are relieved by pale yellow blossoms.

Each piece of furniture is a thing to be considered not entirely alone, but qualities depend in every case on the proper relation to a complete scheme when this furniture finds itself happily at home in a little world of colour and form.

DINING-ROOM

SITTING-ROOM FIREPLACE

SITTING-ROOM

FURNITURE IN SITTING-ROOM

SITTING-ROOM

BOUDOIR AND MUSIC ROOM

FIREPLACE IN BOUDOIR

BAY IN MUSIC ROOM

MUSIC ROOM

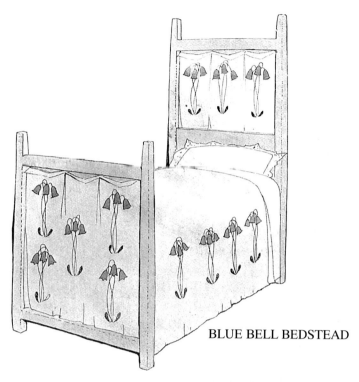

BLUE BELL BEDSTEAD

INLAID SIDEBOARD

DAFFODIL DRESSER

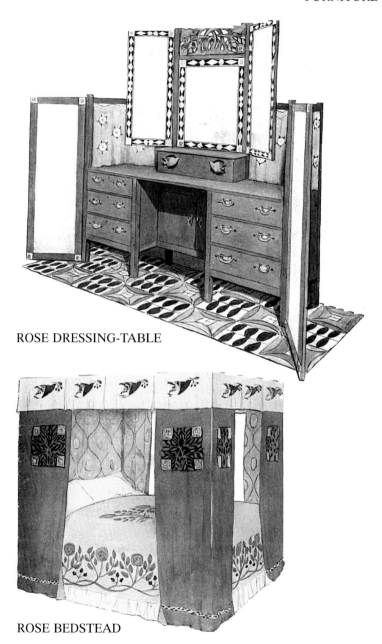

ROSE DRESSING-TABLE

ROSE BEDSTEAD

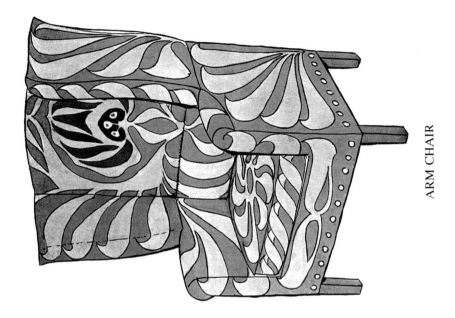

ARM CHAIR

INLAID CHAIR

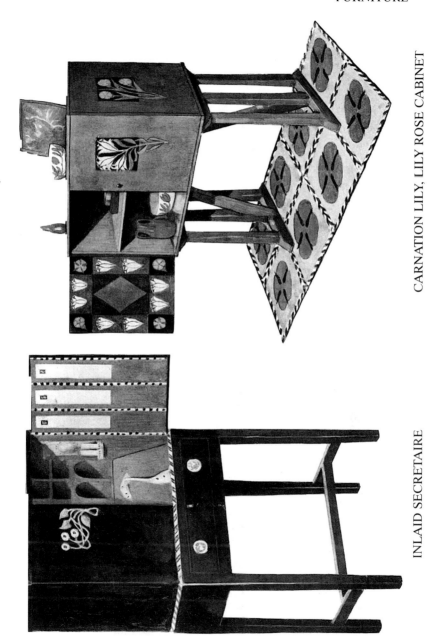

BLACK AND WHITE ILLUSTRATIONS

BLACK AND WHITE ILLUSTRATIONS

BLACK AND WHITE ILLUSTRATIONS

BLACK AND WHITE ILLUSTRATIONS

BLACK AND WHITE ILLUSTRATIONS

The thanks of the author are due to Mr. C. Holme, Mr. Alex. Kock, and Mr. J.P. White for allowing the use of illustrations which have appeared in the 'Studio', 'Inner Dekoration' and 'A Book of Furniture', and to Mr. H. Hulme and Mr A.E. Beresford for assistance in the preparation of plans.